Joseph Pennell, Arthur H. Norway, Hugh Thomson

Highways and Byways in Devon and Cornwall

Joseph Pennell, Arthur H. Norway, Hugh Thomson

Highways and Byways in Devon and Cornwall

ISBN/EAN: 9783337126711

Printed in Europe, USA, Canada, Australia, Japan

Cover: Foto ©Andreas Hilbeck / pixelio.de

More available books at **www.hansebooks.com**

HIGHWAYS AND BYWAYS

IN

DEVON AND CORNWALL.

" *Take these two women to the cage.*" — (P. 222).

Highways and Byways
in Devon and Cornwall

BY ARTHUR H. NORWAY
WITH ILLUSTRATIONS · BY
JOSEPH PENNELL AND
HUGH THOMSON

LONDON: MACMILLAN AND CO., Ltd.
NEW YORK: THE MACMILLAN COMPANY
1897

CONTENTS

LIST OF ILLUSTRATIONS

HIGHWAYS AND BYWAYS

IN

DEVON AND CORNWALL

CHAPTER I

" INSOMUCH," quoth the Reverend John Prince, somewhile
vicar of Berry Pomeroy, summing up in his judiciously impar-
tial way, the merits of Devonshire as compared, or rather as
contrasted, with those of other regions less signally blessed by
heaven," insomuch—without envy be it spoken—what has been
avouched of England in general may be applicable to this
county in particular, ' that she can live better of herself without
being beholden to the rest of the kingdom, than that can sub-
sist without being obliged to her.' "

Now this is the true spirit of the west country, that very
voice issuing from the tomb, which any one may hear to-day,
who takes the trouble to travel into Devonshire or Cornwall ;
and as this modest consciousness of being set (so to speak)
right at the top of all creation is deep planted in the heart
of every West countryman, the quotation is very worthy to be
placed at the front of a work which proposes as its object to
gather up some of the chief aspects of those counties, which

E   B are still distinguished by marked differences from the rest of England.

But we are cutting Mr. Prince too short.   He has more to say on the same subject, and it is very well deserving of attention.   " I would not be thought," he cries anxiously, " to speak so bold a truth of my country out of vanity or ostentation ; but let it be to the glory and praise of the great God, who has so signally blessed us and laid so much the greater obligation on us to gratitude and obedience."   We must believe the good man when he speaks so earnestly and withal so humbly, manifesting so valorous a resolution not to give way to pride in his superior station as a man of Devon.   Let it be so therefore. Neither " vanity " nor " ostentation " shall be mentioned ; but as these vices are ruled out, curiosity springs so much the stronger to find out what it is that instilled into the vicar's heart so deep a sense of gratitude to heaven, and what those blessings are which have been showered down in so great a measure on the West.

There will be no great difficulty in making the discovery. For indeed it is the simple truth to say that Devon contains scenery of a beauty which is not surpassed, and of a variety which is nowhere equalled in all England.   Hills, the beauty of whose outline conceals their want of altitude ; deep and fertile valleys, through which flow streams and rivers of extraordinary beauty, now flashing down swift and brown and foam-flecked from the moor, now gliding among richly wooded pasture, now issuing in harbours where the great tradition of sea power has lain unquestioned during untold centuries ; a coast line, which when low falls into sunny bays of exquisite charm, and when lofty rises into unmatched grandeur ; a stern and rugged upland of vast extent, all glorious with furze and fern and purple heather, a wonderland of tradition and romance, the background of almost every landscape in Devon—could anyone look out over such a noble country without some swelling of the heart, some sympathy with the pride of those who feel it is their own land.

the one in which both they and their fathers before them came to life? And add to this the memory of all the mighty deeds which have come to pass in Devon, or which have been wrought by Devon men elsewhere, how valiantly they fought, how greatly they upheld the honour of England, how nobly they called the tune of that passionate imperialism which sounded first from between the Tamar and the Axe, but which has now swelled to a mighty organ blast, heard and heeded over all the world —why, what need of words to make one sensible that the birth-right of the west country is an inheritance in which the least imaginative man must needs exult, and over which it is easier to rhapsodize with Prince than to write soberly!

"Some shires," says Fuller, "Joseph-like, have a better coloured coat than others, and some with Benjamin have a more bountiful mess of meat belonging to them. Yet every county hath a child's portion, as if God in some sort observed gavel-kind in the distribution of His favours." It is a quaint and pretty saying; and it would be a pleasant task to go round England, tracing out county by county what the "child's portion" is that has fallen to each one. But in Devon every portion is a child's portion, and whether it be a question of fertility or beauty, or accessibility by sea, or wealth of navigable rivers, or mines or timber, or even fisheries, decayed as they are in all directions of the West—in each of these matters Devon has shared the luck of Benjamin, and has been endowed more richly than the rest.

It will appear as this work progresses whether this be true or no. For the present the important matter is to make a start, which will not be managed while we linger here in what are neither highways nor byways, taking general surveys at our ease. There is a great deal of ground to cover and a vast amount to do and say by the way, and therefore, omitting all further preface, it were well to conceive ourselves to be approaching the ancient town of Lyme Regis which, as will be seen presently, forms as good a "jumping-off place" as one can find in going west.

It is scarcely possible to approach Lyme Regis without

passing through or near the very ancient town of Axminster,
which is on the old highway from London to Exeter and the
Land's End, and being the first town which travellers reached
in Devon, as well as a place noted for the manufacture of very
excellent carpets, it retained until 1835 some remnants of its
former consequence. But it has lost all traces of them now, and
has relapsed into the deepest slumber, which it can hardly be
necessary to disturb by any search for objects of interest, seeing
that none exist.   Indeed it might not have been worth while
to mention the drowsy old town at all, had it not been for
friendly feeling towards Prince, our quaint companion, who
assures us with a due sense of gratitude, that at Newenham
Abbey "the author of this discourse, by divine mercy, breathed
his first air."   Newenham was once a very lordly place, though
nothing is now left but a couple of shattered walls near the
river's bank. It is not worth diverging from one's way to pause
upon so slight a fragment, but there is at no great distance the
remnant of an ancient mansion in which "his first air" was
breathed by a man so great and various, so strange a compound
of honour and disgrace, that Ashe House, where the great Duke
of Marlborough was born, must always draw curious pilgrims as
long as English history shall last.

Ashe was the residence of the very ancient family of Drake,
which had won so much distinction before the great Sir Francis
came to life, that even the connection with him, which has been
doubtfully asserted, could add no further lustre to its annals.
Marlborough's mother was a daughter of this honourable house.
His father, Winston Churchill, was a Dorsetshire gentleman,
who, having followed the king when war broke out in 1640, and
borne himself bravely and conspicuously at several battles, was
marked by the Parliament as a dangerous malignant, and
punished by a fine of such amount as involved the surrender
of his estate.   Ruined and homeless, the Churchills sought
refuge at Ashe, and there in 1650 Mrs. Churchill gave birth to
her illustrious son.

Ashe House has suffered so greatly from a fire which almost
destroyed it, about a century ago, that there are scanty traces of
its ancient grandeur.   But the detached chapel in which Marlborough was christened can still be seen, pitifully desecrated,
used as an outhouse to the farm buildings which have usurped
the seat of so much bygone dignity.   The memory of the
peasants has preserved many tales about the house and the
ancient family which dwelt there.   They will tell you with bated
breath, of the wicked Drake who died in punishment, yearning
so sorely to see once more the quiet homestead among the
orchards by the river Axe that not death itself could quench
his longing.   And so his spirit is ever circling round Ashe House,
drawing nearer to its goal with each circuit, and from time to
time by this slow process it gains ground so far that it is almost
home.   Then is the moment for the Church to interfere, and
the restless ghost is exorcised and driven back, and has all the
labour to perform again.   The slightest sign of incredulity on
hearing stories such as this will instantly dry up the flow of
rustic confidence.   But a fit gravity of attention may be rewarded by a second remarkable tale of a lady of the Drake
family, who was betrothed to a sailor, but who broke her troth
during his absence on some distant voyage, and chose another
bridegroom.   The wedding feast had begun and all was going
on quite cheerfully, when the door opened without hands and
every one turned to see what was coming in.   For a moment
nothing entered ; but when the attention of the whole company had been roused, a cannon ball made its appearance
rolling gently along the ball-room floor.   It rolled on steadily
and slowly until it reached the feet of the faithless bride, when
it stopped and rooted itself so firmly to the ground that the
united strength of those present could not make it budge.   It
was clear enough that this remarkable event was a portent
demanding close attention, and the lady very wisely interpreted
it as a gentle hint that she was using the absent sailor rather
badly.   It was not too late to repent ; which she accordingly

did, sending the new lover about his business and herself waiting for him who had the better right to her.

Tales such as these flutter round Devon as plentifully as bats flit across the chimneys of an ancient manor house. There will be occasion to tell many such, as this work goes on ; for in both the Western counties the Keltic temperament has produced its full crop of superstition. There is hardly a cottage in the West where the incidents of domestic life are not affected almost daily by the welling up in the hearts of the people of some belief or prejudice so ancient that no centuries which we can count exhaust its life, but which has risen generation after generation, throbbing to-day as powerfully as a thousand years ago, if more secretly. Those who search openly for these beliefs will seldom find them ; for the people hide them with a sedulous anxiety which springs, partly from pride in the old faiths which have become entirely their own since the outer world rejected them, and partly from timidity lest what they cherish and believe should be laughed at by superior persons. And so not the most sympathetic enquirer will learn much by directly questioning the peasants. He will be met at every turn by " Augh, tidd'n worth listening to by a gentleman," and no persuasions will break down this attitude of reserve. But those who go among the people day by day, hearing when they do not seem to listen, and noticing what is not set before them, are frequently startled by actions or by speeches which, like the opening of a sudden door, set before them scenes and glimpses of an antiquity incredibly remote, proving that the peasants of five centuries ago with their untutored minds, their wild beliefs and their barbarous usages are not dead, but only slumbering in the hearts of those labourers and sailors who go about the world to-day.

However, it is not in this part of Devon that legends and traditions are most often met with, nor superstitious beliefs most commonly practised. There is a somewhat different atmosphere in these border regions, as there is in all others

which are remote from the great central ridge of moors, for it is
roughly true of all Devon and Cornwall to say that superstition
clings to the granite. Certainly it is on, or near, those five
great islands or bosses of granite of which Dartmoor is one, and
to which all the finest scenery of the West is due, that one
meets the strangest survivals of faiths which have perished off
the earth elsewhere; and as one wanders over those lonely
tracts of moor and bog, out of whose sterility man has never yet
succeeded, during all the centuries he has dwelt there, in
producing the means of sustenance for any but the thinnest
population, one understands how it happens that the fancies
born among those solitudes are still nourished by the agencies
which produced them, and are not likely to die whilst the shepherds are left alone all day upon their pastures, as they were
five centuries ago, with no other occupation than the use of
their imaginations, nor any other voices round them than the
soughing of the wind or the rushing of a stony river in the
hollow.

The further one goes West, the wilder and the more plentiful
grow the superstitions, until in some of the moorland districts
of Cornwall there is an atmosphere which is really not altogether
of this world. I must not anticipate these delights of Endor;
but as there are many people to be found who, when they catch
a superstition, proceed to stick a pin through its poor body, and
expand its wings and nail it neatly on a card with name and
date and place of capture scientifically added, I think it well to
say betimes that I mean to do nothing of the sort. I shall not
try to capture any superstitions. I shall hint at them. I shall
let them flutter vaguely by in the half light. I shall abstain from
questionings or analysis; content to be scared from time to
time in company with wiser men. If any man likes to go a
gunning after my devil's wildfowl, he may do it by himself; and
when he has collected all the poor dead things, and stripped
their pretty plumage off, and trussed them up as little like real
life as possible, he may dispose of them in the report of some

learned society, where I doubt not they will meet with all the
attention they deserve.   For my part I would as lief shoot a
kingfisher ; and with these not impertinent observations, I will
resume my way.

We have lingered long enough at Ashe, which is quite out
of the way to Lyme Regis ; and it is time to be getting forward
on our journey, the more so as it is a very hilly one, and takes
time to accomplish.   The hill leading out of Axminster is a
fair sample of what is to come.   Long and steep and winding,
it climbs to a portentous height ; and the traveller who propels
himself by his own exertions, whether on foot or wheels, will
gladly turn before the last glimpse has vanished of the old town
lying in the hollow, and rest himself while looking out over
this lovely borderland of Devon.

Now standing on this hill with our faces to the West we have
behind us all England, but what have we in front?   Two
counties —or, if one must be exact, a county and a duchy—
whose very situation isolates them from the rest, the ancient
land of the Damnonii ; peopled in years before the dawn of
history by that mysterious race whose megaliths and cromlechs
invite us to perpetual guesses on their origin ; occupied again
by the great wave of Keltic immigration ; left unconquered, or
at least only partially subdued, by the Romans ; alternately
befriended and tortured by the Danes ; tamed at least in part
by the Saxons, but not till after they were Christianised ; a
strong fastness held against the Normans ; and in later years
when the strife of races had died out in England, when
conquerors and conquered had fused into that sturdy English
type which won our liberties, which saved our Empire, and
which still holds from day to day, like none other, the advance
posts of civilisation—why then the West became a home of lost
causes, out of which at more than one crisis of English history
there marched a host of brave enthusiasts fighting sturdily for
principles which were dear to them when other Englishmen
were very ready to lay them down.

Here in this corner of Devon, the master key of the West, as is seen by glancing at the map, one looks down on the Great Western Road, a thoroughfare as ancient as any in these kingdoms, which is saying much. For nobody believes any longer that the Romans were our first road-makers. Two thousand years ago, when Cæsar first landed on our shores, the main routes of commerce in this island were well trodden, and had been trodden, for aught we know to the contrary, during many ages and by countless generations. How far this may be true of other great roads in England is not to be discussed here. But this Great Western Road leads directly to the tin-producing districts ; and tin is the one commodity which, according to all testimony, was exported from Britain from the very earliest ages. There is a school of archaeologists who declare that tin-mining is not a very ancient art, and who seek for its origin at a distance of no more than four or five centuries. But if the mines be indeed so modern, there can be no doubt of the vast antiquity of the stream works, any examination of whose age leads one quickly back past all recorded history, so far that geology alone can give even a rough idea of time. In those distant years—who knows how far beyond our ken?—the patient bearers of the tin came toiling out of Cornwall or Dartmoor in the direction of this great highway, plodding on to some harbour on the south coast, whence the metal could be sent to Gaul, and so by a beaten trade route to the Mediterranean. And remote as these old workers are from us, they too had their ancient memories of conquest and the right of settlement torn from a still older people, whose dolmens and great stone circles stirred in them perhaps the same wonder as in us, and were doubtless no less inexplicable, since the names they gave them prove that they knew nothing of their use.

In this road then—let us recognise it—is antiquity many times higher than we can conceive. For it was hollowed by those whom we call ancient Britons, a mere trench or gully

over downs and hills, such as we may see to-day left in lonely
places on the moor.   Then the Romans came and saw it was
the best way, and used it more or less exactly through all its
course.   And next the Saxons took it for a military way ; and
the Normans followed, still travelling in the ancient track ; and
so century went by after century, bringing alternate war and
peace, and travellers of many sorts, and sights of every kind.
Armies marched along it, peasants crowded up in hot and
passionate revolt, ambassadors and Royal progresses jogged
along in all their pomp, and humbler traders followed them.
Mitred abbots came riding up to Parliament ; and merchants
ambled on their mules from Fowey or Dartmouth to make
what peace they could before the Council for some raid on
France or Spain in time of peace, or some foreign trader
unlawfully plundered and detained.   Expresses came pricking
fast to town, bearing foreign news from Plymouth or Falmouth ;
the coaches raced along careless of life or limb ; and so year
after year the pageant swept in some fresh form along the
ancient roadway until that sad hour when all the world
deserted the primrose banks and hawthorn hedges for a dusty
metalled track, and a great silence fell upon the ancient road,
which is hardly lifted yet.   But it lies biding its time ; for it
has seen too many changes of human institutions to believe
that this one will last for ever.

These longwinded reflections have quite beguiled the way to
Lyme.   The steepest hills are past already.   The pretty village
of Uplyme is left behind, and from the ridge along which the
cycle runs without exertion blue sea begins to show itself far
down below upon the left, with glimpses of a high and broken
coast line.   The road is flanked by pretty cottages ; and now
it drops as only Devon or Dorset roads have the face to drop,
steeply, precipitously, heartbreakingly, straight and sheer into
the very heart of the town—and Lyme Regis is attained at
last.

Now, as every one knows, Lyme Regis is in Dorsetshire,

Lyme Regis

with which interesting county this work is not concerned.   But
that is not its own fault ; for at the present moment it is
agitating for inclusion in Devon.   This is certainly a sign of
grace ; and as nothing, not even a soldier's uniform, is more
often altered than a county border, it may very well be that
before these words reach the printers Devon will have gained
what Dorsetshire has lost.   And in any case, even if Lyme
were much more inconveniently situated, we have come here
because we wished to come, which is a reason quite good
enough, and so we will proceed to see the town.

A wide irregular street plunging furiously down a steep place
towards the sea, then swerving sharply to the east where Charmouth lies in a dip of the hills ; a long curve of pebbly shingle,
over which the waves break in calm weather with a monoto-
nous clashing and with a deafening scream when it is rough ; a
pleasant course of sea wall sweeping round a crescent in the
low cliff to the Cobb which the fourteenth century sailors built
when this was a place of note, and held its head up even
among the noble range of ports which flank the western coasts,
—such is Lyme Regis as it stands to-day, an ancient sleepy
town, whose greatness has gone by and whose story is in the
past.   For it is but a tiny harbour which the Cobb encloses,
and the ships in which men go afloat in these days have almost
nothing to say to it.   But it sheltered well and safely those
cockle shells and hoys which were good enough to carry English
sailors when King Edward went to Calais, and still such craft
lie there as safely as of old.   Lyme Regis has not altered.   It
is the world which has moved on and grown used to greater
things ; and so Lyme is left to muse upon the past, and remind
us of Monmouth and Miss Austen.

The last is by far the most pleasant reminiscence ; for the
handsome featherheaded pretender who started from the Cobb
on that short course of royalty which was bought by such a
bitter tithe of blood from all the farms and villages for twenty
miles around, is a figure too tragic to mingle pleasantly with

the recollections of a holiday.   But Lyme retains a distinctive
flavour of Miss Austen.

Who, save those unhappy people, vegetating in ignorance of
the prime joys of literature, who have never read *Persuasion*
can forget the visit which the Musgroves with Captain Wentworth and Anne Elliott paid to Lyme ; or can ever see the
place without thinking of Anne and Henrietta strolling down
before breakfast "to watch the flowing of the tide," and agree-
ing in the flush of their enthusiasm for the ocean on the
eminently safe remark that "with very few exceptions, the sea
air always does good," or of the sad catastrophe which marred
their pleasure when after strolling on the Cobb and finding the
wind unpleasantly high, "all were contented to pass quietly
and carefully down the steep flight except Louisa, who must
be jumped down by Captain Wentworth," and who, in this
sportive occupation, fell and broke her head.   Oh rarely
pleasant trivialities !   Lyme is redolent of leisured unexcited
people ; and even the poor ghost whose penance it is to go
cockstriding up the river to all eternity was reduced to this
dreadful punishment for no more full-blooded sins than selling
water for the price of wine, and combing her hair upon a
Sunday.

In Lyme one is not plagued by any signs of tiresome activity,
the brain rests with the body as one looks about the wide and
empty street, watches the sailors lounging round the piers, or
gazes past the Cobb towards the huge dark precipices of the
eastern coast—where Black Venn and Hardown tower high and
menacing above the sea.   Charmouth lies in a broad low cleft
at the foot of these great hills, and beyond one sees a succession of dark and jagged cliffs which need only a grey sky and
the shadows of a thin mist clinging round their summits to
give them the mystery and grandeur of a mountain line.   Far
away the land creeps down so close to the water's edge that only
keen eyes can discern that the high bluff beyond is not rightly
named the Isle of Portland ; while over this low tongue of

shore the white sails of ships lying in the roadway on the further side gleam softly in the passing sunlight. It is a noble view, and is in truth the greatest charm of Lyme.

But our faces are set the other way, and it is time to be turning westward with a firm resolution not to be led aside from the straight path to dally with any of the associations of Lyme, not with Monmouth, who landed on the Cobb, and set up his standard in the town, nor with Defoe, who came to join him and afterwards regretted it, like many others equally hasty, nor even with that distinguished townsman whose fame old Fuller has most rightly rescued from oblivion on account of his talent for opening other peoples' letters. " He had," says Fuller, lost in admiration, " he had an admirable tact in forcing a seal, yet so invisibly that it still appeared a virgin to the exactest beholder." Evidently a very rare and virtuous person ; but we cannot stay to talk of him, for the way lies westward, and one can only notice in leaving the town how fast the crumbling hillside on which it stands is slipping and sliding to the sea. In every direction one sees garden walls shored up and houses dropping from the perpendicular. Old inhabitants remember when the cliff between Lyme and Charmouth extended half a mile further out to sea than now ; and all along the shore rock falls are perpetually taking place so fast that quarrying is not allowed, nor is it necessary.

Now this frequency of landslips has determined the character of the whole coast line for several miles west of Lyme, and has imparted to it a wild and surprising beauty, casting it into the form of terraces and undercliff, the debris of successive falls which at one time, when the scars were recent, appeared as defacements on the grassy slopes, but in a climate so mild and moist as this, have been quickly converted into hanging gardens. A path winding pleasantly through overarching trees leads by a steep ascent up the first slopes above the town, emerging on a plateau, whence one looks down on the sea washing gently among shattered boulders at the base of a grassy cliff. There are ferns in all the crevices, and trailing ivy on the rocks. The grass is spangled with violets, and here and there an orchid glows deep and red in the increasing sunlight. As one treads carefully along the undulating path which traverses this wilderness of clinging greenery, broken by steep cliffs and patches of well wooded upland, a certain feeling of unrest and insecurity is suggested by the aspect of the undercliff. For here is no trace of that immobility and stillness which brood over the great cliffs further west ; but rather a perpetual slipping and contortion which is so strongly marked, that in looking across any one of these strangely broken slopes one can easily fancy the surface to be still heaving and subsiding as it did once long ago when the great mass slipped away from the bed on which it rested and the boulders came crashing down from the rocky peaks above. And indeed the earth disturbances along this coast have been terrific. At one point especially a catastrophe occurred which has probably had no parallel in England, and which even now, at a distance of more than fifty years, leaves an indelible impression of awe on the minds of those who wander through its ruins.

In 1839, certain cottagers who dwelt on the borders of these cliffs were alarmed by the appearance of little cracks and fissures in their gardens and in the surrounding portions of the cliff. Such alarms are so frequent in that district, and had so often come to nothing, that the peasants reassured themselves, and thought all would be well. But as the year went on, the cracks increased both in number and in size. There were occasional sounds like the snapping of roots ; and pieces of plaster began to tumble from the cottage walls. Doors which used to swing easily could be opened and shut only with difficulty ; and there were mysterious heavings and subsidences of fields which had long been cultivated on the margin of the cliff. On Christmas eve there were merry-makings at a house at no great distance, and the tenant of one of the threatened cottages, returning late at night from the feast, found the path running through his garden a foot lower than he had left it. He went to bed; but was disturbed by loud noises and tremblings of the ground; and when daylight came, he found the path had sunk six feet further, leaving a little cliff up which he had to climb to seek for help. It was both difficult and dangerous to rescue the man's family and goods from the fallen cottage, but it was done; and during the rest of Christmas day no further movement seems to have occurred.

But the catastrophe was near at hand. In the following night two coastguards were on duty on Culverhole Beach, and they observed the sea to be agitated with extraordinary violence; the beach on which they stood surged up and down beneath their feet; there were loud and terrible noises such as neither man had ever heard; a deafening sound of falling rocks was in the air, and through the darkness they could see that some large black object had risen in the waves at a short distance from the land. When daylight came the ruin was revealed. Three-quarters of a mile of cultivated land had crashed down upon the undercliff, carrying with it forty-five acres of arable ground, two cottages, and an orchard. But the land had not fallen bodily in one unbroken surface. It had been wrenched and torn by the violence of the convulsion in the most fantastic manner; here sinking into a cavern a hundred feet below the former level, while close by an isolated pinnacle rose carrying on its towering summit a remnant of the pasture which the day before stretched continuously across the chasm. A bare precipice of enormous height, cut sheer and perpendicular in the middle of a field, showed at a glance the extent of the calamity, and at its feet the fallen surface—still bearing the remains of cottages and orchard—lay broken into ridges and gullies and ravines. It was a strange and awful sight to see the solid earth so twisted; and all men's minds were full of fear, which grew the greater on finding that the very bottom of the sea was changed and upheaved where there had been deep water, for at a little distance from the shore a reef had formed itself forty feet high and nearly a mile long, thrust upwards from the bowels of the earth as the great cliff crashed down upon the shore.

Such was the memorable landslip at Axmouth, a convulsion which in the judgment of Dr. Buckland "far exceeded the ravages of the earthquakes of Calabria," and which remains to-day but little changed from the aspect it presented to the terrified peasants who stood watching for the slow winter dawn sixty years ago. The reef has been washed away by successive storms; but the cliff ruin stands, though its terrifying aspect is disguised and hidden by the adhesion of the most luxuriant vegetation, which has crept thickly everywhere among the ruin, turning the ravines into bowers of moss and trailing ivy, and strewing primroses and violets so thickly on the slopes that one hardly remembers amid one's admiration of such lavish beauty what a murderous agency has been at work. But the memory returns; the sense of awe is dominant; and it is with a feeling of relief that one climbs up the steep path and sets foot once more upon unshaken ground.

CHAPTER II

To those who delight in searching for the picturesqueness of bygone days, it is a little disappointing to discover that in this corner of Devon the harbours are all choked up. For in the two Western counties, so deeply indented by the sea, fronting to both channels, renowned throughout all history both for the number and the quality of their seamen, all that is best and greatest has settled on the seaboard, and unites itself with the coming and the going of ships. There was a time when shipping entered freely into East Devon ; but that is so very long ago that the tale is more for the archæologist than for the ordinary reader.

It is melancholy when one climbs down the steep hill barrier by which the Valley of the Axe is approached from Lyme, to see this wide and open river bottom, so obviously designed by Nature to hold a navy, occupied by marshy river meadows, while the stream, which higher up its course flashes swiftly over a gravelly bed, seems here to have lost its strength, and crawls slowly on beneath the hill, powerless to carry down its silt, or sweep seawards the pebbles which the ocean tosses up. There needs no history to tell us that this was once a place of consequence. At a glance it shows its wasted value, proclaiming loudly how great a part it might have played in the story of England had its waters not been choked and its citizens condemned to idleness when there was need of sailors. As it is,

full four centuries have passed since any active life existed here.
When Leland rode this way in the reign of Henry VIII., he
could only say, "Ther hath been a very notable haven at
Seaton, but now ther lyith between the two points of the old
haven a mighty rigge and barre of pible stones in the very
mouth of it, and the River Axe is driven to the very est point
of the haven caullid Whitclif, and ther at a very small gut
goith into the sea; and ther come in small fisschar boats for
soccur." So far the port had fallen three centuries ago and
more, for want of such protective work as the townsmen were
too idle or too unskilled to undertake. Perhaps it was even
then too late to save the harbour; and certainly now the time
has long gone by when any useful effort could be made. Yet
only in the present century the farmers in the district, moved
perhaps by a sense of the advantages of water carriage, but
more strongly by a certain pride in the ancient maritime consequence of their river, which lingers with curious tenacity even
after all these centuries, agreed to dig it out, and restore its
glories. Entering on this gigantic undertaking without any
true sense of its difficulty they sent each so many of his own
farm labourers, and had actually made some progress, when
there came a flood great enough to destroy all that had been
done, and the farmers, not perhaps unwillingly, abandoned the
unequal task. There is something admirable and rather
pathetic in the spectacle of these rustics setting themselves so
boldly to a public work whose difficulties would tax the genius
of our greatest engineers; and though it failed, so great an
effort of public spirit deserves to be commemorated.

The last occasion on which Seaton influenced the life of
England seems to have been in 1347, when the town con-
tributed two ships to the fleet with which Edward III. set sail
for Calais. If one seeks for other associations, it is necessary to
go back much further, deserting the trodden ways of history for
the mire of archæological discussion. Indeed, this valley is
one over which the antiquaries have gathered like a cloud of

vultures, and inasmuch as no visitor to Seaton will be allowed to escape scot free, it may be just as well to say what all the pother is about.

Nobody who walks along the esplanade at Seaton—unless indeed he is wisely giving all his attention to the cliffs and sea and the fine inland hills—can fail to see the word " Moridunum " written up in large letters on the stone work ; and most people who have noticed it have probably been rash enough to inquire what it means. This question is what the Seatonian has been waiting for. He will promptly buttonhole you, and explain that there is an ancient document called " Antonine's Itinerary," which was in truth to the Roman legions very much what " Patterson's Roads " was to the modern traveller, giving him some more or less accurate ideas of the distances he had to march and the stations he would pass in this far-distant land of Britain. Now of these stations Exeter has been recognised ; and further east is another named " Moridunum," a name over whose signification the quarrel burst out. The older antiquaries, a very credulous set of people full of wild ideas and speculations, decided that " mor " meant " sea," and having settled this, identified Seaton as the Roman station. Other more careful inquirers, since their time, have come to different conclusions, but the Seatonians will not hear of them, and maintain that in the first two centuries of our era their waste harbour was alive with the coming and going of frequent Roman galleys. We had better leave them to fight out the dispute among themselves ; but before passing on it may be said that in this corner of Devon there are almost the only signs of any long-settled Roman occupation which exist west of Somersetshire. Indeed the scarcity of such remains in the former county contrasts strangely with their frequency up to the very border of the latter, and points without doubt to some marked difference in the nature of the dominion exercised by the invaders in the west.

Whatever Seaton may or may not have been in bygone days,

it is now a pleasant breezy watering place, neither so beautiful
nor so interesting as many other towns further west, but noted
all along the coast for the freshness of its breezes and its open
situation.   For the two white cliffs which terminate its bay lie
far apart, and the sea winds sweep up the wide valley without
hindrance, creating a climate which is brisk and stimulating.
The little place is unsophisticated too,—a long beach, a pebble
ridge on which half a dozen boats lie bottom upwards, a few
sailors lounging round them, a good hotel, a couple of streets
running to a point—there is nothing more in Seaton ; and in
search of active memories one strolls on to Beer.

The pleasantest way from Seaton to Beer is over the western
cliff by a steep and broken path.   From the summit of this
crumbling white chalk bluff there is a singularly fine view up
the valley of the Axe, winding in dim luxuriance till it is lost
among the hills of Shute ; and one has scarcely turned away
from this rich prospect of inland beauty before the path drops
rapidly to a deep and narrow cove, hardly seen until one is
immediately above it, and suggesting irresistibly by the
seclusion of its situation certain pursuits which brought to the
fishermen of Beer for many generations more profit than favour
in the eye of the law.   There is no harm in speaking of these
matters now ; for Beer has been this many a day like the
sinner that repenteth, and is rather pleased to detail its former
transgressions, feeling perhaps that a certain spice of devilry
handed down from former days is an agreeable relief to the
more prosaic occupations of the present time.   But it is certainly not more than fifty years since the whole community of
Beer—men, women, and children all alike—was desperately
addicted to smuggling, and found its glory and its chief delight
in eluding the vigilance of the revenue officers ; and it is a
curious instance of the changed conditions of life in England
that law, which never was otherwise than reluctantly obeyed on
the western coasts of England until the present century was far
advanced, has at last succeeded in tying down the restless

energies of the men and women of Beer to the peaceful pursuits of trawling and the manufacture of lace.

Beer, like many other places, bred its hero, one whose wiles were as many as those of Ulysses, and who bids fair to obtain, at least on the South Devon coast, an equal length of memory. "Jack Rattenbury" was his name; and it fortunately happened that he kept a journal, which was published some fifty years ago, so that we are fully instructed, not only about Jack's engaging character as it appeared in his own not too critical eyes, but also about many other circumstances which cast light on the wild life of those times.

"I bought a vessel," Jack says, "for smuggling, in which I made three successful voyages to Alderney; and on my return from the last, thinking all was safe, I went on shore with a few friends to spend an hour at a public-house. In the same room were a sergeant and several privates of the South Devon Militia, and also some horse soldiers, amounting on the whole to some nine or ten in number. After drinking two or three pots of beer, the sergeant, whose name was Hill, having heard my name mentioned by some of my companions, went out with his men, and soon they returned again, having armed themselves with swords and muskets. The sergeant then advanced towards me and said, 'You are my prisoner. You are a deserter, and must go along with me.' For a moment I was much terrified, knowing that if I was taken I should, in all probability, be obliged to go aboard the fleet; and this wrought up my mind to a pitch of desperation. I endeavoured, however, to keep as cool as possible; and in answer to his charge, I said, 'Sergeant, you are surely labouring under an error; I have done nothing that can authorise you in taking me up or detaining me. You must certainly have mistaken me for some other person.' In this manner I contrived to draw him into a parley; and while it was going on I jumped into the cellar. I then threw off my jacket and shirt, to prevent any one from holding me, and having armed myself with a reap-hook

"You are my prisoner."

[To face p. 21

and a knife, which I had in my pocket, I threw myself into an attitude of defence at the entrance, which was a half-hatch door, the lower part of which I shut, and then declared that I would kill the first man that came near me, and that I would not be taken from the spot alive. At this the sergeant was evidently terrified; but he said to his men, 'Soldiers, do your duty; advance and seize him.' To which they replied, 'Sergeant, you proposed it; take the lead and set us an example, and we will follow.' No one, however, offered to advance, and I remained in the position I have described for four hours, holding them at bay. Not knowing how to act, the sergeant at last sent for Lieutenant Durall; but before he arrived, some women ran into the house with a story that there was a vessel drifted ashore, and a boy in danger of being drowned. This tale they told in such a natural manner, that it attracted the attention of the sergeant and his men; and while they were listening and making inquiries about it, I jumped over the hatch, and rushed through the midst of them, without their being able to lay fast hold on me, in consequence of the precaution which I had taken to lay aside my clothes. I then ran toward the beach, and some men got me into a boat and conveyed me on board the vessel, where I immediately hoisted the colours."

It is an agreeable picture which Jack draws for us, and one sees how important was the part which the women played when their husbands were in peril. This kind of thing was going on not only at Beer, but at every creek and inlet on the coast: and as what Jack tells us is thus typical of the scenes enacted at many other places, where for want of a chronicler the memory of them is lost, we may find space for another of his stories, one, moreover, which shows how lustily his wife could help him on occasion.

Jack, it seems, had grown tired of smuggling, and tried to gain an honest living in a public-house. But fortune was against him and drove him back on the career for which his natural gifts so plainly marked him out. It was in 1812, not long after he had taken to the sea again, asking only to be let alone that he might regain what the pursuit of honesty had cost him, that he was chased, cannonaded, and captured by a meddling cruiser stationed in Torbay to convoy the Brixham fishing fleet, but which left her proper duty in order to capture Jack. There was some difficulty in doing this ; and the commander of the cruiser was therefore the more enraged to find nothing more compromising in his prize than a pint of gin in a bottle. Jack affected indignation. " I said, ' You have treated us shamefully. You have taken my vessel on the high seas and retained it, though you found nothing on board to justify you on being so ; and it is, I conceive, an act of piracy.' To this he replied, ' I care nothing about it.' My wife, hearing of my situation, came on board. Our interview was short, but long enough for me to entreat her to get a good boat and come off to me next morning. When she came the second mate had charge of the vessel, the other officers being on shore, which was favourable to my design. As soon as she was alongside I jumped into the boat, and made a motion to my companions to do the same, that we might assist the women on board. One of them did so, and I whispered to him to wait till they were all out of the boat ; and immediately on this, I called out aloud, ' Shove off.' I then put my oar against the side of the vessel, but the second mate caught hold of it and broke off the blade. Being very angry, I threw the remaining part at him, and called to my companions to hoist the sail. He exclaimed, ' If you do, I'll fire at you.' To which I replied, ' Make sure of your mark.' At this he fired, and the shot went through the sails. He was preparing to do so again when my wife wrested the piece out of his hands. Having recovered it he fired again, and the shot striking the rope of the sail, it fell down. He then stopped firing, thinking that we were sufficiently frightened to induce us to return on board ; but in the meantime we had hoisted the sail up again and pushed off. They then got the boat out and chased us, keeping up a continual fire at us; but though the sails were full of shot holes, none of the men received any injury. We put in at a promontory called Bob's Nose;[1] my companions jumped out; I was the last man, having steered the boat; and as I was in the act of doing so a shot passed close to my head, but did not touch me.

" As soon as I got on shore I scrambled up the cliffs, and when I had reached the top I looked back, but could see no one. I then took off my jacket and left it, thinking if they met it they would suppose I had thrown it off to facilitate my speed in getting away. After this I rolled myself down the cliffs, not far from where we landed. At the same time I saw our pursuers following my companions, and several hundred people on Brixham Cliffs looking on. About one o'clock I saw the men belonging to the brig go by and embark, and when all seemed quiet, I started over hedges, fields, and ditches, and got safely to Torquay."

Such was the smuggling life of the western counties within the lifetime of our fathers, or, to speak more accurately, such was one aspect of it. For the west country smugglers were not all Jack Rattenburys; and this jovial, good-tempered duel with the law, this wrestling without ugly throws, this fencing with the buttons on the foils, was by no means the whole story. The play was very often in most deadly earnest, as was natural, seeing that the players were men whose fathers, for centuries untold, had imbibed the fierce traditions of a race of wild sea rovers. Corsairs were their ancestors, and just as we go round the coast, gloating on smuggling stories, so they dwelt with equal glee on the traditions which were then plentiful and living, of Vaughan the pirate, and of Captain Hamond, and of Clinton Atkinson, whose deeds are now forgotten, but were known then to the very children.

[1] Surely he means " Hope's Nose," for which he would naturally make as he was escaping from Brixham.

There will be more to say of some of these people presently. But for the moment we have lingered long enough upon the coast, and we cannot move on to Sidmouth without going up the valley of the Axe, even if it be no further than to Shute, whose dark fir woods catch the eye from every side standing heavily against the sky line. There would be much to say about this fine valley, had we time to climb the slopes of Hawksdown, Musbury, and half a dozen other hills whose crests are topped by very ancient earth-works, or to gather up the memories of the bloody deeds which Jeffreys wrought among the farms and cottages when fugitives from Sedgemoor came slinking homewards through the dusk of the short summer nights. But these scenes are best forgotten; and indeed they seem strangely remote from a land which smiles as this does with springing corn and budding apple blossom, and late primroses and early bluebells in the hedges, while the anglers go up and down the low margin of the river—no brawling hasty stream, like those which tumble over boulders from the moor, but a sedate and quiet water, well loved by those who know it best. There are many interesting places on its banks; Colyford, that ancient borough of some fifteen houses, which confers upon its mayor the least onerous dignity in England; Colyton, which has a remarkable church; Colcombe Castle, where dwelt Sir William Pole, that great antiquary on whose work most of the Devon history is founded; and at no great distance Shute, which still belongs to the descendants of the antiquary, and is in itself a place of interest and note.

At the base of the pine-clad hill which was so conspicuous from the coast, stands an ancient gatehouse, picturesquely draped with ivy, giving entrance to a park within which lies the manor house, "Old Shute House," as it is called, in distinction from the more modern dwelling which was built a century ago on an eminence some half a mile away. The old house is a handsome Tudor building, worn and weather-beaten, but still standing almost as perfect as it was four centuries ago.

High battlemented walls inclose a gray stone courtyard, antique and beautiful, where heavy mullioned windows, which once looked out on knights and gallant gentlemen dismounting, now behold only the farmer's dog stretching himself on the sunny stones, or a rough farm pony clattering under the silent archway.

Here the family of De la Pole has dwelt for three centuries and more since the great Sir William lived. Before them Shute was ruled by the turbulent family of Bonvile, who, in this secluded spot, conspired with such vigour for the Yorkist party that the house became the headquarters of the White Rose in the west. They appealed to the sword, and by it they perished. Lord Bonvile fell in the second battle of St. Albans; his son and grandson were slain at Wakefield. One can imagine how the news was brought to what was thenceforth a house of mourning, for the male line was extinct, and one frail girl remained to carry on the great inheritance. One might roam the whole day long among the woods of Shute, or around its very ancient deer-park, without exhausting its associations, which, indeed, go back to days far more ancient than are mentioned here. But we cannot stay to trace them. The ancient gatehouse, the old church, half hidden by its stately cedars, the deer-park, and the hospitable modern house —on all these we must turn our backs; and retracing our steps to Colyford, mount the steep and winding hill by which Sidmouth is approached.

Alas, poor cyclist! it is a foretaste of much toil to come. " Si quis, suadente diabolo. . . ." It is no use to take a cycle into Devon unless one is prepared to work. And after all, what is a bicycle? Surely a machine for carrying one where one wishes to go! And where could one wish to go more than to a spot whence there is spread out a view so fine as that which meets the weary cyclist when he turns, breathless and hot, to scan the height up which he has climbed? The Axe valley lies beneath, spread open like a map, marked out in squares

and ovals by the prominent hedgerows. Hawksdown, Musbury, and the whole eastern barrier stand in dark shadow
beyond the shining stream, the blue sea breaks on the pebble
ridge of Seaton in a curving line of foam, the white cliff
gleams, and far out beyond the breakers the sunlight catches
the brown sail of a fishing boat, which glows like ruddy
bronze.

From this point onwards there is a good and easy road along
the ridge until one comes in sight of the valley running down
to Sidmouth.   Here there is what is doubtless the worst hill
in the county ; but having once got down it, the road runs
pleasantly among pretty villas, and through tidy streets out
upon a long parade skirting round a beach of pebbles which
curves inland between two lofty cliffs of that deep red sandstone which gives so rich a colouring to nearly the whole of
the South Devon coast, and which from this point is hardly
broken till Torbay is reached.   Pleasantly the little town lies
there fronting its sunny bay, the blue water ripples round the
base of the blood-red cliffs, the wet pebbles shine with divers
colours, the wind blows warm and softly in this sheltered spot,
a southern atmosphere of idleness pervades the town, the very
river makes no sound as it slips out to sea.

Sidmouth is a happy place to idle in, but it has not much to
tell us ; and having loitered for an hour on the parade we turn
our backs upon it and pass on up the pretty valley and across
the hill to the valley of the Otter, whence an easy road leads
to Ottery St. Mary, which very ancient town is both famous
and beautiful, and well deserves description.   But I vow
that I am weary of description, and will describe no more, but
push on by Otterton and Bicton till I reach a spot at which I
needs must pause, for one of the very greatest names of Devon
is closely linked with it.

This is the village of East Budleigh, the birthplace of Sir
Walter Raleigh, the most interesting, if not the greatest
among that group of strangely gifted men, whose fiery energies

and passionate pursuit of vast ideas shook the world out of its
faith in Spanish greatness and set England once for all in the
forefront of colonising nations. Of this vast work Raleigh was
the very soul. His seething brain conceived the notion of a
colony in Virginia ; his was the restless energy that fashioned
and maintained it ; his the knowledge of the Court that
smoothed the obstacles thrown in its way by jealous rivals ; and
his the purse that made good its huge expenses. And though the
settlement of which he dreamed had never any vigorous life,
though it withered and died like a thing born prematurely, yet

Budleigh.

it did not pass away as if it had not been ; or the idea was
one which could not fail, animated by a vitality far exceeding
any temporary collapse, and destined, though Raleigh did not
know it, to expand in a measure worthy even of the great mind
which conceived it.

" Inspired by a restless genius," Prince says of him, " he
designed nothing but what was extreme." And, indeed, it is this
note of extravagance in Raleigh's character which wins for him

the interest and love of men to-day, as it did that of the Virgin
Queen three centuries ago. In all things Raleigh was magnifi-
cent, a man of vast ideals and of schemes which neither he
nor the rest of the world were then able to execute. He
dreamed and planned and toiled, and failed, leaving his bones
by the wayside, but bequeathing to his countrymen a heritage
of great ideas, to which they owe no small part of the material
fortune which has been won since the weary dreamer laid down
his head upon the block, which an ungrateful and subservient
monarch had prepared in recompense for unforgotten services.

Hayes Barton, where Sir Walter was born, was not the original seat of the Raleigh family. Their ancestral home was at
Farwell, near Cornwood ; and it was only on the marriage of Sir
Walter's father, with Joan Drake of Exmouth, that he removed
to Hayes, which house, besides its proximity to his wife's relations, stood conveniently near his own two manors of Withycome
Raleigh and Colaton Raleigh. It is no great distance from the
village to the house. One passes out of the street by a road
near the church, which runs half a mile or so along the side of
a valley, and brings one out at length upon a little hollow where
the old house stands at the foot of the hills, apparently not
much altered since the Raleigh's left it. It is a long thatched
house of two stories with many gables and a picturesque
projecting porch. A farmer occupies it now, and will show the
room in which Sir Walter was born.

Here we can imagine him, an eager child, poring over such
books as he could command, or sitting on the beach at Budleigh
Salterton, as Millais has drawn him for us, listening rapt to some
story told by a swarthy sailor of wild adventure on that ocean
which in those days was still the pathway to wonders in which
a child's imagination could rove at will, or five miles away at
Exmouth, where the greatest estuary of the west is filled twice
a day with great salt floods, bringing up ships from many lands.
The lad must have found endless stimulation for his seaward
fancy, in wandering round the quays, and talking to the tarry

sailors. It was there, doubtless, that he acquired a deep knowledge of all naval questions which distinguished him through
life, even when he stood among seamen such as Drake or
Frobisher, or that terrible John Hawkins who was so great in
the very qualities that Raleigh lacked.

From Exmouth into Topsham is a rather hilly road without
much that is interesting to detain us by the way. And the
case is not very different when we arrive at Topsham, though
the old town, deserted by its former consequence, lies pleasantly enough along the low shore of the estuary, and retains
many ancient houses that speak plainly enough of past prosperity. For a long time Topsham was the chief seat of Exeter
commerce, the largest ships unloading here in preference to
going up the river; while, independently of its great patron,
the little town had a large and valuable trade with Newfound-
land. There was thus a very busy active life upon the quays
which are now so quiet; and Topsham sailors held their own
in many a fierce sea fight whose memory is lost.

Chance, however, has preserved for us, in a scarce tract at
the British Museum, the story of a fight so grim and deadly
waged by one Robert Lyde, a Topsham man, two centuries
ago, so full of living details, and so eloquent of that firm faith
among the Puritans that God was on the side where they would
have Him be, guiding their hands at every onstroke, and sus-
taining them when the force of battle went against them, that
its interest as a human document is of the highest, and I regret
that I cannot quote it in full.[1]

It is evident that Topsham was full of detractors; for Lyde
says in his Preface, "What I have written . . . had never

[1] The title of the work is as follows :—"A True and Exact Account of
the retaking a ship called the *Friend's Adventure* of Topsham from the
French . . . where one Englishman and a Boy set upon Seven Frenchmen,
killed Two of them, took the other Five Prisoners, and brought the Ship
and them safe to England. Performed and Written by Robert Lyde, Mate
of the same Ship. 1693." Since these lines were written it has, I understand, been published in full by Mr. Arber.

appeared in print were it not to vindicate myself, and to free
myself from the many calumnies of unreasonable men . . . who
tell the world I attacked the Frenchmen in cold blood and
murdered the two men I fairly killed, and that the spirits of
them have haunted me ever since, and will till I am hanged."
After which embittered protest, he proceeds to tell the true
story as it happened.

Harking back a little to make his tale the clearer, Lyde tells
us that in February 1689, he shipped on board a pink of 80
tons at Topsham, bound for Virginia, and on the way home
was taken by a French privateer and carried to St. Malo, where
"we were used with such inhumanity and cruelty that if we had
been taken by the Turks we could not have been used worse.
For bread we had six pounds and one cheek of a bullock for
every twenty-five men for a day ; and it fell out that he that
had half of a bullock's eye for his lot had the greatest share."
Even a century later than the time of which Lyde writes,
prisoners of war were treated, in this country no less than in
France, with what we think barbarity ; but Lyde quotes details
which are certainly shocking, and adds, "These and other their
barbarities made so great an impression on me as that I did
resolve never to go a prisoner there again, and this resolution I
did ever since continue in and by the assistance of God always
will."

This resolution took absolute possession of the man.   In
1691, having regained his liberty, and stayed awhile at home,
he was again afloat, and not long passed before he was once ·
more captured by a French privateer, which having plundered
the unlucky *Friend's Adventure* took out all her crew save Lyde
and a single boy, and put her in charge of a prize-master with
six other men to be navigated to St. Malo.

And now Lyde's heart began to burn within him.   He saw
himself almost at the gateway of his former prison, and all the
sufferings he had endured once more at hand.   His first idea
was to make the Frenchmen drunk ; but this failed, and he

then determined to attack them, but hung back till he could win over the boy to join him. The boy hesitated, as well he might : and before any plan was settled, the ship arrived off a small harbour near Brest, and the French fired a " pattereroe " for a pilot to come off. " Whereupon," says Lyde, "considering the inhuman usage I formerly had in France, and how near I was to it again, struck me with such terror that I went down between decks and prayed to God for a southerly wind, to prevent her from going into that harbour, which God was most graciously pleased to grant me, for which I returned my unfeigned thanks."

Thus strengthened in his faith that the Lord was on his side, he became so eager that he could hardly stay his hand from striking. " At eight in the morning all the Frenchmen sat round the cabin table at breakfast, and they called me to eat with them ; and accordingly I accepted of their invitation, but the sight of the Frenchmen did immediately take away my stomach, and made me sweat as if I had been in a stove, and was ready to faint with eagerness to encounter them, . . . but could stay no longer in sight of them, and so went betwixt decks to the boy, and did earnestly entreat him to go up presently with me into the cabin, and stand behind me, and knock down but one man in case two laid on me, and I would kill and command all the rest presently." But the boy would not ; whereupon Lyde, half resolved to attempt the business himself, applied himself to prayer, and " desiring God to pardon my sins which I had committed and to receive my soul to mercy, I prayed also for my enemies who should die by my hands, because they may not have time to call for mercy themselves ; I prayed also that God would strengthen me in my design, that my heart fail not in the action." And then he detailed to the boy all the hardships of his cruel imprisonment ; whereupon " the lad said, ' If I do find it as hard as you say when I am in France, I will go along with them in a privateer.' These words of his struck me to the heart, which made me say,

' You dog; what, will you go with them against your king and
country and father and mother? Sarrah, I was a prisoner in
France four months, and my tongue cannot express what I
endured there, yet I would not turn Papist and go with them.
If I should take my brother in a French privateer after he had
sailed willingly with them, I would hang him immediately.' "

The lad was wavering; and on the morning after this conversation he agreed to join.   The moment was propitious; for
of the seven Frenchmen two were lying asleep in the cabin.
What followed must be told by Lyde himself.

"Then the boy coming to me, I leapt up the gun-room
scuttle, and said, 'Lord be with us and strengthen us in the
action'; and I told him that the drive-bolt was by the scuttle
in the steeridge, and then I went softly aft into the cabin, and
put my back against the bulkhead and took the iron crow and
held it with both my hands in the middle of it and put my legs
to shorten myself, because the cabin was very low. But he
that lay nighest to me, hearing me, opened his eyes, and perceiving my intent and upon what account I was coming, he
endeavoured to rise to make resistance against me, but I
prevented him by a blow upon his forehead which mortally
wounded him; and the other man, which lay with his back to
the dying man's side, hearing the blow, turned about and faced
me; and as he was rising with his left elbow on the deck, very
fiercely endeavouring to come against me, I struck at him, and
he let himself fall from his left arm and held his arm for a
guard, whereby he did keep off a great part of the blow, but
still his head received a great part of the blow.

"The master lying in his cabin on my right hand, rose and
sat in his cabin, and seeing what I had done, he called me
'Boogra!' and 'Footra!' But I having my eyes every way
I push't at his ear betwixt the turnpins with the claws of the
crow; but he falling back for fear thereof, it seemed afterwards
that I struck the claws of the crow into his cheek, which blow
made him lie still as if he had been dead. And while I struck

The Church at Topsham.

at the master, the fellow that fended off the blow with his arm
rose upon his legs, and running towards me with his head low,
I push't the point at his head, and stuck it an inch and a half
into his forehead ; and as he was falling down, I took hold of
him by the back and turned him into the steeridge.

" I heard the boy strike the man at the helm two blows after
I knocked down the first man, which two blows made him lie
very still ; and as soon as I turned the man out of the cabin,
I struck one more blow at him, thinking to have no man alive
further aft than myself, and burst his head, so that his blood
and brains run out upon the floor.

"Then I went out to attack the two men who were at the
pump, where they continued pumping without hearing or
knowing what I had done ; and as I was going to them I saw
that man that I had turned out of the cabin into the steeridge
crawling out upon his hands and knees upon the deck, beating
his hands upon the deck to make a noise that the men at the
pump might hear, for he could not cry out nor speak. And
when they heard him and saw his blood running out of the
hole in his forehead, they came running aft to me, grinding
their teeth as if they would have eaten me ; but I met them as
they came within the steeridge door and struck at them ; but
the steeridge not being above four foot high, I could not have
a full blow at them, whereupon they fended off the blow and
took hold of the crow with both their hands close to mine,
striving to hawl it from me ; then the boy might have knocked
them down with much ease, but that his heart failed him. . .
The master that I thought I had killed in his cabin, coming to
himself, came out of his cabin and also took hold of me " . . .
Then ensued a desperate fight, in the midst of which the boy,
thinking his champion overthrown, cried out for fear. "Then
I said, ' Do you cry, you villain, now I am in such a condition ?
Come quickly and knock this man on the head that hath hold
of my left arm.' The boy took some courage, but struck so
faintly that he missed his blow, which greatly enraged me ; and

I, feeling the Frenchman about my middle hang very heavy, said to the boy, 'Go round the binikle and knock down that man that hangeth on my back'; so the boy did strike him one blow on the head, and he went out on deck staggering to and fro. . . . Then casting my eye on my left side and seeing a marlin speck hanging with a strap to a nail in the larboard side, I jerkt my right arm forth and back, which cleared the two men's hands from my right arm, and took hold of the marlin speck, and struck the point four times into the skull of that man that had hold of my right arm, but he caught the strap and hauled the marlin speck out of my hand. . . . But through God's wonderful providence it either fell out of his hand or else he threw it down; for it did fall so close to the ship's side that he could not reach it again.

"At this time I said, 'Lord, what shall I do now?' And then it pleased God to put me in mind of my knife in my pocket; and although two of the men had hold of my right arm, yet God Almighty strengthened me so that I put my right hand into my right pocket and took out my knife and sheath, holding it behind my hand that they should not see it; but I could not draw it out of the sheath with my left hand, so I put it between my legs and drew it out, and then cut that man's throat with it that had his back to my breast, and he immediately dropt down and scarce ever stirred after."

Such was the end of this most murderous fight. The French lost heart, and the uninjured men sued for quarter. In another hour Lyde had five living prisoners under hatches, and had set his course for Topsham. It would be too long to tell of all the perils of the voyage, of the heavy weather he encountered, and his suffering for want of sleep, and how, when at last he reached Topsham bar and was in sight of home, the pilot for whom he signalled did not dare come off, but lay inside the bar just out of sight, fearing some trap; while Lyde, not venturing to take the ship in himself by night, was blown off the coast again; but at length made home and told his tale, where, as we have seen, his reception was not quite what he had expected. Probably most who read the story now will do so with mingled feelings; but whether we admire the man's desperate courage or shudder at his murderous contempt of human life, the story illustrates well enough the hearts and spirit of the Devon sailors two centuries ago. Such men they were, and in such a way they fought.

It is time to pass on from Topsham, that ancient sunny little town; for the river Exe, as Risdon observes, "runneth a long course with his crooked cranks," and there is a great deal to see and think about before entering on that region beyond the wide estuary, in which some men maintain that the west country properly begins. Beyond the wet sands of the river, that lovely country rises into high hills, over which the evening sunlight falls most richly, picking out with its mellow glow every mansion and white farm and low-thatched cottage that stands among the yellow woods or in the fertile fields below. Midway in the river a pair of herons stand pluming themselves and arching their long graceful necks upon a sand-bank. The stream has just begun to flow. It comes up with a gentle ripple, carrying a string of heavy barges bound for Exeter. The ferry-boat from Exmouth ploughs across, leaving a golden track upon the water; and presently the light and colour fade away from the widening river, the hills turn gray and cold, and the last few miles of the journey into Exeter are ridden in the dark.

Exeter.

CHAPTER III

THERE are not many towns which stir the imagination as much as Exeter. To all west countrymen she is a mother city, one who during untold centuries has been their head and capital, and fought their battles and suffered with them when the luck was bad. At times opposing them, like every other mother, she has never lost their hearts; and there is not one among them, however long absent from the west, who does not feel when he sets foot in Exeter that he is at home again, in touch with people of his own blood and kindred. And this is true as much of the Duchy as it is of Devon; for there is no town in Cornwall which has ever held a similar position. Bodmin is too small, Truro too lately elevated; and neither can hope to rouse a similar attachment till it has fought and suffered with the Cornishmen during eighteen centuries, as Exeter has done.

In Exeter all the history of the west is bound up—its love of liberty, its independence, its passionate resistance to foreign conquerors, its devotion to lost causes, its loyalty to the throne, its pride, its trade, its maritime adventure, all these many strands are twined together in that bond which links west countrymen to Exeter. There is no incident in their past history which does not touch her. Like them she was unstained by heathendom, and kept her faith when the dwellers in less happy cities further north were pricked to the worship of Thor and Odin at the point of Saxon spears. Like them she fought valiantly against the Norman Conqueror, and when she fell their cause fell with her. And since those days what a host of great and stirring incidents has happened here, from Perkin Warbeck beating on the gates with his rabble of brave Cornishmen, to William of Orange going in high state to the cathedral, welcomed already as a deliverer to that throne which it lay almost with Exeter to give or to withhold.

The city streets are steeped in memories. " Ther be divers fayre streetes in Exeter," says Leland, " but the High Streete that goethe from the west to the east gate is the fayrest." Unhappily, both west and east gates are gone ; and the street itself is sadly modernised. Yet still, as one looks along its slanting length, one is arrested constantly by some fine old timbered house, whose rich carved gables take one back to the days when trading companies were great and powerful in Exeter, and when the " Society of Marchantes Adventurers of the Citie of Excestre, trafiquing the Realms of Fraunce and Dominions of the Frenche King," swept all the foreign trade of the ever faithful city into its own net, and turned fiercely on such as dared oppose it. Here, in some one of these old houses, the " marchantes " dined in solemn merriment ; while below stairs, the big rough-bearded captains from Topsham or from Exmouth waited till summoned up to receive their orders to " lade wines for Juberaltare or Sherys." There, too, is the highly picturesque guildhall, whose gabled roof and fine projecting porch are linked with so many pageants made to

honour kings and queens whom the loyal magistrates received
there. From beneath that porch doubtless rushed out in
towering wrath that mayor of whom Prince tells us, whose
sense of dignity was outraged by the spectacle of a "haffing
captain" marching through the High Street with his colours
flying and his pipes playing, *en route* for Plymouth, where his
men were to form part of some great expedition. The mayor
vowed that he should go by more quietly, testifying respect for
the civic dignity, or else should not go at all. The "haffing
captain" swore great oaths which he had learnt abroad; and
forgot himself so far as to threaten to "garter the mayor's
hose with his bowels"; but in point of fact did not do so, and
did obey the plucky mayor's commands. Here, too, is that
which was formerly the "New Inn," a hostelry as ancient as
any in the city, which is saying much, and one, moreover,
which was very noted as the headquarters of the trade in
woollen cloth, from which, not Exeter alone, but the whole
county of Devon, reaped a golden harvest. There is a finely
plastered chamber in this old building, now a draper's shop,
where merchants from every part of England used to meet for
the sale or purchase of this cloth, while the stables down below
were full of carriers, and their pack mules which had plodded
patiently up from Totnes, Ashburton, and a dozen other towns,
carrying the produce of the cottage looms, and the winter's
work wrought in lonely farms and homesteads upon the moor.
A surprising amount of cloth was brought in by these carriers.
In 1725, the Dolphin Inn, another very famous hostelry,
remained without a tenant for a week, and accounts were kept
for the benefit of the trustees. In this single week, carriers
came from Yeovil, Moreton, Ashburton, Totnes, and Okehampton, having among them no less than fifty-six pack-horses.
And of this Dolphin Inn a story is told which shows that there
was quite another life in Exeter than that of the grave merchants
who met to chaffer at New Inn. The story is told in the
Transactions of the Devonshire Association, and is as follows:—

"On a January night in 1611, there was staying at the
Dolphin Sir Edward Seymour of Berry Pomeroy. He was in
an upper chamber playing cards with some friends, when the
party was joined by Master William Petre, and by John and
Edward Drewe of Killerton. One of the Drewes wore a white
hat and cloak, the other was in black. Edward carried a short
sword and John a rapier. These three gallants, already flushed
with wine which they had drunk at the 'Mermaid' and the
'Bear,' drank a pot or two of beer and some more wine with
Sir Edward Seymour. After tarrying an hour and indulging in
a rude practical joke upon the tapster, they remounted their
horses, dropped in at a few more taverns, and rode out of the
city by the east gate. Here Will Petre spurred on at a reckless pace up the broad highway of St. Sidwell, and was lost in
darkness. The Drewes gave chase, but stopped at St. Anne's
Chapel and shouted to him. Receiving no answer, they groped
their way to a house where a light was burning, but the woman
of the house had seen nothing of Will Petre. They rode on to
his home at Whipton House, and found his horse standing
riderless at the gate. Edward Drewe took the horse by the
bridle, and with his foot, as he sat on horseback, knocked at
the gate, whereupon a servant of the house came forth and
opened the gate. He then willed of him to take his master's
horse ; and then the servant demanded where his master was.
Drewe contented himself with the answer that he would come
presently, and rode off with his brother to their home at
Killerton. The dawn of Sunday morning showed the dead
body of Will Petre lying by the causeway near St. Anne's
Chapel, with a ghastly wound on the head. The hue and cry
was raised, and the two Drewes were taken as they lay in bed,
and brought before the city justices on the charge of
murdering their friend."

I am sorry that I cannot give the upshot of this pretty
business ; but for that the reader will properly blame the author
of the paper quoted, who might have made more search, rather

than me, who made no search at all ; while, on the other hand,
I shall deservedly reap the credit of giving wider publicity to
the scandal. But in the absence of further information, we
may fairly say that the story told by the Drewes was very lame,
and there will not be much injustice done in observing that
many a man has been hanged on weaker evidence.

The side streets of Exeter are full of charm. They are
tortuous and winding ; they bring you face to face with
fine old churches, with little ancient chapels and hospices
built of crumbling stone. Sometimes they drop steeply to the
river's bank ; and then one sees the Exe swirling dark and
rapid through some gut so crowded and overbuilt with houses
that it seems a piece of Rotterdam or Leyden ; and again the
winding alleys mount the hill, and one comes by the little
College of Priest Vicars to the Close, where the old red brick
palace nestles underneath the south-west angle of the great
cathedral, redolent of memories of great bishops in the past,
among whom not the least was he whose personality is still a
household word in all his diocese, Henry Phillpotts, more widely
known as " Henry of Exeter," a bold, strong ruler in days when
such a man was needed in the Church. For when he mounted
the steps of that wondrous carved oak throne, which was built
six hundred years before, by a bishop as great as he and far less
fortunate, the murdered Stapledon, he looked forth on a Church
which had gone pitifully to waste in the solitary districts of the
west ; a Church in which those parishes were counted happy
whose clergy were simply careless, while the worst that could
result was seen in the lives of men such as Parson Chown,
whom Mr. Blackmore has drawn but too truly in *A Maid of
Sker ;* or in many another of whom stories still pass from mouth
to mouth in the country sides where they disgraced their
calling.

One instance will serve as well as fifty : " My good woman,
can you point me out the vicar of your parish ? " was asked of
an old peasant from a certain parish on the moors. " Did'ee

see a man goo by on a white harse ? " " I did." " And was a blind drunk ? " " He was certainly rolling in his saddle." " And was a cursin' an' a swearing fit to burn his tongue out ? " " He was using very shocking language." " Augh, then that's our passon, an' a dear good man he be." This story, which is quite true, could be capped by many another of the same individual ; and he was not alone in the life which he affected ; so that when Phillpotts, a bold, stern fighter, came to set God's house in order, he found those to deal with who could not be changed, but only broken ; and setting his strong will against theirs, he did break many of them, and left his charge far better than he found it. Peace be with his memory, for he had storms enough in life.

Well, he lies now in the great cathedral, adding another to the countless memories which cluster in the shadow of that ancient building, which is the one thing standing permanent while Norman walls and mediæval houses pass like the changes of a dream. You will scarcely trace the walls of Exeter now. Of the gates not one is standing. You may search some time before you find the castle. The greater part of the old city is clean gone. But here in the cathedral is Exeter of every age, the old immutable, the modern mellowing in its turn, the rest and silence out of all the centuries that have passed so stormily elsewhere, the same almost in appearance as when the people crowded in to see the Prince of Orange new come from Brixham with his growing army, while "sundry men with halberds " kept the way, that his Highness might not be unduly thronged. " And as he came all along the body of the church, the organs played very sweetly . . . and being set, the quire began to sing Te Deum, for the safe arrival of the Prince of Orange and his army in England."

Ah, " ever faithful city " ! Was it a Dutchman who so dubbed thee ? Alas, walls and fortresses are not the only ideals of past days which decay and change so very swiftly !

Now there are many writers who have praised Exeter for

this and that, some selecting one of her manifold charms and
dignities for especial comment, while another gives the meed
to something else ; but there is one which has been neglected
strangely, and as it will come cropping up time after time as we
go on westwards, we may as well refer to the matter now.
Exeter has for generations, if not for centuries, been the head-
quarters of west country witchcraft.

Of course it is notorious that the west is full of witches.
There are few towns or villages of any consequence which do
not boast some man or woman skilled more or less deeply in
necromancy, and able to furnish charms against the evil eye ;
while in addition to these regular practitioners, there are many
travelling gipsies and vagabonds who derive a comfortable sustenance from the black art.   Now most of these witches will
refer difficult cases to Truro, Plymouth, or to Exeter, the white
witch at the ever faithful city being a sort of acknowledged
chief among them all ; and as these are things not generally
known, it may be well to give the facts of one such case in
which the prescription was singular and doubtless derived from
some very old tradition.   The particulars are taken from the
Transactions of the Devonshire Association.

A man and his wife in South Devon, having had a run of ill-
luck, came to the conclusion that they had been overlooked ;
and they suspected that it was a certain relative of the wife
who had " cast her eye " over them.   The wife accordingly
posted off to Exeter, and consulted the white witch, who
thoroughly confirmed her suspicions both as to the nature of
the mischief and the individual who had caused it.   Fortunately the charm could be broken easily enough ; and the
witch advised the woman on returning home to buy a large
beeve's heart.   Having done so, she and her husband were to
rise from their beds at midnight, lock, bolt, and shutter all
their doors and windows with the greatest care ; and when they
were secure, put the beeve's heart into the fire.   The woman
who had bewitched them would then come to the house, and

use every effort to get in. If she succeeded, the charm would not be broken, so that it was absolutely necessary to keep her out.

It happened exactly as the witch had said. In the dead of the night, when the beeve's heart was burning in the fire, the woman whom they suspected came to the door, beat upon it, rattled at the windows and did everything in her power to get in. But the bewitched couple were firm, if terrified; and resolutely kept her out till the heart was completely burnt away, when she ceased her efforts, the spell was broken, and the ill-luck vanished with the smoke of the burning heart.

It is far from my desire to give the white witch a gratuitous advertisement; but all candid persons must admit that this is a remarkable cure, one difficult enough indeed to make the reputation of any specialist. As this work proceeds we shall have facts enough to excite the envy of Endor itself.

And now, to finish up with Exeter witchcraft while we are about it, we may as well relate the sad story of Mr. Jacob Seley, which set all the ever faithful city gossiping so long ago as Monday, September 23rd, 1690, and is very worthy to be remembered even yet. Mr. Seley, it appears, set forth from his own home in Exeter on the day just named, with the full purpose and intention of riding to Taunton in Somerset. As far as we can gather he jogged along quite comfortably for a considerable distance, following the road through Hinton Clist to Blackdown, at which place there is a public-house called Cleston, "where the coach and waggons usually lodge on that road." Here Mr. Seley stopped some time, and refreshed the inner man. Perhaps he was a thought imprudent; for after he had called for a pot of beer, he had also a noggin of brandy; but if there was excess, surely even rigid moralists will admit that his punishment was more than he deserved. For when he at last resumed his journey, (the quotation is from a tract entitled "Strange and Wonderful News from Exeter,") "he met with a country-like farmer, being about seven or eight at night; and

the country-like farmer persuaded Mr. Seley to ride back a
mile and a half to lodge, telling him there was very good
quarters, but at his return, he supposed it to be about three
mile ; and then he brought him to a plat of ground near the
house, and the country-like farmer and his horse vanished
away."

This of itself was sufficiently startling to a tired man, and
might serve to point the moral how rash it is to ride back
upon your road with people whom you do not know. But
mark the sequel. " Immediately near 100 or 200 appeared to
him, men, women, and children, some like judges, some like
magistrates, some like clergymen, and some like country
people ; and the country people had spears who made at him,
and then he made use of Scripture, but they made him no answer.
Then he did abjure them." We may pause to remark that it
might have helped him more if he had abjured noggins of
brandy. " He did abjure them in the name of the Father, the
Son, and the Holy Ghost ; for it is written, the seed of the
woman shall bruise the serpent's head." However, there
seemed to be something wrong in the abjuration, for Mr. Seley
did not succeed in bruising the serpent's head, though having
laid about him with a hanger which he wore, he formed the
conclusion that he had cut off some of its fingers. At any
rate there was blood upon his hanger, and then the enemy
hung over his head "something like a fishing net," with what
purpose exactly does not appear, but no doubt it was a wicked
one. All this went on by Mr. Seley's account in a plat of
ground not above four yards square. " At last he lighted off
his horse, and his horse laid his nose on his shoulder as if he
had been a Christian." But even this sorry comfort poor Mr.
Seley did not long enjoy ; for the spirits gave his horse
" something like treacle, and then he let go his horse and never
saw him after."

There is a good deal more of this story, prepared doubtless
for the consumption of Mrs. Seley when her lord returned.

But where Mr. Seley really was all this time is a matter of pure speculation.

There is no doubt that the whole Exe valley is extremely beautiful. Less striking than the valley of the Axe, if one regards the altitude and grouping of the hills, it has a greater richness, and a sweeter luxuriance of tranquil beauty. The way out of Exeter is not defaced by any such deformities of mean and squalid streets as encircle many of our ancient cities. A single street of quiet houses brings one down the hill through a suburb which changes fast to absolute country; and a short two miles of pleasant winding lane leads to Cowley Bridge, where the River Creedy, flowing down from Crediton, joins the Exe, and the two rush swiftly underneath a stately bridge, and through wide level water meadows of lush grass which occupy the bottom of the valley. There is a weir beside the bridge, which fills the air with the sound of rushing water; and there the birds, rejoicing in the tall trees which grow so straight in that sheltered situation, seem to sing both earlier and later than they do elsewhere.

At this spot there is a parting of two roads. The way to Tiverton lies through a shady wood upon the right, and one has followed it but a little distance when an opening of the trees give an outlook across the river to a square red house, standing among pleasant gardens on the side of a hill, which will be long remembered as the dwelling place of one who was not the least among that race of fine and cultured gentlemen of which the long succession has never failed in the west, a man whose life is never spoken of without admiration, nor his end without a pang, such as all men feel when a finely tempered instrument is broken in a strain to which it should not have been put,—Sir Stafford Northcote, first Lord Iddesleigh. It is easy to comprehend the feeling held by him and all its natives for this lovely valley through which the river winds so sweetly, now rippling up to the very margin of the road, now swirling away across the meadows or coursing swiftly underneath

a hillside where dark woods grow steeply down to the water's
edge, and trailing willows drown their lower branches in the
stream. Sometimes the road ascends a little hill and then one
sees the river slipping by at the foot of an old orchard; and
again it drops to an ancient bridge, where some smaller stream
comes hurrying down a second valley, clattering and gushing
over a stony bed, and at last one sees close by the river's bank
an old house almost hidden up with ivy, set at the foot of a
well-planted hillside, and looking up a reach where the water
flows more rapidly than we have seen it yet, black and broken
into foam, rushing like a moorland stream from beneath the
arches of an ancient bridge which spans the valley with its
pointed piers somewhat higher up. This is Bickleigh,
the birthplace of a rarely famous vagabond, Bampfylde Moore
Carew, now sleeping in the red churchyard on the hill.

"Never," says the biographer of this extraordinary man,
"never was there known a more splendid appearance of
gentlemen and ladies of the first rank and quality at any
baptism in the west of England than at his"—an ingenuous
remark which is doubtless quite as true as many others made
about its subject. However there was naturally a large company
of well-born people; for the child to be baptised was born into
as good a family as any in the west; and they were moreover all
very merry over the wrangle between the two destined godfathers
as to which of them should have the precedence in naming
him, which important point was settled by spinning a coin.
The toss was won by Hugh Bampfylde—the same who, as
Prince tells us, riding too fast down hill not long after,
"ruthfully brake abroad his skull,"—and he accordingly rushing
off in triumph to the font gave the child his own name first.
Perhaps he was sorry afterwards that he had been so eager, for
though Carew's biographer spends vast labour in seeking to
persuade us that his friends were always glad to see him, however
like a scarecrow he was looking when he turned up, we remain
incredulous to the end. However, all went on very well for a

E

good many years. Bampfylde's father, who was rector of the parish, sent him to school at Tiverton, designing him for the Church; but though the lad seems to have picked up some odds and ends of learning, which afterwards served him well in his impostures, he was chiefly distinguished among his fellow scholars for a "remarkable cheering halloo to the dogs," and for the discovery of an important secret, thitherto unknown, for enticing anybody else's dog to follow him.

These acquirements promised future eminence; and it was not long before Bampfylde planted himself firmly in a walk of life where they were of service to him. For having got into a scrape for hunting a deer with his "cheering halloo" over a number of fields which were ripe for the reapers, and not feeling disposed to face the irate farmers who had called at the school in a body, Bampfylde with one or two chosen friends played truant till the storm should be overpast, and in the meantime joined a company of gipsies whom he found regaling themselves in an alehouse on "fowls, ducks, and other dainty dishes." With these vagabonds he seems to have gone away without giving any news of himself to his parents who, we are told, "sorrowed for him as one that was no more," until, after hearing of their grief at intervals for full eighteen months, his heart rather tardily "melted with tenderness," and he went home to Bickleigh, where "joy gushed out in full streams" when his parents recognised him, and there was "nothing for some time but ringing of bells with publick feastings and other marks of festive joy."

This is very pleasant to read about; but the long-deferred flogging might have done the boy more good than public feasting. The wild, free vagabond life had caught his fancy deeply; and ere long he had cast off home and friends once more, and was gone without farewell. Thenceforth he became the Prince of Beggars, renowned throughout the kingdom not only from the oddity of finding a man of birth and family choosing such an occupation, but even more through the

singular genius which he possessed for disguise, and which
enabled him to impose with ease even on those who knew him
best. Sometimes a shipwrecked sailor who had lost his all,
sometimes a grave clergyman who had given up his benefice
for a scruple of conscience about the oath to Government, and
then again an honest miller whose house, mill, and all his
property had been burnt by the carelessness of an apprentice,—
there was no end to the characters he could assume, and in
each one of them he collected rents from society with such
success, that when the excellent old Clause Patch, who for
many years had occupied the gipsy throne with dignity and
credit, was snatched away from his people by death, Bampfylde
was elected in his stead,—so at least his biography assures us
and the tale seems to be accepted.

Bampfylde Moore Carew, King of the Gipsies, is a legendary
hero in this lovely valley. By far its most famous inhabitant,
he has earned an immortality much like that of Robin Hood.
Through half the countries of Europe he begged and jested,
cheating people with a zest and humour which disarmed their
anger, saved frequently from prison by respect for his descent,
and welcomed almost everywhere for the sport and merriment
he brought with him. The following anecdote may serve to
drive home the recollection of his singularities before we leave
him and pass on to Tiverton.

It was hardly knavery, but a healthy love of mischief, which
drove him to this freak, and for that reason it leaves a somewhat better taste in the mouth than many of the pranks
recorded of him. " Dressing himself in a checked shirt, a
jacket and trousers, he goes upon Exeter quay, and with the
rough but artless air and behaviour of a sailor inquired for
some of the King's officers, whom he informed that he
belonged to a vessel lately come from France which had
landed a large quantity of run goods, but that the captain was
a rascal and had used him ill, and d——n his blood if he
would not . . . He was about to proceed when the officers,

who with greedy ears swallowed all he said, interrupted him by
taking him into the Custom House and filling him a large
bumper of cherry brandy, which when he had drank they forced
another upon him, persuading him to 'wet the other eye,'
rightly judging that the old proverb 'In wine there is truth'
might with equal propriety be applied to brandy . . . But
that no provocation should be wanting to engage him to speak
the whole truth, they asked him if he wanted money.   He
with as much art answered very indifferently, 'No !' . . . They
then ordered him to go to the Sign of the Boot in St. Thomas'
in Exeter, whither they soon followed him, having first sent an
exciseman to ask what he would have for dinner and what liquor
he would drink.   A fire was lighted upstairs in a private room, a
couple of ducks roasted, and wine and punch went cheerfully
round ; they then thrust four guineas into his hands, which he
seemed at first unwilling to accept, which made them the more
pressing.   He at last acquainted them that the crew to which he
belonged had landed and concealed part of a valuable cargo
in the outhouse of Squire Mallock of Cockington, and the
remainder in those of Squire Cary at Tor Abbey—both which
houses, upon account of their situation at the seaside, were
very noted for such concealments.   The officers having now
got the scent were like sagacious hounds for pursuing it forthwith, and thought it proper the sailor should accompany them ;
but to prevent all suspicion, resolved he should change his
habit.   They therefore dressed him in a ruffled shirt, a fine
suit of broadcloth belonging to the collector, and put a gold
laced hat upon his head ; and then mounting him on a very
fine black mare, away they rode together, being in all seven or
eight of them . . . Being arrived in Tor town, they demanded
the constable's assistance, who was with the utmost reluctance
prevailed on to accompany them in making this search, Squire
Cary being a gentleman so universally beloved by the whole
parish, to whom he always behaved as a father, that every one was
very backward in doing anything to give him the least uneasiness.

"Being come to the house, they all dismounted, and the collector desired the sailor to hold his horse, but he replied he would go round the garden, and meet them on the other side of the house, to prevent anything being conveyed away, and that it would be proper he should be present to show the particular place in which everything was deposited.

"This appeared quite right to the collector; he therefore contented himself with fastening his horse to the garden rails, and proceeds with the rest of the officers in great form to search the dog kennel, the coal house, dove house, stables, and all other suspicious places, expecting every minute to see the informing sailor, who by this time was nearly got back to Newton Bushell, having turned his horse's head that way as soon as he got out of sight of the collector; he stopped at the Bull, where they had been the preceding night, and drank a bottle of wine; then ordering a handsome dinner to be got ready for his company, whom he said he had left behind because his business called him with urgent haste to Exeter, claps spurs to his horse, and did not stop till he reached that city."

From Bickleigh to the very ancient town of Tiverton is no more than four very pleasant miles, following the river through a richly wooded valley. Of the town itself, a description so eloquent and plaintive is contained in a little pamphlet, now not often met with, that I shall make use of it in preference to writing a new one of my own. The author calls his work "The Lamentable Spoyle of Teverton," and the use of it has this advantage, that it introduces us at once to all the history of Tiverton, which really consists of very little more than of being burned down and builded up again.

"It is not unknown to many," says this eloquent brochure, "that the town of Teverton in Devonshire was the chief market for cloth, that is in all the west parts of England; pleasantly situate on the clear running river of Exe, garnished with many costlye and goodlye buildings, inhabited with divers rich and

wealthy marchants, and so well peopled as no other town of the
same bignesse in all those quarters could compare therewith ;
and by reason of its market, kept therein every Monday fo.
cloth and other commodities, it was greatly frequented of all
the country people, . . . where they were sure of sale and to have
present money for their commodities, were it never so much,
where always before dinner they had theyre coyne truely payde."
Oh, excellent and honest place, where the necessity of having an
untroubled mind when sitting down to meals was so clearly
seen.   Yet not even this availed against an adverse fate.   " But
such is the mutabilitie of fortune," our author goes on, in
pained surprise, " that no man can make assurance of that he
hath, nor warrant his own welfare one minute of an hower, . . . for
when they thought themselves secure, in prime of the bright
day, . . . not when they were asleep or naked in their beds, but
when they were awake and apparelled for any business, . . . lo,
then, I say, sodenly came that great griefe upon them, which
turned their wealth to miserable want, and their riches to
unlooked for poverty ; and how was that ? Marry sir, by fyer ! "

Fyer it certainly was ; and what grieved the unlucky people
of Tiverton was, that what consumed their goods, their houses
and themselves was "no fyer from Heaven, such as worthily
fell on the sinful cities of Sodom or Gomorrah."   There was
not even the consolation of deserving the calamity, which was
produced merely by " a sillie flash of fyer blazing forth of a
frying pan."   It happened thus : " Ther was dwelling in a little
lowe thatcht house a poore beggarly woman who had got a
companion fit for the purpose, and they together went to bake
pancakes in the strawe, . . . and as they were busied about the
cooking, sodenly the fyer got into the pan, which also caught
present hold on the strawe lying hard bye, . . . and by this means
in less than half an hower the whole town was set on fyer, . . . at
least ther was four hundred houses on fyer at once, . . . most
dreadful was the noise which was then heard in every corner
and streete of the town, women piteously screcking, maydens

bitterly crying and children roaring out of measure." Indeed
a very lamentable scene; and unhappily little more than
"screeking" could be done, for the town possessed no means
whatever of extinguishing the flames, and the consequence was
that in a very little while our author, whom we must assume to
have been an eye witness of the calamity, had nothing more
important to do than to indulge in a sort of swan song over the
smoking ruins. As this effort is poetical, we append it here or
rather the latter part of it, for the whole is a trifle long-winded.
"Oh, Teverton," he chants lyrically, "well may thy friends cry
over thee, saying alas, alas for that proper town of Teverton,
that wealthie and rich town, for at one hour is thy judgment
come; thy marchants may now weep and mourne, for no man
buyeth ware in thee any more."

This extremely low-spirited view of the position was probably
adopted to stimulate subscriptions, which did in fact flow in
with great rapidity, so much so indeed, that in fourteen short
years everything was in full swing once more and the place
quite ready to be burned down again, which it accordingly was
on the 5th August, 1612. This time the fire broke out through
the carelessness of an apprentice, and destroyed six hundred
houses, goods and merchandise to the value of £200,000,
with almost all the machinery and implements of trade in the
town. But happily the eloquent scribe was at hand again, for
it could be none but he that penned the pamphlet entitled
"Wofull Newes from the West Partes of England, being the
Lamentable Burning of the Town of Teverton in Devonshire
upon the fifth of August last 1612," and sent it flying round
the country embellished with a woodcut of a house flaming
terribly from the roof, while from an upper window a mother
suspends her baby by the neck, and the elders of the town toss
their aged hands into the air in evident regret that they cannot
catch it. A heart of stone would bleed at the sight of this
picture; and the result was a fertilising stream of bounty
flowing from all England towards Tiverton which, if in some

quarters it provoked the answer given to King Bampfylde, when
he tried to play this game in connexion with a fire at Crediton,
"Damn Kirton, there has been more money collected for
Kirton, than Kirton was ever worth," yet proved quite effectual
enough to replace everything destroyed by the flames, so that
in three years business was as brisk as ever.   But the habit of
being burned to the ground at short intervals is not easily lost
when once acquired ; and Tiverton indulged itself again in
1661, as well as in 1731 and 1794, and probably on many other
occasions which I have not counted.

   There is a fine church in Tiverton ; there is also the ruin of
an ancient castle ; but what interests us more than these is the
old school-house where the gipsy king was educated, with
many another man of note, and among them our dear friend
John Ridd, whose life has been so worthily set forth by Mr.
Blackmore.   Who can forget his description of this place?
"The school-house stands beside a stream, not very large
called 'Lowman,' which flows into the broad river of Exe
about a mile below.   This Lowman stream is wont to flood into
a mighty head of waters when the storms of rain provoke it ;
and most of all when its little mate, called the Taunton Brook
. . . comes foaming down like a great roan horse, and rears at
the leap of the hedgerows.   Then are the grey stone walls of
Blundell on every side encompassed, the vale is spread over
with looping waters and it is a hard thing for the dayboys to
get home to their suppers. . . and in the very front of the
gate, just without the archway . . . you may see in copy-book
letters done a great P. B. of white pebbles.   Now it is the
custom and law that when the invading waters, either fluxing
along the wall from below the road bridge, or pouring sharply
across the meadows from a cut called 'Owen's Ditch' . . .
upon the very instant when the waxing element lips though it
be but a single pebble of the founder's letters, it is in the
licence of any boy, soever small and undoctrined, to rush into
the great schoolrooms, where a score of masters sit heavily,

and scream at the top of his voice ' P. B.' Then with a yell
the boys leap up or break away from their standing ; they toss
their caps to the black beamed roof, and haply the very books
after them ; and the great boys vex no more the small ones,
and the small boys stick up to the great ones ; one with another,
hard they go to see the gain of the waters. . . . Then the
masters look at one another, . . . with a spirited bang they
close their books, and make invitation the one to the other for
pipes and foreign cordials, recommending the chance of the
time, and the comfort away from cold water."

Such is John Ridd's inimitable description of the scene ;
and inasmuch as no better ever has been, or ever will be, written,
I make no apology for having quoted it. But it is time to
leave old Tiverton. The spring sun is sinking low. The
valley is full of warm golden light, warning us of the distance
back to Exeter and the near approach of dark. And so the
cycle races back through the lovely valley ; for not all Devonshire is hard rough riding, and here at all events is a road as
pleasant as could be wished. The lights are out in Exeter as we
mount the last long hill ; and the sleepy porter rubs his eyes
and grumbles as he wheels the muddy cycle into the coach-
house of our hotel.

CHAPTER IV

THERE are many grander roads than that which passes out of Exeter by the banks of the wide estuary, but it would be difficult to find one of more charm. On a bright spring morning one meets the keen sea air blowing up across the warren before the town is left behind ; and in passing onwards through the budding orchards which clothe the first slopes of the hilly country lying further west, the salt flavour of the wind grows more perceptible, and one tastes the sea even in the midst of this rich farming district. Whenever the road rises it gives a prospect over the great tideway and the waste bare sandbanks to Topsham or to Exmouth lying backed by ruddy hills ; and presently it sweeps out on the shore itself at Starcross, which little village is a thing of naught when the tide leaves it, but a pleasant spot to loiter in when the sea returns. There is one great object too in staying there long enough at any rate to see the park at Powderham, the chief seat of that great family of Courtenay, whose name is bitten in so deeply on the history of Devon that it can never be obliterated like that of other families which have come and stayed and passed and been forgotten by all men save by antiquaries. I would fain stay to speak of this famous house, and its park of yellowing oaks which sweep so finely up the hill behind, but time and distance warn me to proceed on my way, and I may not stop until I come to Dawlish, which besides being a pretty

Teignmouth Bridge.

seaside place, hemmed in among the warm sunshine by high
red cliffs, possesses two remarkable island rocks, the Parson
and the Clerk, now sadly damaged by the sea, but still rising
sufficiently above the surface of the water to attest the truth of
the following story, which the townsmen tell with bated breath.

Centuries ago a bishop of Exeter was lying on his deathbed ;
and the worthy priests of Devon were already tormenting themselves about the succession. Among them was one who had
ridden up to Exeter to ask how near the old man was to death ;
and turning homewards with a mind more bent on ambitious
hopes than on following the trackway, had lost himself on
Haldon, that lofty spur of hills at the foot of which both
Dawlish and Teignmouth lie. The night was stormy; the
clerk, who was his master's guide, was utterly at sea ; and the
priest, after wandering about among trackless country till he
was weary, broke out impatiently and cursed the clerk, saying,
" I would rather have the devil for a guide than you." He
had hardly spoken when a peasant rode up whom he had not
noticed till that moment, and volunteered to lead them to
shelter. The offer was eagerly accepted ; and ere long the
guide had brought them to a lonely house where great revelry
was in progress, for the windows were lighted brightly, and the
sound of wild songs sung in chorus made itself heard above
the storm. Master and man were too glad to be under cover
to feel disposed to criticise their entertainment ; and they were
soon at supper with a party whom they might have seen cause
to fear had they been less weary. As it was they accepted the
whole crew in good faith, drank and jested with them, joined
lustily in the chorus of their songs, and spent such a merry
night, that when tidings of the bishop's death were whispered
to the priest, his brain was none of the clearest. Yet he remembered stupidly that he had work to do now the stool was
actually vacant ; and he rose up and called for his horse. The
whole party came to the door to see the guests mount. Master
and man swung themselves heavily into the saddle in the dark,

and spurred their beasts. But the horses did not move. The
priest slashed them cruelly with his whip, but still they would
not budge ; and for the second time that night the priest used
the name of Satan. "The devil's in the horses," he cried,
" but devil or no devil, they shall go." Whereupon there was
a roar of wild laughter, the house vanished, the company
turned into devils capering with glee, the waters of the sea rose
round the two wretched men, now clinging to the flanks of
their horses for dear life ; and in the morning the drowned
bodies of the parson and his clerk were found on the two
rocks which bear their name, while the horses were wandering
quietly upon the sands at Dawlish.

I do not know whether it was this same priest or another
like him whose memory clings round Ladywell, under these
same Haldon Hills, and who decoyed poor women to his
chapel, slew them cruelly and threw them down a well. He is
very well remembered in the neighbourhood, as is natural,
seeing that the ghosts of the poor murdered women and
children are to be seen hovering round the opening of the well
on almost any night when the moon is not too bright ; while as
for the monk himself no one seems to know what became of
him.

These two attractive stories form the past history of Dawlish.
It has nothing more to tell, though it has existed for a good
many centuries ; and it lies now on its warm and sunny shore
unconcerned with anything but the entertainment of visitors,
which it must be said it does extremely well, showing the
advantages of concentration on a single object, for every one
likes Dawlish, and carries away some pleasant recollection of
its ruddy beaches and the clear cool water lapping on them, or
of the long sea wall which makes so easy a stroll towards
Teignmouth. It is better not to think of this parade as one
goes out of Dawlish on a bicycle ; for the road is inf. . . . . . ,
well, it is not level, and the parade would be much nicer.
However, the distance is short ; there are some fine views to

console the perspiring rider ; and when he comes warily down
the last crooked hill, he will doubtless find Teignmouth looking
extremely beautiful.

For it is not in midsummer when the air is thick with heat,
and sky and sea are of a steady blue, that this coast is at its
best.   It should be visited in the spring, while the sky is still a
trifle watery, while the clouds floating over Haldon have
density and weight, and their shadows lie darkly here and there
upon the sea.   Then the colour of that wide and sunny bay is
at its loveliest.   Far away in the east the white cliffs of Beer
and Seaton gleam and shine, and a soft blue line behind them
can be followed out to sea till it is lost in haze just where we
know that the Chesil beach and the Isle of Portland lie.   In
the nearer distance a curving line of low red rock sweeps
round past Budleigh to the wide estuary out of which we came
this morning ; and nearer still the blood-red promontory of
Dawlish ends in an island rock, pierced by a natural arch,
through which the blue sea glimmers warmly.   On the other
hand one does not see the harbour, but the red bluff that
marks its opening, and which here is called " The Ness," stands
up finely bearing woods which are cool and dark in the deep
morning shadow ; and beyond, far away to Hope's Nose and
the Leadstone, stretches a long black line of coast, waiting the
veering of the light which will bring it all to sparkle with life
and colour.

To some of us who love the west it seems as if it were at
Teignmouth that it properly begins.   For here is the first of the
true west country ports,—a little town huddled in the warmest
corner of the hills, where neither west nor east wind can bite it
or molest it, a tidal estuary left almost bare twice every day, a
harbour of floating seaweed and green limpid water, where
half a dozen ships lie canting over in the shallows, a race of
honest kindly slow speaking people, to whom the soil and
climate seem to have communicated their own warmth and
geniality—such is Teignmouth, a place of which the very

memory carries with it a warm ray of sunshine, and the salt
odour of the wind that rushes up the valley when the tide
begins to flow.

Teignmouth has not the glorious past history of Plymouth,
Fowey or Dartmouth.   Nature denied it a deep water harbour;
and unless the entrance has altered vastly for the worse, the
sandbanks which leave only a shifting channel must have been
an effectual impediment to any such greatness as was attained
by those ports which the largest ships can enter at any hour of
day or night.   And so Teignmouth was not the starting-place of
great expeditions; nor does it seem to have tasted the fearful
pleasures of private war, such as often drew Fowey and
Dartmouth into battle with the French when the rest of
England was at peace.   However, the town had its share of
tribulations, having been burnt in 1340, "about Lammas," by
some French who are naturally described as "pirates," though
knowing what we do about the gentle ways of Devon sailors in
past ages, we need not set down the piracy as existing only on one
side.   It was three centuries and a half before the French were
seen again in Teignmouth, at a moment of deep shame for
England, when her captains having sallied out together with
the Dutch to fight De Tourville, held aloof and left the
Hollanders to be crushed.   Devotion to the Stuarts was
probably the motive of this base action, for William of Orange
was newly seated on the throne, and the allegiance of the
people was divided.   Never had the coasts of Devon been in
greater danger; but the peril roused the courage of the west;
and what happened may be told in the words of a broadside
headed " Great Newes from Teignmouth, Torbay and Exon,"
which was doubtless written by an eyewitness of the events.

" The French fleet," says this brown old document, " having
been on our coast for several days past, sometimes coasting
about, other times at anchor in Torbay, has had this good
effect, as to put us in a very good posture of defence.   On
Saturday morning about daybreak, the whole fleet, being with

their galleys, about one hundred and twenty sail, weighed
anchor and stood in for a small fishery village called Teignmouth.   About five o'clock the galleys drew very near the shore
of the said place, their men of war at the same time played
their cannon on the shoar for the space of about an hour or an
hour and a half, which scared the poor inhabitants from their
cottages, they first taking with them what of any value so short

Teignmouth Harbour.

a warning and great fright would permit them.   The inhabitants
being fled, the invaders immediately landed their men in their
long boat to the number of one thousand foot, who being no
sooner come in shoar but they presently set the town on fire ;
which was soon done, there being never a house in the place
but was thatched except the parson's, which was covered with
Cornish slate.   They likewise burnt two or three fishermen's
boats in the river and the beacon, and plundered some other
straggling houses.

" Upon the news of this villainous attempt and bold
invasion, the militia of the county, horse and foot, immediately
made a body and marched after the invaders, shewing a great
deal of zeal and resolution to serve their Majesties and country
upon this extraordinary occasion. . . . The invaders having
intelligence by their scouts of the posture of our forces and that
we were moving towards them, they immediately prepared for to
return to their ships. . . . They landed seven or eight small
pieces of cannon just by the shoar side to play on our horse in
case we came too quick upon them. . ."

Thus ended this small invasion ; and may all invasions end
as well, which is as much as to say, in other words, may all
invaders land in Devon or in Cornwall.   But it is time to pass
onwards, crossing the harbour by its long wooden bridge,
traversing the little village of Shaldon, and climbing the hill
road which crosses the shoulder of the Ness.   There is an easy
way which may be followed through Newton Abbot to Torquay ;
but it lacks the great beauty of this undulating coast road,
which sweeps round the very margin of the cliff across a ridge
so lofty that the view extends not only far out to sea on the
one hand, where fishing boats plough to and fro across winding lanes of beryl green round banks of watery indigo, but on
the other stretches out over a fine broken country of hill and
valley rising at length, on the blue horizon, into that great
barrier of jagged Tors which hides the wonderland of the moor.
There are the twin peaks of Heytor. Rippon Tor and the Saddle
tower further west among a number of lesser hills, all barring
access to that great boss of granite, that wild central table-land,
out of which Devon draws its rivers, its keen fresh breezes, and
the greater part of its vast store of tradition and romance.

Now this road in which we are engaged is most dangerously
seductive.   Here is Labrador, when we have hardly got up the
first hill, calling us off the road to clamber down its steep cliff
path and sit in the pretty tea house, where so many lads and
lasses go from Teignmouth on summer evenings to eat cream

and whatever fruit may be in season, and talk of heaven
knows what, while looking out over a sea view as fine as any it is
possible to find in this region of rocks which, to use Barham's
pungent expression, "Look like Anchovy sauce spread upon
toast." It is so rare to find culinary language fitting scenery
that the acute perception and nice taste for colour shown in
this comparison deserve ungrudging recognition. We have no
sooner torn ourselves away from Labrador than a lane appears
upon the other hand inviting us to stray down to the lovely
villages seen nestling among trees at the foot of the ridge, and
having sturdily pushed past this peril, there is a constant
succession of diversions,—Maidencombe, where there is a
waterfall upon the shore, Watcombe, which owns the best red
potter's clay in England, as the Romans knew, who used it
largely, and Babbacombe, where man has tried to paint the
lily, and has spoilt it in the process, as he always does. All
these are places where everybody lingers, and lingers wisely ;
for indeed there is no end to the sunny beauties of this warm
red coast, whose peculiar property it is to break into inlets of
shape more exquisite than can be seen elsewhere from Portland
to the Lizard.

We must go past them all, past even Anstey's Cove, that
exquisite bay which, if seen when a warm sun is sinking low
on a still evening, seems fitter for some unsubstantial fairy
land than for a portion of this solid earth, and so one passes on
towards Hope's Nose, and stands at length upon the point
itself, looking down upon the great expanse of all Torbay
lying at one's feet.

It is a very noble and moving view which lies below. High
precipices of limestone wall the bay upon the nearer side,
broken into masses of green verdure, and cut by terraces and
lovely gardens over which the eye runs from point to point still
catching some new beauty, still dwelling on some fine contrast
of rich plantation and dark crag and gloomy pinewood skirting
the rich purple of the ocean, till wearied by the gleam of the

white rock, it drops upon the sea, all smooth and oily, unbroken
by the faintest ripple save two long trails which follow the wake
of a white yacht creeping in around the Leadstone.   Far across
the wide bay a few smoking chimneys catch the eye ; and
looking closer, one recognises Brixham, and thinks of how on
that great day three centuries ago when the Spanish cannon
went roaring up the Channel, and the sound echoed all round
this empty bay, Drake brought in the huge galleon *Capitana*,
the first prize captured in that terrible series of engagements,
and left her with all her treasure in charge of the Brixham
fishermen, staying only to tear out of her clumsy hold the
powder which at that moment was more to him than treasure,
and send it flying after the English ships in the swiftest of the
Brixham fishing boats, famed then as now for their fine sailing.

As one glances over the wide expanse of sheltered anchorage
which lies between Hope's Nose and Berry Head, the wonder
grows that until quite modern times no other towns planted
themselves upon this noble bay than little Brixham, which has
never conceived any higher destiny than fish, or still smaller
Paignton, which was an ordinary sleepy seaside village.   One
might have looked to find some great city on a site so fit for
shipping, sending forth its argosies into all lands and amassing
riches by successful commerce.   And such a city might have
stood upon Torbay had not the entrance been so wide.   For
in those early days when seaport towns first rose along this
coast, the seas were so unsafe that the first consideration was
defence ; and in the long desultory wars which Devon and
Cornwall waged with Brittany, when each side ravaged the
other's territory without mercy, slaughtering and plundering for
the mere joy of pillage, the houses in a port whose entrance
could not be blocked would have been the first to smoke, and
would have been ravaged by every corsair who sailed out from
St. Malo.   For this reason the early ports grew in places like
Dartmouth or Fowey, where a spacious harbour is approached
through a channel narrow enough to be barred by a chain

swung across nightly from side to side ; and Plymouth in those
distant times confined her shipping to Catwater, which was
secured by a chain in just the same way. And because this was
impossible at Torbay, this noble haven lay waste and idle all
through those centuries, and worse than idle because its shelter,
which could not be utilised for commerce, was freely open to
those who preyed on commerce. Pirates and privateers of
every nation could enter safely into this wide bay ; and as the
anchorages under Berry Head were most convenient stations
on which to lie in wait for shipping which went or came to
Dartmouth, it was a common thing a century or two ago to see
strange vessels lurking there of such appearance that prudent
captains gave them a wide berth. Nay even the French fleet
which, as told above, ventured to burn Teignmouth, did not
hesitate to anchor in Torbay, where it rode quite safely for
some days ; and indeed the bay gradually acquired a reputation
for being a place where almost anything in reason might go on
without fear of interruption, which doubtless explains why the
Prince of Orange chose to land there. After he had come and
gone other less reputable characters continued to haunt the
bay. It was seen in the last chapter that the barns of Mr.
Cary at Tor Abbey and Mr. Mallock at Cockington were often
packed with smuggled goods, doubtless without the connivance
of those gentlemen, but none the less to the exceeding profit
of some person or persons unknown and to the loss of that
common enemy the revenue. Jack Rattenbury too was well
acquainted with Torbay, which must have been a merry playground for him and for his kind ; and not to dilate further on
those wild old manners of which we shall never know the details
now, it may be said generally that the quick growth and
adolescence of the town of Torquay has put an end to a life
far more romantic than its own, and those who find health and
amusement in its pretty streets and drives must balance such
gains against the loss of all chance of witnessing a fight with
smugglers or of being abducted by a pirate.

Need I say that Torbay is like the bay of Naples? Why stick at such a statement when you hear it all about you. All English bays are like the bay of Naples. Swansea bay resembles it with singular exactness, even to the smoke of Landore ironworks, which is so like Vesuvius. Bideford bay is like it too, and yet is not at all like Torbay nor Swansea bay, while St. Ives bay which is very different from all the rest, is as like Naples as twin sisters, having even a little Capri at the entrance. What could be more exact? Why go abroad when all the beauties of the Mediterranean are five hours from town?

I do not wish to carp, but I am weary of hearing of the Bay of Naples. Torbay is far too beautiful to need the help of any such comparison, and need wish nothing better than to be like itself. Of Torquay, so modern and so beautiful, there is not much to say, it is a town of bands and pleasure parties, and high cliffs and pretty gardens, of tennis parties and pleasant picnics, and other forms of butterfly existence which are charming to take part in, but apt to seem a thought too trivial when written down.

Now the weight of historical associations in Torbay is all upon the western side, at Paignton and at Brixham, and in both cases the best known memories are those of the third William, who landed at the latter place rather more than two centuries ago, and of whose march there are still plenty of living recollections. But before we begin to speak of them there is another subject that claims attention. For it is not William of Orange who forms the chief glory of Paignton ; nor is it Miles Coverdale, who is fondly thought to have translated the Bible in an ancient tower by the church. Still less is it the church or the exquisite chantry it contains, or the memory of any one of the ancient families connected with the place. Of all these distinctions the man of Paignton is modestly conscious ; but what makes him swell with pride is the recollection of the Paignton Pudding.

It is in a note on the MS. autobiography of Dr. James Yonge, so Mr. Worth tells us, that we find our first reference to this mighty dish. " Paynton " says the doctor, who flourished about

1680, "Paynton was anciently a borough town, and, as is sayd, held her charter by a Whitepot—whence Devonshire men are soe called—which was to be seven yeares making, seven baking and seven eating." Now the doctor may or may not have been right in saying that the term " Whitepot" adhered to men of Devon. Certainly the Cornish call them " Dumplings " when much irritated, and the Devon men retaliate with the injurious epithet of " Pasties," and then peace is no longer worth hoping for, but both sides proceed to argue with their fists, as actually happened not long ago when the militia of the two counties were called out for training on the same ground. But to return to the pudding. It may or may not be a "Whitepot," but it certainly does not occupy seven years in either making, baking or eating. In fact it is only once every fifty years that the construction of the pudding is undertaken. It was made in 1809; and it may be interesting to append the recipe. The ingredients were as follows :— 400 pounds of flour, 170 pounds of beef suet, 140 pounds of raisins, and 240 eggs. Picture what a mountain it must have made ! This gargantuan pudding was kept constantly boiling in a brewer's copper from Saturday morning to the Tuesday following, when it was placed on a car decorated with ribbons, evergreens, etc., and drawn along the street by eight oxen. Thus far a newspaper of the date just mentioned. Fifty years later, namely, in 1859, the pudding had grown even larger. This time it required twenty-five horses to draw it round the town ; and, having been found a trifle stodgy on the last occasion, it was baked instead of boiled. There were a number of navvies working in the town, and all these worthy men walked behind the pudding, pleasingly clad in white, waiting anxiously the moment when each would get his share, and the great pudding melt in their expectant mouths.

Paignton is a pleasant place, irrespective of its pudding, possessing a long open beach where the air is vastly fresher than at Torquay ; and a fine old church of ruddy sandstone, in which is a screen of white Beer stone closing in the Kirkham chantry, which screen is so richly and exquisitely carved that its like is not to be found in any parish church in Devon. A modern town is growing fast around the ancient village; but one can still find the streets and buildings of the older time, the inn where William of Orange slept, and many a thatched cob cottage, in one of which that old sailor, William Adams, may have dwelt, of whom Prince tells so strange a story, collected doubtless by himself on some summer evening when he had strolled down from his vicarage at Berry Pomeroy to talk with the sailors on Paignton beach.

Adams was one of those "Turkish captives" of whom so many were languishing in Algiers two centuries ago, and who, there is little doubt, were specially in the minds of the authors of the petition in our Litany, "For all poor prisoners and captives." Indeed those miserable men were in sore need of the prayers offered in their own village churches by their happier friends at home; and it may very well be that Adams' name was coupled with this prayer on many a Sunday in Paignton Church; for the agony of his captivity lasted full five years. "At the end of that time," says Prince, "he and his companions resolved to contrive the model of a boat which, being formed in parcels and afterwards put together, might form the instrument of their deliverance. One of them was allowed a cellar and in this they began their work. They provided a piece of timber twelve feet long to make the keil; but because it was impossible to convey a piece of that length out of the city, they cut it in two and fitted it for jointing just in the middle; then they provided ribs, after which, to make the boat water-tite, because boards would require much hammering and the noise would be likely to betray them, they bought as much strong canvass as would cover the boat twice over. Upon the convex of the carine they provided also so much pitch and tar and tallow as would serve to make a kind of tarpauling cere-cloth to swaddle the naked body of their infant boat. Of two pipe-staves sawed across from corner to corner they made two things to serve for oars ; and for provision they got a little bread and two leather bottles full of fresh water, and remembered also to buy as much canvass as would serve for a sail. They carried out all these things in parts and parcels, fitted them together in the valley, about half a mile from the sea ; into which four of them carried the boat on their shoulders and the rest followed them. At the sea side they stripped, put their clothes into the boat, and thrusting her so far into the sea as they could, they all seven got into her, but finding she was overladen, two were content to stay on shore."

One would willingly know the names of these two noble fellows, but Prince has not recorded them. Adams was one of the five left on board. " June 30th, 1644, they launched out into the deep, where they saw the wonders of God," and after immense suffering, which Prince describes as if he loved it, they landed at " Mayork," where they were well treated by the Spaniards and assisted home to England.

" A most bold adventure," Prince says it was ; but we might more truly call it a counsel of despair, to which men could be driven by nothing but the imminence of awful suffering, and this is what makes the story interesting after all these years ; for the fate which Adams and his companions dared so much to escape was that of great numbers of poor seamen, as will appear more clearly when we come to speak of the ravages of the Sallee rovers. As for Adams who in the judgment of his eulogist was "a very honest sensible man," he died " in the year of our Lord 1687, "and his body, so like to be buried in the sea and to feed fishes, lies buried in Paynton churchyard, where it feasteth worms." Dear old Prince. How fond he was of charnel-houses !

There is a pleasant road from Paignton along the western cliff to Brixham, crossing the golf links at Churston, and a high spur of ground beyond them, whence it drops into the ancient town of Brixham, where the houses cling in true west-country fashion to the sides of a wide cleft falling steeply to the harbour. The streets are narrow, winding, and obviously very old; there are little flights of steps ascending here and there to higher levels, fish cellars jutting out over the dwelling-house below, wide quays filled with empty crates and baskets smelling horribly of fish, a harbour where, when it is not packed with trawlers, the seagulls fight and scream all day for the refuse scattered by the fishermen—it is just such another town as Newlyn, or Mevagissey, or Port Isaac, though the Brixham men, who are not among the most modest of God's creation, would resent highly the comparison. For does not Brixham produce the best fish along the coast? Have not its fishermen become lords of the manor? Did they not give a king to England, whose statue, to say nothing of his footprint, stands to this day on Brixham quay, testifying to the favour he showed that Protestant town of very evil savours by landing there? What if Brixham had prevented him from landing? Where would England have been then? And to descend from high state policy to art—if that be indeed a drop—is it not well known how greatly the Brixham men have excelled in all generations for sweet singing? What says the ancient song?

> In Brixham town so rare,
> For singing sweet and fair,
> None can with us compare;
> 　We bear away the bell.
> Extolled up and down
> By men of high renown,
> We go from town to town,
> 　And none can us excel.

It is their own testimony; but let us take it, and have no more comparisons; for there is a good deal to say about King William's landing, and we have not time to wrangle with the fishermen about their own superiority.

Most people are aware that it was on the 5th November, 1689, that the fleet carrying the Protestant deliverer approached the shores of Devon. From the diary of one Whittle, who

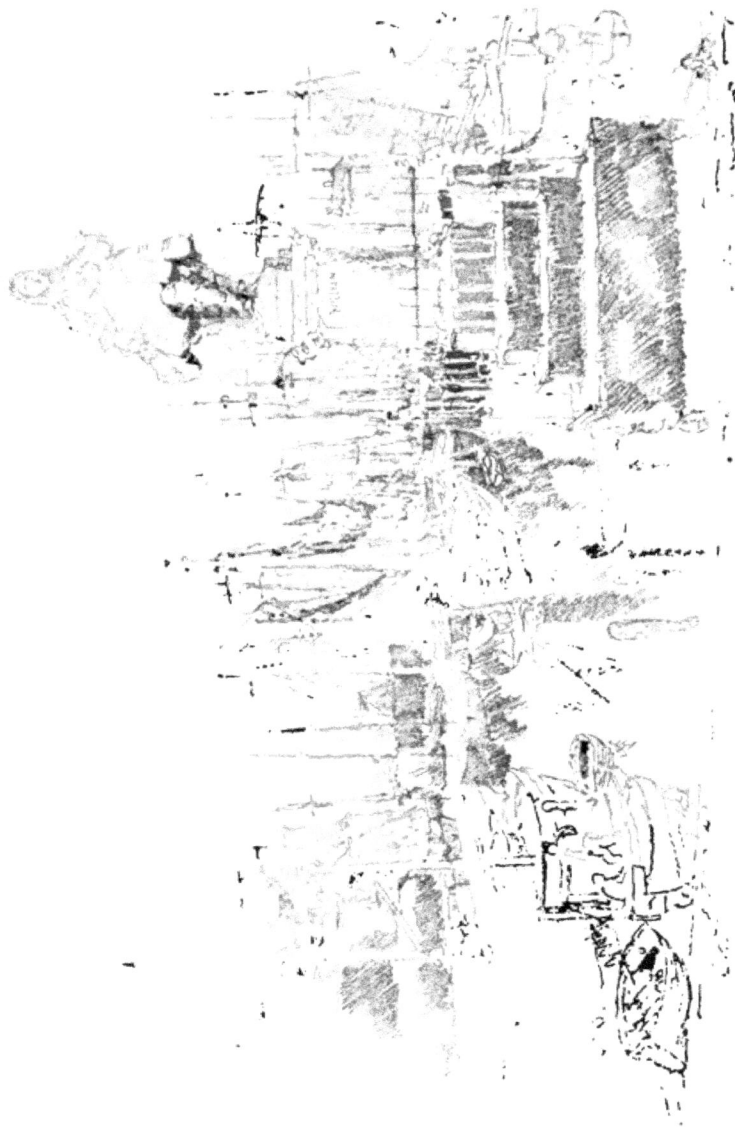

Brixham—Statue of William of Orange.

was a chaplain of the fleet, we learn that it was a foggy morning; but ". . . the sun, recovering strength, soon dissipated the fog, insomuch that it proved a very pleasant day. Now every vessel set out its colours, which made a very pleasant show. By this time the people of Devonshire thereabout had discovered the fleet; the one telling the other thereof, they came flocking in droves to the side or brow of the hills to view us; some guessed we were French because they saw divers white flags; but the standard of the Prince, the motto of which was "For the Protestant religion and liberty," soon undeceived them. . . . The major part of the fleet being come into the bay, boats were ordered to carry the Prince on shore with his guards; and passing towards the land with sundry lords, the Admiral of Rotterdam gave divers guns at his landing. The boat was held lengthways till he was on shore; so after he had set his foot on land, then came all the lords and guards, some going before the Prince's sacred person and some coming after."

Whittle does not tell us the stock story of the Prince's landing,—how he paused at some distance from the quay, saying, "If I am welcome, come and carry me ashore." Whereupon a little man plunged into the water and carried his future monarch to the steps of the pier, and afterwards rode before him bareheaded all the way to Exeter. But he adds a picturesque description of the scene as he saw it. "The people came running out at the doors to see the happy sight. So the Prince, with Mareschal Schomberg and divers lords, knights and gentlemen, marched up the hill, which all the fleet could see over the houses, the colours flying and flourishing before his Highness, the trumpets sounding, the hoit-boys played, the drums beat, and the lords, knights, gentlemen and guards shouted, and sundry huzzas did now echo in the fleet from off the hill, so that our very hearts below in the water were even ravished for joy thereof."

Meantime, while they were getting on thus cheerfully in

(To face p. 76.

They came flocking to the side of the hills to view us.

Protestant Brixham, equal satisfaction was being felt in Catholic quarters near at hand, though with less reason. "At the upper

Brixham Harbour.

end of Torbay," Whittle tells us, "there is a fair house belonging to one Mr. Carey, a very rigid Papist, who entertained a priest in his house. This priest going to recreate himself upon the leads, it being a most delightsome day, as he was walking there, he happened to cast his eye upon the sea, and espying the fleet at a distance, withal being purblind in his eyes, as well as blinded by Satan in his mind, he presently concludes that 'twas the French navy come to land the sons of Belial which should cut off the children of God . . . and being transported with joy, he hastened to inform his own disciples of the house and forthwith they sang Te Deum."

It cannot have been long ere the exultant Catholics were undeceived; for twenty-six regiments had been landed at Brixham before night fell, and the news was spreading far and wide.   It is curious to see how little fear was inspired by the landing of fifteen thousand foreign soldiers.   People actually walked over from Totnes after morning service the next day to see the army, in absolute confidence that no violence would be offered them; while as for the peasants, they did their utmost to bring in supplies for so great a number of men, and coming to the top of the hills set apples rolling down into the town, where the soldiers scrambled for them.   Surely never in all history was the work of an invader so fully done from the moment of his landing.   The country was won.   The county magnates were already meeting in secret to decide their attitude; and those who were for supporting King James were few.   A few days of hesitation and anxiety ended in the accession of Sir Edward Seymour of Berry Pomeroy, and thenceforth the game was won.

Some five-and-twenty years afterwards the Duke of Ormond took it into his head that as Queen Anne was just dead, and the people of England might be supposed to be something less than elated at receiving a sovereign from Hanover who did not know their language, it might be worth while to see whether another invasion could not be brought off at the same spot where the last had been so brilliantly successful.   Accordingly he repaired to Brixham in a French ship, and on coming off the port fired three guns, as a signal for the gentry to rise to his assistance. Unfortunately nobody paid the least attention, except the Custom-house officers, who asked prosaically chilling questions ; and the end of the Duke's enterprise was that he was nearly drowned in going back to France.

CHAPTER V

THERE is but one course to set on leaving the infinite beauties of Torbay. One road only leads to the upper waters of the Dart, that famous stream which has in all ages so touched the imagination of the dwellers in the west that they still personify it, and speak of it as if it lived, not as a dead thing haunted by a demon, but as possessed itself of life, a sentient creature conscious of its actions, one to be feared and loved. To the peasants who dwell upon its banks the Dart is "He," and is so spoken of with a conscious undertone of awe, such as one might use of a beautiful savage animal whose caresses were apt to be broken suddenly by moods of anger which not those who knew him longest could foretell. And this is exactly the character of the Dart; for the clear, brown noisy river is sometimes swollen by sudden freshets from the moor so high that the shallow fords through which carts are used to drive with ease are changed quickly into raging torrents, and the black waters leap down, boiling angrily six or seven feet deep where half an hour earlier one could see the spotted trout glancing by between the sunny boulders.

A stream so passionate and changeable may well seem to be endowed with life. And it comes, too, charged with all the odours of the moor, brown and sparkling, carrying down the scents of furze and purple heather and the keen air of wide stretching uplands, and all the infinite traditions of that wild region where the fears and fancies of mankind have run riot during countless generations ; and so comes leaping down the valley through cool shady pools where trout and salmon

Street in Totnes.

slumber through the heat, and goes splashing over weirs and by deep overhanging woods till at hoary old Totnes it is swallowed by the salt tide rushing up from Dartmouth, and so

G

ends a course of which not one mile is tame or dull, but from
source to sea it is all beautiful and charged with memories of
famous men.

Now Totnes being the limit of the salt water in the Dart,
the parting line of river and estuary, is the place to which one
naturally turns ; and it is approached from Paignton by one of
the pleasantest of roads, undulating for the most part easily
enough. When the first high ground is reached, there is an
outlook over a country gloriously undulating, a land of warm
red earth, over which the springing corn is casting its first
green flush. The rounded hills are cultivated to the summit,
rich and fertile, the same hills on which old Prince looked
forth when he penned his immortal boasting preface which
still contains so large a measure of truth. " Heretofore more
than now," he tells us, " Devon was aspera et nemorosa, rough
and woody, hilly and mountainous, wild and rocky. But now, by
the matchless labour and industry of its inhabitants, it yields a
great abundance of all things which the earth, air or water can
afford for the use of man. And that not only as to necessaries,
but delicacies also ; and what might be desired by a Helio-
gabalus or an Apicius may here be found."

On what had Prince been banqueting when he wrote these
words ? His vicarage lies down there upon the left at Berry
Pomeroy, but little changed since its most famous tenant was
carried to his sleep under those old arches where his voice had
been heard so many Sundays of his life. We will go down and
see the place ; for he who told the lives of so many worthies
was himself not the least worthy of them all ; and if one
sometimes reads his great work with a smile, it is far more
often with an answering throb of sympathy for that strong
local patriotism which in Devon, as elsewhere, was the fount
of noble deeds, and may be so again, when the county wakes
from its long slumber, and begins once more to remember how
it led all England, not once or twice, but for many generations.

The best road to Berry is that which turns off on the right

within a mile of Totnes ; and from the parting of the ways it is but a little distance down a gentle hill to the old red church, which like all others in this part of England shows a few fragments of an earlier and more interesting building worked in among the eternal Perpendicular which is so common in the west. It is a tiny village shaded by huge chestnut trees, a pleasant nook where life goes easily and all things seem to breathe that gentle optimism which made the good man declare that he "delighted not in that stinking employment of weeding men's lives, and throwing the nauseous trash upon their tombs," but inclined him to gentle judgments and soft excuses such as we may hope he dealt out among his parishioners.

A steep hill leads up past the church towards the castle, which was long one of the first estates in Devon and is still its finest ruin. It stands among high woods on the shoulder of a hill, over which the road drops so steeply that it seems to be descending to the very bottom of the valley. It is not so, however, for the castle is built on a bluff so lofty as to give colour to the tale told by the guides of some old Pomeroy who, at the end of a long siege, finding that his castle must needs fall, mounted his horse in full armour, and blowing his bugle in token of surrender, leapt down the precipice and was dashed in pieces.

This is the story of "The Rime of the Duchess May," and is probably told of many other castles. But there is another tale which is peculiar to Berry, and which may very well preserve the memory of some actual tragedy occurring in those days when there was none to question any action that the Pomeroy thought proper to commit. There are still to be seen beside the ruined gateway of the castle the overgrown remains of the old pleasaunce. Tall trees have sprouted now and grown to maturity among the flower beds ; but in the days when the winding walks were cleared and the sunny corner underneath the walls was gay with flowers, a son of the

Pomeroys surprised his sister in an arbour with an enemy of
their house.   How or where he slew them is not known ; but
there is a winding passage just within the castle entrance which
after running for some distance through the thickness of the
walls, widens out into a deep recess, and here it may be that
the deed was done.   For on moonlight nights, the silvery
glimmer falling through a high embrasure, reveals two shadowy
figures, man and woman, parted by the width of this recess,
pitifully struggling to reach and touch each other across the
empty space, but held back by some power stronger than
their love, still withholding from them after all these years of
death that satisfaction which the cruelty of Pomeroy denied
them in their life.

The ruin is a curious mixture of baronial strength with the
peaceful grandeur of Tudor domestic architecture.   Behind the
grim old Norman gatehouse rises a mere shell of empty
windows, through which the blue sky shines, making the
shattered wreck a far more lovely sight than it could have been
in the days of its magnificence, when it was the work of one
servant merely to open and shut the windows daily ; and the
great family of Seymour kept here a state which was almost
kingly.   It is all very still and silent now ; and the jackdaws
chatter away among the ivy quite undisturbed.   The people regard
the scene of so much dead life with a little nervousness, and
are not very fond of going there after the light begins to change.

We have hardly travelled back to the point at which we left
the main road before we catch sight of Totnes lying on the
hillside just above that point where a greater richness of
vegetation marks the position of the river, and straying some
distance down towards the bank.   In coming down the hill
the valley opens on the right, and we see the pretty bridge
spanning the wide stream, and the winding course which it makes
downwards from the hills.   And here one hesitates like the ass
between the two bundles of hay, having the Upper Dart on one
hand and the estuary with Dartmouth on the other, a choice

which it is better to resolve by going up the river first, and
leaving Totnes itself to be seen on the way to Dartmouth.

And so we turn off the main street of Totnes a little distance
from the foot of the town, and follow a pretty winding road,
past the station and up the valley, skirting rich woods, and
bordering the river till Dartington is reached and passed, and a
small *détour* brings us down to Staverton, where the river flashes
brightly underneath the arches of a gray stone bridge, casting
off the smooth even surface with which it slipped beneath the
bridge at Totnes, and breaking more and more with every reach
it makes into the character of a mountain torrent.   Here where
the cool shadow of the bridge interrupts the sparkle of the
sunshine, and the ivy trailing from the parapet is reflected leaf
by leaf in the transparent pool below, left as the water swirls
round a boulder, it is already possible to understand how great
the force must be with which the river rushes down when it is
angered by cloud bursts among the hills.   Some years ago, not
far above this point, a farmer and his wife were crossing in a
cart by a ford which was well known to them, and usually as
safe as the high road, when they saw a freshet coming.   The
farmer tried to turn his horse and regain the bank, but the
effort did no more than seal their fate.   The rush of water
struck the cart, and carried all away.   It was three weeks before
the man was found.   The woman's body was taken from
a tree which overhung the bank, while the cart and horse were
found floating under Totnes bridge.

> " River of Dart, river of Dart,
>   Every year thou claimest a heart."

The note of warning in this traditional couplet is not to be
despised ; for the Dart has all the treachery of a beautiful wild
animal ; and the force of its current cannot be estimated from
the bank.   In these lower waters the danger is less than on the
moor, where there is a resistless force in the steady glassy slides
which from the shore look so smooth and safe.

When, leaving Staverton behind, we rejoin the road to Buckfastleigh, the river is our close companion, clear and brown and noisy. Sometimes one hears it splashing out of thick woods deep down below the road ; and then again the two are running side by side, and one sees the fish leaping where the flies are thickest. Already the road has run out of the low rounded hills of the South Hams, and has brought us into a country of steeper eminences ; for we are near the foot of the great barrier which we have watched so long ; and the time has come when we must climb it and face the steep unridable roads beyond, or lose the most exquisite country in Devon. The latter alternative is out of the question now that we have come so far ; but it is better to cross the barrier on foot than on a bicycle.

Far back in this work it was observed that as a general rule superstition clings to the granite. It is true. The granite district of the moor is the chief source of wild traditions ; and so many relics linger there of an age which has passed away elsewhere, that one who knew it better than any other living man was used to say there was to be found upon the moor almost every form of superstition which Bishop Bartholomew of Exeter condemned in his Penitential in the twelfth century. Still when a child is scalded the mother will lay her thumb upon the spot and repeat three times, " There came two angels out of the west, one brought fire, the other brought frost. Out fire, in frost. By the Father, the Son, and the Holy Ghost, Amen, Amen, Amen." And if any accident causes blood to flow, the bystanders may possibly send for a doctor, but they are more likely to undertake the cure by the aid of certain verses from the 16th chapter of Ezekiel, " And when I passed by and saw thee polluted in thine own blood "— here give the name of the person in full—" I said unto thee when thou wast in thy blood, Live, &c." The common faith in this remedy is profound. " A little while ago," said an old man, " my wife's nose burst a-bleeding in the night. She called me to say the prayer ; so I caught hold of my own nose, and brought in her name, and it very soon stopped."

The faith in pixies is dying out upon the moor, but the wild story of the Yeth hounds who hunt among the tors in stormy weather with blue flame playing from their mouths is very firmly credited, and there are many people still who have heard their baying. Indeed it is easier to believe these stories than to doubt them in the dusk evenings on the lonely roads which cross the moor ; where the very rivers make a strange moaning sound that fills the hollows of the hills, and echoes among the gloomy boulders.

But we are straying into superstition much too early. It is now high noon and the sun is shining warm and glorious upon the hillsides. Here is the town of Ashburton, ancient if not picturesque, but not worth staying for when there is so much to see and so very far to go. The town is at the foot of the hills, and the last houses are hardly left behind when the road mounts sharp and almost straight towards Buckland Tor. It is no use to speak about the gradient ; those who set themselves to climb mountains must not complain if they are steep. But at the top there is a recompense for all. The last ten minutes' climb has been among dense beech woods ; and it is worth the climb only to see the sunlight shining through the tender foliage, and falling on the mossy wall below. The road drops into what seems an absolute solitude. A fresh cool wind blows upward from the valley. On the one hand rises the high slope of Buckland Tor ; while on the other every opening in the trees gives a fresh glimpse of rough hillside and rugged valley far below. It is a country of dark and misty depths, of rough rounded hills now clothed with oak coppice all brown and golden in its first spring splendour, now no better than mere waste moorland, of which the desolation is increased by a few stunted trees. On the sides of these valleys the shadows lie dark and heavy ; the sun hardly seems to penetrate them. Another steep pitch down the winding hill, and the distant view is lost. The road is dropping through thick woods again; and somewhere close at hand there is the splashing of a brook. The bottom of the valley is almost reached, and there a mossy bridge is thrown across the stream which comes splashing down a narrow ravine among trees so thick that it is absolutely hidden till it flings itself impetuously through the arches, and washes swiftly round the boulders. A couple of thatched cottages flank the stream with sloping gabled roofs and diamond windows; it is such a deep and cool and shady spot that one turns reluctantly to the road leading forth into the hot glare again.

This is Buckland-in-the-Moor. The ancient little church lies on the hill just beyond these woods; and when one climbs above it only a short way, one sees a grand expanse of lofty rounded hills and undulating down lands, and far away in what appears to be a hollow, the tower of an old gray church standing up conspicuously. That is Widdecombe, a place popularly supposed to be a favourite haunt of the devil.

There are many stories which connect his Satanic Majesty with Widdecombe, all dating more or less from the great thunderstorm of 1638, which was certainly terrible enough to set the most careless thinking of the devil. Prince tells the story with even more than his usual impressiveness. "In the year of our Lord 1638, October 21st, being Sunday, and the congregation being gathered together in the parish church of Widecombe in the afternoon at service time, there happened a very great darkness, which increased to that degree that they could not see to read. Soon after a terrible and fearful thunder was here, like the noise of many great guns, accompanied with dreadful lightning to the great amazement of the people, the darkness still increasing that they could not see each other; when there presently came such an extraordinary flame of lightning as filled the church with fire, smoak, and a loathsome smell like brimstone; and a ball of fire came in likewise at the window and passed through the church, which so affrighted the

congregation that most of them fell down in their seats, some
upon their knees, others on their faces, and some one upon
another, crying out of burning and scalding and all giving
themselves up for dead. . . . One Mr. Mead had his head
suddenly struck against the wall in his seat with such violence
that he also died the same night. . . His son sitting by him had
no harm.   At the same instant another man had his head cloven,
his skull rent in three pieces and his brains thrown upon the
ground whole ; but the hair of his head, through the violence
of the blow, stuck fast to a pillar near him, where it remained
a woful spectacle a long time after.   Some seats in the body of
the church were turned upside down, yet those who sat in them
had little or no hurt.   One man going out of the chancel door,
his dog ran before him, who was whirled about towards the
door and fell down stark dead, upon which the master stepped
back and was preserved.   The church itself was much torn
and defaced with the thunder and lightning, a beam whereof
breaking in the midst fell down between the minister and clerk
and hurt neither.   The steeple was much wrent. . . a pinnacle
of the tower being thrown down beat thro' into the church.
There were in all four persons killed and sixty-two hurt,
divers of them having their linen burnt, tho' their outer
garments were not so much as singed.   The lightning being
passed and the people in a terrible maze, a gentleman in
the town stood up and said "Neighbours, in the name of God
shall we venture out of the church ?" To whom Mr. Lyde, the
minister, replied, "Let us make an end with prayer, for it is
better to die here than in another place."   But the people
looked about them, and seeing the church so terribly wrent and
torn over their heads, durst not proceed in the public devotions,
but went out of the church. . ."

And now for the explanation of this terrible storm.   It
appears that on this very Sunday a rider on a coal black steed
called at the inn at Poundstock and asked his way to Widdecombe.   The innkeeper's wife directed him, and brought him
a glass of ale, which to her vast terror hissed and sputtered as

it went down his throat as if it had been running over burning metal. The rider galloped off in the direction she had given; and reaching Widdecombe fastened his horse to a pinnacle of the lofty tower, and rushed into the church, where service had begun. An unfortunate boy had so far forgotten himself as to fall asleep, and this gave the devil his opportunity. He dashed at the luckless youth, caught him in his claws, and flew with him through the roof to the pinnacle where his horse was fastened, dislodging bricks and beams and the very pinnacle itself in his headlong flight, and so rode away through the air with a roar and rattle of thunder.

Now, since every one who visits this district will naturally desire to see the spot selected for so stern a reproof of a vicious habit to which many of us have yielded, it may be well to add some observations on the way thither. The plain truth is that it needs a cheerful temper and a stout heart to visit Widdecombe; and if it be indeed a fact that the stranger who called at Poundstock Inn on the day of the great storm rode away at high speed, or at any pace above a walk, the landlady who served him must have been very dull if she did not at once know him to be the devil, for nobody else could do it. It would be quite easy to write volumes on this subject. There is no vice within the reach of roads in which these byways do not wallow. They are steep beyond description. They are never level. They are covered with loose stone, so that it is impossible to ride a bicycle either up or down them. They start suddenly round sharp corners as if shying at their shadows, and then plunge madly into the ravine, resolved to cast you headlong to the bottom. There is a song known to most people born in the west, and to some who had not that good fortune, which is, properly read, neither more nor less than a parable of Dartmoor roads. It goes thus, with a comic lilt inexpressibly grateful to the ear :

> Tom Pearse, Tom Pearse, lend me thy grey mare,
> All along, down along, out along Lee ;

"*Tom Pearse's old mare her took sick and died.*"

[*To face p.* 91.

For I want for to go to Widdecombe Fair
  With Bill Brewer, Jan Stewer, Peter Gurney, Peter Davy, Dan'l
    Whiddon, Harry Hawk, Old Uncle Tom Cobleigh and all.
      Chorus: Old Uncle Tom Cobleigh and all.

Now Tom Pearse was inclined to make objections, but they were overruled with the assurance that the beast would be restored "by Friday soon, or Saturday noon." But it was not so. Tom grew anxious; and the song proceeds:

So Tom Pearse he got up to the top of the hill,
  All along, down along, out along Lee;
And he seed his old mare down a making her will,
  With Bill Brewer, Jan Stewer, Peter Gurney, Peter Davy, Dan'l
    Whiddon, Harry Hawk, Old Uncle Tom Cobleigh and all.
      Chorus: Old Uncle Tom Cobleigh and all.

It is plain enough that the poor brute had been spavined: nothing else could be expected on such roads. In fact, even that was not the worst of it, for the animal was at the point of dissolution.

So Tom Pearse's old mare her took sick and died,
  All along, down along, out along Lee;
And Tom he sat down on a stone and he cried,
  With Bill Brewer, Jan Stewer, Peter Gurney, Peter Davy, Dan'l
    Whiddon, Harry Hawk, Old Uncle Tom Cobleigh and all.
      Chorus: Old Uncle Tom Cobleigh and all.

It is thus that repentance ever comes too late; but the vivid picture drawn in this pathetic verse of eight grown men sobbing over the carcase of an old gray mare is a warning too expressive to be forgotten against the cruelty of taking a dumb animal, or even an inanimate cycle, to Widdecombe-in-the-Moor. If a man will go, let him go on foot.

Over deep ruts and jutting shoulders of the rock the road bumps along to Leusdon, and at last it rises on a kind of terrace sweeping round an exquisite valley filled with furze and bronzing oaks and sloping fields, up which sheep are grazing. Far off, yet not so far that one cannot see the jags and clefts of the riven granite, towers the lofty breastwork of the moor, its great slopes parted into fields both red and green, for these fringes of the moor are by no means barren. It is setting towards late afternoon. The glitter has gone out of the sunlight, and a tinge of purple is being blown across the hills. There is a sound of rushing water in the air, which leads one on down the most precipitous of slopes, beneath the shadow of a fine mass of rock made glorious with bluebells and with springing ferns, to a point where the river valley takes a double reach, and the stream is seen both right and left, a wide brawling torrent, filling the bottom with its hoarse voice. On the nearer side there are wide marshy meadows, over which a drove of forest ponies go snuffing the short grass ; but beyond the stream the woods are steep and high, their spring foliage all bronze and gold and tender green, while here and there tall clefts of gray rock break the mass of colour with a touch of sternness. It is absolutely solitary by the stream. There is no sound but that of the river, sinking now into a low murmur, now rising to a loud noise almost like a scream, as the water tears over some stonier impediment.

Just at the highest point of the bow into which the stream is forced by the jutting of the hills, a gray stone bridge is thrown across it. This is New Bridge ; and the level grass by the ivied parapet was a very famous haunt of pixies in the days when that frolicsome little people still held their antics on the moor. Farm lads returning late from harvest work on summer evenings on the uplands used to see them often dancing in the moonlight in rings beside the river, and hear their sweet silvery choruses rising on the clear air. These were the true fairies of romance, not imps or gnomes such as are more common in Cornwall, but pretty little people clad in green, more fond of doing kindness than of mischief. And where on the wide earth could they find a playground more beautiful than this?

The coppice surges down from the hilltops like a cataract of golden water. On every side the tors fall deep and scarred into the narrow winding valley. The bridge is stained with a thousand shades of brown and orange lichen, its buttresses are cushions of soft moss ; and underneath its arches long trails of ivy and of wandering Jew droop in the cool shadow towards the gleaming pebbles, brown, red, green, and purple, which lie sparkling underneath the clear, dark water.

Ah, exquisite New Bridge ! How often in the dust and glare of city streets the roar and murmur of the river returns upon the ear !

Among the tales of Dartmoor pixies collected by Mr. Crossing in *The Western Antiquary* there is one so weird and so truly illustrating the strange thrill produced in even unimaginative people by the approach of winter twilight in this valley, through which the rushing of the river seems to rise and fall like a sighing wind, that it may fitly terminate this chapter ; and with slight omissions, I shall give it in Mr. Crossing's very picturesque words.

"At Dartmeet the east and west branches of the river mingle, and the course of the united stream is through a deep and narrow valley. On the left rises the conical hill of Sharp Tor, and on the slope of this hill stands a solitary farmhouse called Rowbrook, overlooking the valley below. At this farm a boy was once employed to tend cattle, a quiet inoffensive lad. One winter evening he came hurriedly into the kitchen, exclaiming that he heard some one calling, and imagined it must be a person in distress. The farm labourers round the fire rose with alacrity . . . quickly gained the spot and paused to listen. Nothing but the sound of the rushing river met their ears, and the men declared the boy must have been mistaken. He however declared he was not ; and as if to bear him out . . . a voice was suddenly heard at no great distance calling out 'Jan coo, Jan coo.'

"The men shouted in reply, when the voice ceased. Lights

were procured and they searched round the spot ; but no trace
of any one could be seen ; and so after spending some further
time in calling . . . they re-entered the house, not knowing what
to think. The next night . . . the boy rushed in with
the information that the voice might again be heard. Up
jumped the men, and running to the spot intently listened.
Out on the stillness of the night came the voice calling again
' Jan coo, Jan coo.' They looked at each other, but shouted
not in reply . . . and again upon the night air came the cry
' Jan coo, Jan coo.' At which they gave a lusty shout, but
waited in vain for any answer . . . 'Tes the pisgies, I'll warn '
said an old man . . . ' Ees, that's what that is, vor sartain ; an'
us had better let un bide an' not meddle wi un,' said another,
and it was consequently determined to take no further notice
of the strange voice.

"The winter had nearly passed away . . . when the lad with
one of the labourers was mounting the slope that stretched from
the house down to the river. Suddenly the voice was heard in
Langmarsh pit on the opposite side of the river, calling as before,
' Jan coo, Jan coo.' The boy instantly shouted in reply, when
instead of the calls ceasing as on the occasions when the men
had replied to them, they were heard again, ' Jan coo, Jan coo.'

" ' I'll go and see what it is,' exclaimed the boy, and
commenced to run down the hill towards the river. The
many boulders in its rocky bed afford crossing places at
certain points known to those in its vicinity, and to one of these
the boy made his way. His companion watched him but a
short distance, for in the deepening twilight he was speedily
lost to view, but as the man continued his ascent of the hill the
voice still came from Langmarsh pit, ' Jan coo, Jan coo.' Again
as he approached the farmhouse could he hear it, and as he
neared the door the sounds yet rang in the valley, ' Jan coo,
Jan coo.' Gaining the threshold he paused before entering
with his hand on the string that raised the latch and listened
for the voice once more. It had ceased. He waited some

time, and seeking the kitchen he related what had
happened . . . hour after hour passed away, but the boy came
not.   No tidings of him were ever heard, and from that time
the voice ceased its nightly calls."

NOTE.—The reason of the omission from this chapter of all mention of
the Buckland Drives and the " Lover's Leap," is that the owner of the
property has recently forbidden access to pedestrians as well as to cyclists ;
and has thus restricted the opportunity of visiting those famous spots
to invalids and children, or to others who travel as they do.

CHAPTER VI

THE town of Totnes, as was stated in the last chapter, has strayed out of the girdle of its old enclosure of walls and towers and wandered down to the bank of the lovely river. But by this rambling it has not lost the shape or aspect of a fortified town; for the first sight that strikes a visitor who has crossed the bridge and sets foot in Fore Street, is the arch of Eastgate, spanning the steep roadway half way up the hill, testifying to the old importance of the place. And when he passes through the gateway he will find a town whose house fronts still bear witness to that fine taste in architecture and carving which distinguished English merchants three centuries ago. Indeed the antiquity of Totnes is literally fabulous. For does not Geoffrey of Monmouth cut straight back past all history of Norman, Saxon, Dane or Early Briton, past even Roman influence, to the very origin of Rome itself, and base the history of Totnes on a sure foundation of the coming of the Trojans? For Brutus of Troy, having wandered much further than did pious Æneas, though he found no poet to sing his fame, came at last to the inlet of the Dart, guided surely by some goddess to this lovely spot, and having landed at Totnes declared with striking good sense,

"Here I am, and here I rest,
And this town shall be called Totnes."

Thus says tradition, backed by Geoffrey of Monmouth ; and since there be those who snap their fingers at tradition, and declare that Geoffrey lied, the townsmen have done well to prove the story true by preserving the very stone on which the Trojan Prince sat when, tired of wandering, he made his famous

High Street, Totnes

declaration.   There it lies in the pavement outside No. 51 Fore Street, a venerable relic, to the confusion of all sceptics, and the perpetual glory of Geoffrey of Monmouth.

We have no time to trace the history of Totnes, which is all to be found, very nicely done, in the County guides ; but Trojan pedigrees are so rare in English towns, that it was worth while to pause on this. Besides, even sceptics will admit that the Brutus story is probably an indication of some very early invasion and conquest of the aboriginal tribes ; and it must be borne in mind throughout Devon and Cornwall that their situation, facing directly to the west and south, exposed them to the first impacts of those successive waves of commerce and of civilisation which radiated from the Mediterranean in ages far beyond the range of history. Very scant and few are the records of early voyages among these northern seas ; but those writers are rash who disregard them, or who pretend to set limits to the enterprise of sailors of whom all we know is that they were bold and daring, and had no difficulties between them and Britain save such as they were well able to overcome.

However all this is speculation ; and he who gropes in the half-lights of early history is very likely to stumble over something and break his knees. We will get back to modern Totnes therefore, which is, unhappily, a thing of naught beside the ancient borough, a place where life beat high in old days but stagnates now, except at cattle markets, when the old streets and the merchants' piazza are thronged with burly farmers who pass the day in cracking jokes and telling stories of their bullpups on those flags where the talk used to be of seaborne commerce and of bold adventures into half-known lands. At other times the place is silent and looks a little lost, much like a garrison town when the soldiers have marched away elsewhere and the townsmen look each other in the face and wonder what they shall do.

However, dead or alive, sleeping or awake, Totnes is a beautiful and interesting town, how beautiful one does not know without going up the keep of the old Norman castle on the hill, climbing up to the battlements, and looking out over the rich soft country which stretches far and wide, a land of swelling hills and richly wooded valleys and green corn springing over the red earth. Northwards on the skyline, the Dartmoor hills lie blue and seeming infinitely distant in the

light morning haze ; while when one turns in the opposite
direction, one sees a long straight reach of river, set most
sweetly among the hills, up which the salt tide is pouring from
Dartmouth so rapidly that it grows wider every moment, and
the bitter sea air which travels with it from the Channel reaches
as far as the battlements on which we stand. Up that reach
the Totnes merchants, standing on these old walls, used to
watch their argosies sailing with the tide, homeward bound
from Italy or Spain, laden with precious wines and spices.
But no one comes to watch for vessels **now** ; the battlements
are deserted all day long.

And **now** the moment **has arrived when I** must say something of the **Dart. It will** make **but** little difference to that
famous river to know that **I** judge its **beauties** to have been
overrated ; much **rather, as** I fear, the disparagement will
recoil on me, and **I** shall be set down by half the Devonshire
men who read this **work** as one devoid of taste and power **of**
appreciation. **And yet I** do not know how any one who has
seen both Dart and Tamar can blind himself by any but the
strongest local prejudice to the far superior beauty of the
latter. I name the Tamar with some confidence, **since** it is **a**
stream which, in Prince's choice expression, "amorously smiles
upon" both counties, which may therefore lay aside all jealousy
concerning her. **Were it** not that **I fear to** be charged with
excess **of** county feeling, I would mention **the** Cornish Fal also
as excelling the Dart ; but let that pass as **prejudice.** I stand
to my guns in declaring that no house upon the Dart is as
finely placed as Pentillie on the Tamar, as romantic as
Cotehele, nor is there any crag which **it** is other than idle to
compare with the Morwell Rocks.

There, I have done with heresy. I have entered my protest
against the article of faith **which** claims for the estuary of the
Dart so much more than can be reasonably maintained ; and
having done so, **I am** ready to profess my admiration with the
rest. For while I have been protesting, **the** steamer has

H 2

reached Sharpham and is ploughing along close in shore
beneath cool woods which rise from the very edge of the
water high and dark to the summit of the hill, a perfect blaze
of bronze and gold where the sunlight touches them upon the
hilltop; but here they are in deep shadow, so that one has to
look and look again before discovering the bluebells which
make all the dusky hollows steam with azure mists.   On a
waste bank in the river stands a heron, preening its feathers
and arching its long neck ; and presently it rises on wing and
circles round the boat in search of some new fishing ground.
Sharpham Woods are scarcely left behind before the river
loses itself in a maze of creeks and inlets, among which only a
well-skilled pilot can select the proper channel, and the
slightest error involves the certainty of being left suspended on
a mud bank by the falling tide, when the youth of half a
dozen villages will surely come and shoot out the tongue of
the scorner at the careless voyager who has gotten himself
in such a plight.   And so picking our way among alternate
banks and channels we pass by Stoke Gabriel and Dittisham,
famous for very succulent damsons, and many another village
lying in soft hollows by the stream.   In a little while we see
Sandridge where John Davis was born, most early famous
among Arctic voyagers, if not absolutely first ; and then comes
the ancient house of Greenway, the home of those two gallant
gentlemen, Humphrey and Adrian Gilbert, whose high
imaginations wrought and shaped such noble schemes as fired
all men's minds with their own enthusiasm, and charged their
memories with so strong an affection and respect, that now,
after three centuries, their names are household words as much
as Philip Sydney's.   And then, that we may omit no one
among the points of interest upon this famous stream, we will
call attention to the Anchor stone, a black rock in mid river,
which was a most useful public institution in ancient Dartmouth.   For thither the shipmen used to convey those
scolding women and disobedient wives, who in other towns

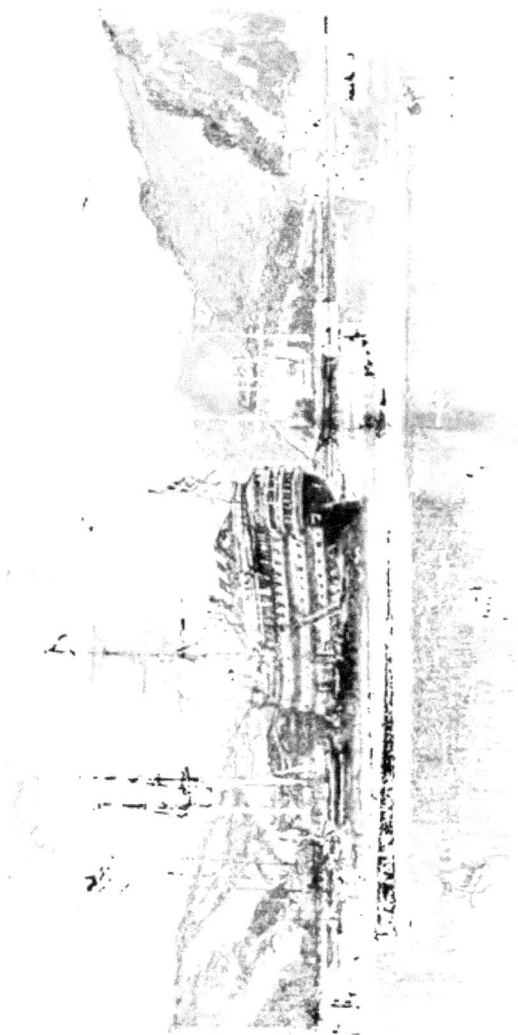

Training Ships, Dartmouth.

were, and are, so very hard to deal with.   An hour's sojourn on
the Anchor stone with a rising tide was often quite enough to
restore obedience to her seat ; and if not, why the stubborn
woman could be left there.

By this time the brown river water is turning green, and the
beginnings of Dartmouth are in sight.   First come a few ship-
building yards, and then, lying a little way off shore, those two
old battleships, linked together by a gallery, which all England
knows as the *Britannia* ; and before one has done gazing at
these hulks, and marvelling at the gracious acts of Providence
whereby the reckless youngsters bred on board them are alone
preserved from cutting short their careers beneath the paddles
of the steamer, before, I say, we have quite realised that the
river has been left behind and the sea is come, we are in mid-
harbour, enclosed on every side by hills so steep and lofty
that the comparison which leaps into one's mind is that this is
the deep crater of some extinct volcano into which the sea has
forced an entrance on one side.

I hope nobody will suspect me of starting a new geological
theory.   I am merely seeking for some similitude which may
convey the true aspect of this strangely situated town, of which
an Italian spy sent to report on it in 1599, when a Spanish
invasion was once more planned, said, " It is not walled.   The
mountains are its walls."   It is an apt expression, well de-
scribing how the old town lies at the water's edge, and how
the hills sink down so straight and deep that they do in fact
resemble walls, rendering other fortifications on the landward
side almost needless.   And now the entrance, which was
blocked by the jutting town of Kingswear on the further bank,
comes full in sight, a deep and narrow gorge, with a castle low
down upon a rocky point, whence in old days a chain was drawn
nightly to the other shore, blocking the entrance against all
vessels.   For there are here no intricacies of channel to perplex
an enemy.   There is deep water almost everywhere, " at low
water five yards," the Italian spy reported ; and he went on

to describe the fortifications by which the mouth of this great
harbour was guarded when he saw it. "At the entrance a
bastion of earth with six or eight pieces of artillery; further in
a castle with twenty-four pieces and fifty men, and then
another earth bastion with six pieces." Such were the
armaments which were maintained at Dartmouth in the years
close following the rout of the great Armada; and if at that
time of perpetual alarms they were a trifle greater than was
usual, there must always have been some strong forces at the
entrance, otherwise the citizens could never have slept in
safety.

For the men of Dartmouth were a strong and lusty race,
eager to fight on the slightest shade of provocation, and no
more troubled with scruples than other seamen of their age,
which is as much as to say that they had none at all. Few
stories would be more interesting than the tale of the settlement
and early struggles of Dartmouth; but the mists of time have
closed around it, and are not broken till within the last eight
centuries. However, nothing is more certain than that Dartmouth men were using their hands to keep their heads up and
down the Channel much earlier than this; and indeed, when
one looks at the harbour, so large, so safe, so easily defended,
one cannot but think that men must have been very dull in
those early days if they did not see how unequalled were the
facilities which it offered to a band of corsairs. Never was a
place more obviously designed by Nature for a stronghold of
pirates; and as a matter of fact, whatever may have been the
character of the first settlers, the reputation of those who
dwelt there when recorded history begins was exactly what
might have been expected of a corsair origin. It was a wide
and well-known reputation too; showing that it had been won
and earned through many generations, otherwise Dan Chaucer,
who drew only typical characters among his Canterbury
Pilgrims, would not have selected a Dartmouth captain to ride
to Canterbury side by side with the Franklin and the Prioress,

and the "Poure Persoun of a Toun," and all the rest of that company, where in small space are preserved for ever the chief aspects of social England in the third Edward's time. And what does Chaucer say of this sea captain? The passage has been often quoted, but it is essential to our theme:

> A schipman was ther, wonyng fer by weste;
> For ought I woot, he was of Dertemouthe.
> He rode upon a rouncy as he couthe,
> In a gowne of faldyng to the kne.
> * * * * *
> And certainly he was a good felawe,
> Ful many a draughte of wyn hadde he ydrawe
> From Burdeux Ward whil that the chapman sleep,
> Of nyce conscience took he no kepe;
> If, that he faughte and hadde the higher hande,
> By water he sente hem hoom to every lande.

Now let us see what Chaucer has told us. Doubtless it is some actual Dartmouth seaman who is thus made to live before our eyes; and what are the characteristic actions chosen to delineate him? First a certain freedom in construing the laws of honesty, drawing his wine from "Burdeux Ward," while the chapman in charge of it was asleep; and secondly, a pleasant knack of disencumbering himself of captives taken on the high seas by sending them home by water, in other words availing himself of an ingenious apparatus much in vogue from the earliest days of piracy, consisting of a single plank hinged in the middle upon the bulwarks, and dropping on the deck with a slope so gentle that even frightened people could walk up it with very slight assistance till they passed the middle, when the natural tilting of the apparatus saved them all trouble in going down.

> Four-and-twenty Spaniards,
> Mighty men of rank,
> With their Signoras,
> Had to walk the plank.

So sings a joyous bard rescued from oblivion by Mr. Leland, unless indeed it were his own very clever pen which produced a verse so accurately reflecting the habits of Channel seamen in the Middle Ages. Does any one regard this as a slander on Dartmouth seamen? Let him ask himself and inquire carefully what were the origins of seamanship; and remembering well the broad facts of human nature in all ages, let him ponder what must follow by strict necessity when bold seamen find themselves in a well-armed ship, controlled by no sort of maritime law which there is any means whatever of enforcing on them, and see a weaker vessel approaching laden with a valuable cargo. What should hinder them from taking her, plundering her cargo, and as a mere measure of prudence, sending her crew to their account? Law—there was none to enforce it. Conscience—it is a modern growth, and was exotic in those days. All seamen were alike. West country, East country, Bretons, Flemings, Spaniards—the law of the jungle was that which ruled the ocean. The stronger preyed upon the weaker, and fell in his turn before one who was mightier than he. The ocean was a lucky bag, into which you thrust your hand and pulled out the best thing you could find. If the thing belonged to your neighbour, and he would not let it go, you slew him, if you could. If not, he slew you, and got it back again.

Whether this was wrong or right is a question which I leave to those whose business it is to teach morality. My concern goes no further than pointing out that it bred a race of exceptionally bold and hardy seamen; and so far as Dartmouth is concerned, it was fortunate both for her and England that it was so. For on the opposite coast of the Channel lies Brittany, a country pierced like western England by a plenitude of deep coves and inlets, offering exactly similar facilities for a life of acquisitive sea-roving. And following that inherent predatory instinct, which is as strong in man as in the lower animals, the Bretons were a corsair nation, so bold and fierce and numerous,

that it would have fared ill with Devon had her sailors been
mere peaceful traders, fighting only when attacked.   But being,
as they were, a race of fighters inferior to none that has ever
roved the ocean, they met the Bretons joyfully half-way, and
rushed out eagerly to fight, the women bearing themselves as
lustily as the men whenever the fighting was on shore.
Walsingham in his Chronicle preserves the memory of one of
these engagements.   A Breton armament had been fitted out
by "Dominus de Castellis," more commonly known as Du
Chatel, a Breton knight, who, finding the men of Dartmouth a
thorn in his side, took a valiant resolution, like Fhairson in
"Bon Gaultier," that he would "extirpate the vipers," and
having done so, he meant to make a pleasant little tour of
burning and ravaging all round the western coasts.   Perhaps
he might have succeeded if all his followers could have held
their tongues, but somebody blabbed, and so it fell out, as
Walsingham remarks, "otherwise than he hoped."   For when
the Bretons came to land, hoping to take Dartmouth in the
rear, they found six hundred men in waiting for them, strongly
entrenched behind a deep ditch which they had dug upon the
shore, and supported by numbers of women, who seem to have
fought like wildcats, having charge of slings with which they
made such capital practice, that the Breton knights and men-at-
arms went down by scores into the ditch, where the men
finished them off, misunderstanding their cries for mercy, as
Walsingham would have us believe; or, as we may more
probably surmise, forgetting in the heat of battle that it was
more profitable to hold a man of birth to ransom, than to club
his brains out in a ditch.   However, when the fight was over,
and the shattered remnant of invaders had regained their ships,
there were still a goodly number of captives in the hands of the
defenders,   out of whom they doubtless made sums large
enough to keep the whole town feasting till that dark day next
year when the Bretons returned more secretly, and falling on
Dartmouth unawares burnt it to the ground.

So the see-saw of existence went on along the Channel coasts. One day Brittany was uppermost, another Devon, but whether returning home exultant over a rich booty, or weeping beside the smoke of burning homesteads, Dartmouth was never at peace, her sailors were never idle, but ranged the seas perpetually, and the fighting was most fierce and fell. A proud impatience was the natural outcome of this lusty life, and in 1385, when great preparations were being made in France for the invasion of England, and the admirals to whom the defence of England was entrusted, were risking all by their slothful indolence, the men of Dartmouth, with their staunch allies, the men of Portsmouth, took the matter into their own hands, and sallying forth without instructions dashed into the Seine, where the French ships where lying, sank four of them, carried off four others, and brought away too the barge of one De Clisson, "cui par non erat in Angliæ sive Franciæ regnis," which had not its like in the realms of France or England, stored as it was with every kind of splendid booty, "enough," says Walsingham, "to satisfy the greediest."

This latest expedition was exceptional in the annals of Dartmouth, in that it bore some relation to the politics of the rest of England. More commonly the warfare of this, as well as of other western seaports, was regarded as a sort of private quarrel, by no means necessarily accompanied by hostilities for other towns. And this attitude was in some degree sanctioned; for in the *Libel of English Policie*, an invaluable and a very spirited declaration of the true policy of remaining mistress of the narrow seas, we are told that Edward III., after vainly representing to the Duke of Brittany that his liege subjects should be kept in better order,

> . . . Did dewise
> Of English townes three, that is to say
> Dartmouth, Plymouth, the third it is Fowey,
> And gave them help and notable puissance
> Upon pety Bretayne for to warre.

Great and noble seaports all three of them, and needing small inducement to do what in fact they had been doing with zest and enjoyment all their days. Still, the king's warrant was not without its value, as will appear when we come to speak of the evil that fell on Fowey in other days for want of it.

So far as we know at present the authentic records of deeds wrought in those early years are few and bald ; and if, therefore, any one is minded to declare that the particular Channel port in which he is most interested conducted its life with full regard to latter-day morality it will be hard to refute him. But it can be said quite certainly that the ordinary sailor of the Channel was what Chaucer tells us, bold, unscrupulous, absolutely master of his profession.

> Hardy he was, and wyse to undertake,
> With many a tempest had his beard been schake ;
> He knew wel alle the havenes as thei were
> From Gootlond to the Cape of Fynystere.

If he was cruel he is not to be reprobated, seeing that he was born into a world of cruelty, and sucked down blood and slaughter with his mother's milk. If he robbed, it was because mankind which learnt so slowly on the land how to distinguish between mine and thine, had not even begun to think of this distinction on the sea. If he struck at others it was because he knew they were but waiting to strike at him, and he had not learnt that it is a Christian virtue to wait till you are kicked. When a sheep dog harries a flock of helpless wethers, it is a cruel and a cowardly abuse of strength ; but a wolf fastening his teeth in other wolves, setting his own life on the cast of skill and courage, is quite another sight ; and such were the Channel sailors of the Middle Ages.

Now all this has been set forth at some length, because it is very often forgotten that on this foundation of generations of piracy and fierce sea-fighting the naval greatness of the days of Elizabeth was built. It was in this lusty life of action and acquisitive self-interest that those qualities were shaped and moulded which set England at the head of the world when the time arrived to use them on a larger field, and all the nations of the narrow seas were spreading their wings in the same moment to those fabled regions of the west, of which the gates, closed since the foundation of the world, were suddenly swung back by Columbus, opening, in the full gaze of the startled nations, a vista over unknown lands, of beauty so bewildering and wealth so boundless and accessible as made all men's senses reel, and shook their purposes, and made them dead to all other thoughts than those of the rich tropical forest, the fireflies flitting in the dusk of gorgeous creepers, the gold and jewels to be grasped so easily, and set their hearts on fire to possess those glorious riches and to slay all men who tried to seize them first.   Cast a bone among a pack of dogs and they will tear each other in pieces for the prize.   Open fairyland to a group of sailors, and the first thought of each will be to cut the other's throat and gain the whole inheritance.

So all the western nations fell a-fighting, and that nation won which had been longest used to flesh its weapons upon all and sundry.   From this moment the roving on the narrow seas was dropped for larger interests.   Not all at once, nor indeed for many a generation, did the old practices die out. The calendars of State Papers are filled with entries relating to pirates who infested the entire coasts of Devon and Cornwall. Vaughan, Clinton Atkinson, Captain Hammond, and many another found their lurking places in lonely creeks around both counties ; and as years went by, and law was gradually enforced upon the sea, those lawless energies which had made the pirates wealthy found an outlet in smuggling, the child and blood descendant of piracy, which died only in our own days.

The Reformation dropped one more ingredient into the nature of these formidable sailors.   It instilled into their hearts a profound faith that God was with them fighting on their side with the full force of heaven, that their enemies were His enemies, and their ends His ends. In the story of Robert Lyde, told in the second chapter of this work, we see the outcome of this blend of piety with inherited ferocity. It produced the very deadliest fighting animal the world has ever seen. " Then said I, ' Lord, what shall I do now ? ' " he appeals with absolute confidence to the Creator ; and swift and murderous the answer comes, " Then the Lord was pleased to put me in mind of my knife in my pocket." No better illustration of the temper of the seamen of the age could possibly be found.

Now this is a long discourse, but it was necessary for the better comprehension of the sea life not of Dartmouth only, but of Plymouth, Fowey, and other seaports of less mark, where we shall pause as we come to them. In the meantime something should be said of all the great associations in which this famous port is steeped.

Dartmouth was much in favour with our early kings. More than eight hundred years ago Richard Cœur de Lion collected in its deep-cliffed harbour the fleet with which he sailed for Palestine ; and a century before that crack-brained expedition William Rufus came hither bound on a more sober journey to Normandy. John Lackland also seems to have found his way to Dartmouth twice, doubtless perceiving in the acquisitive habits of the turbulent old port something congenial to his own predilection for seizing other people's kingdoms. And indeed the value of Dartmouth was so clearly seen by the monarchs of this country that they included the port in the estates of the Duchy of Cornwall, a connection with royalty which is not broken yet.

But it is not of these Norman kings that one thinks as one wanders round the quays and ancient streets of Dartmouth. Their memories are effaced by those of greater men ; of Adrian Gilbert, the lofty enthusiast who dreamed night and day of that north-west passage to Cathay and India the search for which has left the bones of so many valiant sailors whitening

among the icebergs by the Polar Sea. "Forasmuch," wrote
the Virgin Queen, having been duly wrought up to interest by
the anticipation of glory for which she cared a little, and of
profit for which she cared much, "forasmuch as our trustie
and well-beloved subject Adrian Gilbert of Sandridge in the
county of Devon. . . To his great costes and charges hath
greatly and earnestly travailed and sought, and yet doth travail
and seeke, and by divers meanes indevoureth and laboureth that
the passage unto China and the isles of the Moluccas by the
northwestward may be known and discovered, known and
frequented by the subjects of this our realm. . . Now we . . ."
Well, it amounted to this, amid much verbiage, that he might go
on labouring to achieve this good, and was not to be deterred
from risking his life, or the lives of any other persons in the
search by the fear of her royal and virginal displeasure. Thus
fortified against the only danger that they feared, Adrian and
"certain other honourable personages and worthy gentlemen of
the court and country, moved," as Hakluyt tells us, "with
desire to advance God's glory and to seeke the good of their
native country," called in one John Davis, likewise of Sandridge
on the Dart, "a man very well grounded in the principles of
the arte of navigation," and one whom Adrian must have
known from his boyhood. The strong, brave, simple sailor
was doubtless a character immensely attractive to the dreamer,
who saw in him the instrument he needed to carry out the
project seething in his brain. And so in London and at
Greenway, and doubtless in Dartmouth also, there were long
sittings over maps and plans, and discourses stretching far into
the night, and all the while in a little dockyard on the harbour
two little cockleshells, no larger than a modern pilot boat,
were being overhauled and fitted staunchly out of Devon oak.
So one day early in June there was a leave-taking on Dartmouth
quay; and the two cockleshells, quaintly named the
Sunneshine and the *Moonshine*, the latter a half
anticipation of the futility of the quest, slipped out beneath

the two old castles and bent their sails on that far voyage to the north where were neither maps nor charts nor any save the vaguest tales of former voyagers. Doubtless there were those who went to the cliff above the castle to watch these little craft pass out of sight hull down on the horizon, and whose hearts failed them as they went homeward to the town lest the day should never come when gallant John Davis and his handful of brave men should bring back to Dartmouth the spoils of those unknown icy regions. Now how he sailed into the Polar seas, and drove his little ships into the teeth of floating icebergs, and all the perils of the Polar pack " still nursing the unconquerable hope," brave forerunner of a long procession of enthusiasts less fortunate than he ; and how he traded with the Esquimaux, and a thousand other things of interest, must be read in the pages of old Hakluyt, from which I shall not borrow them, lest I should turn away one reader from that wondrous book, the true English epic, the immortal poem of our great sea life. There those who care to read will find it written how he came and went again, and yet a third time made the voyage, and afterwards sailed into the southern seas, earning great honour for himself and Dartmouth, and so was slain at last by pirates at Malacca.

If I were to try to speak of all the great associations of Dartmouth I might write a volume, and still not finish. But the conclusion of the story is that the sailors of this port, which now appears to have but little mission in the world, filled manfully and nobly their part in that great duty of the dwellers on the Channel coast which was seen and realised more than four centuries ago as clearly as we know it now.

> Cherish marchandize, keepe the Admiraltie,
> That we bee masters of the narrow sea.
> The ende of battaile is peace sikerly,
> And power causeth peace finally.
>
> Keepe then the sea, about in special,
> Which of England is the town wall ;

Keepe then the sea, that is the wall of England,
And then is England kept by Goddes hand.

" Keepe then the sea ! " the cry is as old as Agincourt, and still it is the last word of modern statesmanship. " Keepe then the sea," that is to say no more than "follow in the way of Dartmouth, Fowey and Plymouth," which kept the sea so nobly in the old days when they had to fight the battle almost single-handed, and there was neither central law nor comity of nations to back them up. They kept the sea. They were the guards and sentinels on the town wall of England ; and when England forgets them, or ceases to read their histories with emulation and to visit their towns with reverence, her day will indeed be past, and she will herself have earned forgetfulness in her day of need.

CHAPTER VII

I SEE I have been descanting so long on the greatness of Dartmouth, and yet have left the story more than half untold, that I have said but little of her beauty ; and I hardly know whether this may not be resented, for when the larger issues of life are lost, vanity flies lightly in ; and Dartmouth has this many a day had little else to think about. Her harbour is as good as ever, her sailors, one would hope, are not less gallant than when John Davis led them. But the spell of the briar rose has fallen on her, with nearly all the western seaports. They are but so many chambers in the enchanted palace, wherein those that should be doing mighty deeds lie slumbering until the coming of him who shall hack down the thorns, and break the spell, and stir the sleepers into life.

There is one seaport over which drowsiness has never crept, but which is still imperial, and we shall reach it ere nightfall. But first we will stroll round Dartmouth, going out upon the quay, where a light breeze is ruffling the water of the harbour which last night lay so smooth and oily, and a couple of yachts are forging slowly out beneath the castle, hoisting their sails that they may catch the wind when they pass out of the shelter of the hills. A few boatmen are plying to and fro ; the ferry boat comes heavily across from Kingswear ; a dirty black steamer goes belching filthy smoke up the blue river,—and that is all there is to see of man's activity in

Dartmouth on this fine fresh breezy morning. We turn away from the quay, and ramble over to the Butter Walk, where we are still haunted by the aspect of former greatness. For here half a dozen houses with projecting upper stories constitute a piazza supported on rich carved pillars, the whole forming a covered way of singular interest and beauty; and in a richly panelled room, adorned with the royal arms carved in old dark oak, Charles the Second is said to have held his court when he came to Dartmouth. Certainly it must have been a grand and stately life that was lived in the ancient seaport when houses such as these were built; and when we pass on to St. Saviour's church there are fresh proofs of the wealth and consequence of the town. There, between his two wives, lies in brazen effigy old John Hawley, chief among all the trader princes of the town, one whose deeds were great if not too scrupulous, and who, as Mr. Worth remarks, "whenever he felt aggrieved, whether with his own countrymen or foreigners, he always kept the law, because he made it himself to suit the occasion." A simple plan, which answered admirably, so well indeed that a jangling couplet ran in all men's mouths :

> Blow the wind high, or blow the wind low,
> It bloweth still to Hawley's hawe.

There are none living now who will take Hawley for a model. Let us leave Dartmouth. The savour of the old days has taken the relish of the new ones out of our mouths, and left us carping and dissatisfied. Perhaps it is really progress which has drained away the lifeblood of Dartmouth, and the lost forces may be operating elsewhere. It is hard to think it, but let us try to do so as we climb the hill, that worst of hills, up which never yet has cyclist ridden, nor ever will until that perfect cycle is produced which will race up a gradient of one in three.

The coast road on which we have embarked is probably the

finest in all Devon. From the moment when one comes hot
and toiling over the backbone of the ridge which rises so
steeply out of Dartmouth, and catch glimpses of blue sea
across a falling country, and the breath of a wind cooled by
the passage of the whole wide Channel, until one turns away
inland at Torcross,—for seven miles of hill and valley skirting
lofty cliffs and sunny sands alternately, this lovely road winds
onward by the sea, at times so close that it would be easy to
drop a pebble into deep water ; at others running a field or
two inland, but never out of sight of the travelled highway up
which the ships of twenty nations are coming and going both
day and night.

There is a high point of cliff upon this road where some old
sea captain has builded him a house, that he may watch this
great stream of commerce sailing on to the greatest market in
the world ; surely there can be no place like it in the
kingdom for a sailor's dwelling, when the time comes for him
to cease from following the sea ; and just below it is another
house, clinging to the very face of the seafront, which, the
country people tell you, the sailor built because the first was
too far inland, though even that must have been washed by
the spray in stormy weather. Between the two a look-out
place is formed upon a bit of cliff, whence the sea view must
be unrivalled. For from the road one looks across the whole
width of Start Bay to the low keen promontory of Start Point,
a glorious range of broken cliff; and on the other hand there
lies at one's feet a lovely little bay out of which the road has
just climbed steeply, and which has witnessed many strange
encounters. For on that curving beach of white sand was
fought out that grim fight with the Breton invaders of which
the tale was told in the last chapter. And there too landed the
great Earl of Warwick, the Kingmaker, bent on undoing the
Yorkist king whom he himself had lifted to the throne on
Towton field nine years before.

Not long ago there was found among these sands a hoard of

gold coins of the mintage in vogue at the date when Warwick
landed here, supplied, as De Commines tells us, with both
arms and money by the French King, Louis XI. Doubtless
it was the purse of some noble who came with Warwick, and
shared in the glories of those marches which within a week
made him master of the kingdom. Thus strangely are those far
distant days linked with this quiet spot.

And so the road goes rising and falling more beautifully
than one can describe till it plunges down its last descent, and
runs away from the hilly country right out upon the sea shore,
traversing a belt of narrow sands which run between the sea
and one of those freshwater lakes which are sometimes found
so strangely near the ocean. This lake is Slapton Lea ; and it
is very famous ground, for both the fishing and the fowling are
good, and the comfortable Sands Hotel which stands between
the salt water and the fresh, has always a cosy corner, and a
cheery welcome for sportsmen, and generally one even for
duffers who have no other end in view in coming there than
to swallow as much as possible of a salt and breezy air which
is not to be excelled in all the width of Devon.

At Torcross the road turns inland, and runs onward
towards Kingsbridge through a gently undulating country
which until the opening of the new railway to that town, was as
remote from communication with the rest of England as any
place in the whole West Country. This is the heart of the
South Hams, a district not very clearly defined, but including
the greater part of the country which lies south of the moor
between Exeter and Plymouth. It is a cider country, very
famous once for the quality of its liquor, and still noted for its
excellence ; though it somehow happens that cider does not
fetch the price it did, and farmers are making less and less.
There is a very ancient ceremony which used to be performed
in this district when apple orchards and their crops were more
valued than they are now. On the eve of Epiphany the farmer
with all his workmen used to go to the orchard bearing a large

pitcher of cider ; and then dancing solemnly round the largest and best bearing tree, they drank to it three times, singing at each draught

> Here's to thee, old apple tree,
> Whence thou mayst bud, and whence thou mayst blow,
> And whence thou mayst bear apples eno,
> Hats full, caps full,
> Baskets, bushel, sacks full,
> And my pockets full too, huzza.

Meantime, the women had bolted the doors of the farmhouse, and when the men returned from their libations, they were kept out in the cold, until some one among them guessed what it was that was roasting on the spit. The lucky guesser had the tender morsel as his reward ; and then the evening passed cheerfully with song and feasting. The farmers care little for honouring their orchards in this picturesque way now, while as for the labourers—they much prefer the vile beer which is commonly found in country taverns, and any one who calls for cider at Ivybridge or Salcombe stands an excellent chance of being offered a tumbler of sour and muddy fluid, with a shame-faced explanation that it is so little asked for.

However, if good cider is becoming scarce in the South Hams, there is another liquor on which the thirsty traveller can fall back, somewhat uninviting in appearance, it is true, but of very high and ancient repute at Kingsbridge, where it is chiefly made. If it be indeed true, as some inquirers have held, that "white ale" was once the staple drink of western England, we may fairly congratulate ourselves on having given one proof at least of progress in shaking off our national attachment to this thick and heady liquor, which perhaps is the same as appalled good Andrew Borde who tried to penetrate into wild Cornwall 350 years ago, but found the ale so bad that he had to give it up. It looked, he said, "as if pygges had wrasteled in it."

And what is this delectable drink ? Why, that is declared to be a secret, known only to one family, and jealously guarded through successive generations. All the outer world knows is that eggs are in it, as well as some mystical ingredient called " grout " ; that it looks like some extremely nauseous doctor's draught ; that it flies quickly to the head ; and that the sooner the South Hams grow as wise as Cornwall and the rest of England, and consign all this nasty liquor to the limbo of the past, the better will be the judgment formed of their good sense. For it would be a rare and monumental folly to lose cider, and retain white ale.

I do not know what can be said of Kingsbridge. It is a little town said to be thriving, but the main fact which strikes a visitor is that its Mediterranean trade, which two generations ago employed 150 vessels, has slipped out of its grasp, and now brings scarce a dozen up the muddy channel of the river. The mudbanks in the estuary are covered with an unwholesome green growth. The hills which flank it are low, and by no means striking ; and indeed it is not until the river opens round its last bend into Salcombe Harbour that one sees any adequate recompense for the journey down the stream.

For if Kingsbridge has lost its Mediterranean trade, the Mediterranean itself seems to have come to Salcombe, so blue and soft is the water of the harbour, and so rich the vegetation of the sunny hillsides. There is an ancient town of no sort of modern consequence, which is alone a striking charm, when it happens to be on the coast, for the same thing inland is intoler-able, the landsman's idleness being as unlovely as the seaman's is picturesque, and his lying, which we know to be the fruit of idle-ness, being about big cabbages and four-pound trout, and uneasy lying too even on such easy subjects, while your unoccupied sailor will lie with grace and charm the whole day long about moving perils which befell him while he was safe in bed, and monsters which rose out of the deep, what time he was reeling homewards from the "King of Prussia." There is therefore no dulness in a seaport town, and no library of entertaining fiction either so cheap or so readable as that you buy for next to nothing on the quay. Of course this attraction is not peculiar to Salcombe ; but what no other town in South Devon possesses, nor indeed more than one or two on any other coast, is a headland so high and dark and jagged at the entrance of the harbour. Indeed to the traveller who has come to Salcombe from the east along a coast which is more often beautiful than grand, the magnificence of Bolt Head is a vast surprise. It is wild and rugged like a Cornish headland ; and the walk across it to Bolt Tail is the finest between Portland and The Lizard. From it there is seen the first glimpse of Cornwall which one has in going west.

Salcombe holds the honour of having been the last place in Devon to hold out for the King in the great civil wars ; and the battered shell of its old castle, on a rock half surrounded by the sea, will recall the memory of a grand defence as long as the winds and weather shall leave it standing. There were no more honourable terms granted in all the war than those which Sir Edmund Fortescue made with the besiegers ; for he and all his men marched out with drums beating and flying colours, while all the officers kept their arms, and every man had three months in which to make his peace with Parliament or else leave the country, in which the cause of the king was absolutely lost. Salcombe and Pendennis, Fortescue and Arundel—with the fall of those strongholds and the loss of those two captains, the last embers blackened and the hearth grew cold on which such a mighty blaze of loyalty had been kindled in the west.

We have struck the end of the story before its opening chapter, though that matters little where the tragedy is unforgettable. But there is another association to be gathered up in Salcombe, the memory of one who loved Devon as he loved England, and that was with a whole-hearted passion which has never been surpassed. How joyously James Anthony Froude told the tale of England's greatness ! How many loved her as they read his glowing pages who had loved nothing great before, and indeed if only a tithe of those who

caught a spark of his enthusiasm were to pass it on to others
undiminished, there would never fail in England a race
absolutely worthy of the traditions into which they are born.
If the spirit of old days should awake in Devon it is to Froude
that men will largely trace the impulse ; and if it be not so, if
Devon merely turns uneasily upon her bed, still many a year
will go by before the long veranda running round the low
white house, and the study windows giving on the quiet garden,
cease to be a place of pilgrimage to those who love either
English history or its subject.   England may wait long ere she
gives birth to another writer so capable as he of clothing the
dead bones of history with flesh and setting them before us in
their full-blooded energy of life.   For one who can do this
there are born a dozen dusty pedants, whose lengthy volumes
contain not one throb of passion ; and so there are many still
who keep a tender memory of him who stirred their hearts like
no other writer, and never gave them a low or mean idea.

What is here said has been summed up so beautifully in the
following lines, published, I know not by whom, in the *St.
James's Gazette*, about the time of Froude's death, that I cannot
refrain from quoting them.

> Now when heroic memories pass
> Like sunset shadows from the grass,
> When England's children cry and stir
> Each for himself and few for her,
>
> We may think tenderly of one
> Who told, like no unworthy son,
> Her history, and who loved to draw
> Champions a younger England saw.
>
> We act no critic's part, and when
> They rank him less than lesser men,
> We feel the golden thread that goes
> To link the periods of his prose.

Perhaps our busy breathless age
That leaves unopened history's page
Had need of hands like his to strike
Imperial chords, Tyrtæan like.

It may be said of all the country between the estuaries of
the Dart and Tamar that it suffers from the accident of its
position.   On either flank it is dominated by a town so great in
its history and so striking in its beauty that its more ordinary
charms are lost and hidden ; and the traveller who wanders
through it with his knapsack, or races round upon a bicycle,
retains no more definite memories than those of a prosperous,
peaceful country life.   When he turns his mind backward, he
thinks of deep green lanes between banks of furze and bracken
and nodding bluebells ; he remembers wandering arms of some
great estuary reaching far up the fields, and bringing in amid
the hedgerows the cool gleaming of wet sand and the fresh
breezes which accompany the flowing tide.   White rustic
cottages come before his recollection all glowing with early
stocks, and shady farms where life goes easily and the guineas
flow in, if not so readily as of old, yet fast enough to make
existence a contented rumination and life a pleasant game.   He
remembers orchards budding freely with fair promise of ruddy
cider in the autumn.   He recalls visions of market towns so
sleepy that chickens grovel all day long in the centre of the
main street, and all life save that of lazy prosperity seems to have
died long centuries ago.   Such only are the memories which
return upon the traveller who takes stock of what he has
gathered in the South Hams : or such they would be were it not
that the district is touched on one side by the sea, and on the
other by the moor.

All the Devon rivers are beautiful ; but those which issue
from the moor are exquisite.   It is towards one of these, the
Erme, that the road runs by which we are moving on Modbury,
most ancient and drowsy of country towns, whence it is but a
little way to Ermington, and then in a short two miles more the

road emerges at Ivybridge, at the very foot of the great rock rampart of the moor.

Every one who has travelled through South Devon, even by train, knows the exquisite hollow in which Ivybridge lies ; and has seen it filled at evening with a golden mist, or basking in the thick noonday heat. But only those know its beauty who descend there and make their way down to the river, not going towards the town, for there a lovely glen has been spoilt by the paper mills which absorb its water, but going upwards into the heart of the ravine, through the dense woods which occupy its deep recesses.

Down the stony slopes of this rockwalled gorge the Erme, a slender stream, is cast headlong over little precipices, whence it falls in mimic cataracts between crags and boulders on which the richest ferns and moss are nourished by the moisture, and grow seldom troubled by the sunlight. For into this deep wood the sun rarely finds his way. A richer light glows among the upper branches and one knows that he is there. A dappled gleam wavers over the brown water and is gone again, a sparkle glances on the foam, a sudden warmth of colour glows amid the moss and polished ivy on the shady bank. But the glare of sunlight never reaches the valley bottom ; and the river flows on in the shadow, clear and brown and cool, from one basin to another, now brimming gently over with a light noise of dripping, now splashing to the lower level with the impetuosity of a true mountain torrent.

There is no end to the infinite variety of this stream. But the Erme is no more than one among a family of lovely sisters ; and the Yealm, a few miles west at Cornwood, is no less exquisite, while on the east the Avon runs a course which is quite as beautiful. It is a vain effort to search for words which express the infinitely changing beauties of these streams ; and we will therefore leave them rushing down from their rock barriers, and pass on through the lower country, by Ermington once more toward the coast. Half a mile out of Ermington the river Erme, which has been straying at some distance from the road, approaches it again ; and at the same time the hills close up, so that the stream flows onward to the sea through a rather deep and very richly wooded valley, the whole of which is occupied by the private grounds of Fleete House. There is, however, no difficulty in obtaining permission to follow the road which skirts the river's bank ; and it is not long before the water which at the outset was hardly larger than a brook, widens out into a channel which is clearly no longer that of an inland stream, but is salt and marshy, and drowned twice daily by the flowing tide. And so the drive passes onward, undulating on the side of wooded hills, until the river's bed is filled with sand, and another turn brings an outlook over Mothecombe, a little harbour enclosed by low red cliffs, between which the river flows but wearily, no longer strong enough to cut a channel, but letting its waters flow where they will, so that even before it is strangled in the breakers, there is hardly any other trace of river than a brighter gleaming on the sunny sand. A small schooner is discharging her cargo on the beach ; and half a dozen carts are plodding to and fro. The sea is of the deepest blue, broken only by the white flashing of the wings of a pair of gulls which are busy fishing near the shore.

It is a beautiful and lonely spot, unchanged like so many others on this solitary coast since that July morning three centuries ago, when the Spanish cannon roared and echoed over these still sands ; and the fishermen having heard all day the noise of battle further down the coast, saw at last when the stormy evening darkened down the huge galleons moving up the Channel in a heavy sea, like tall stags among a crowd of yapping terriers. And hardly one of those who witnessed that great spectacle, however confident in the might and seamanship of England, could have dreamt that in a short week that proud fleet would be driven headlong through the narrow seas, having no more cohesion than a herd of frightened sheep

shrinking from the colley's bark, and fleeing only to meet a
pitiable death on seas which they had never sailed, and among
a people who knew no mercy for shipwrecked enemies. One
cannot escape from memories of those great days when one
travels along this coast of which every creek and inlet saw the
battle ; and still less can one set the tale aside when one is so
near Plymouth, which of all the harbours in the West played
the greatest part on that stage. In this corner of England, so
removed from the lines of traffic between west and east, so
little fitted by Nature to play any but a minor part on the stage
of history, the one great memory excludes all others. It
haunts us all day long as we ride through the rich country,
catching glimpses of the sea perpetually above the hedgerows ;
and when at last we reach the Laira estuary, and enter the old
town near Sutton Pool, the abiding thought is still of the
handful of ships which lay here on the stormy summer evening
three hundred years ago, of the shouts of the sailors and the
creaking of the spars and cordage as the goodly ships were
warped out one by one beneath the light of great cressets
flaring in the gusty wind.

CHAPTER VIII

In speaking of Dartmouth it was remarked that among the long list of western seaports which have lost their consequence, there remains one which is still imperial. It is not necessary to name it. Plymouth leaps into one's mind before the question which it is has shaped itself. For many a century she was no more than first among her equals; but it is now long since she has waked while they have slumbered, going on from strength to strength, while Fowey and Dartmouth have shed their greatness plume by plume; and now she stands a living example of that law, that those who help themselves to grow shall grow even beyond their own endeavours, recognised long since as the chief naval port of England, and winning fast the recognition that of all the English harbours there is none more suitable for commerce also.

There are so many towns in the West whose story is obviously told, and so many more which seem to have no care to struggle any longer for their place, that it is a keen pleasure to walk round busy, active Plymouth and to see on every hand the signs of growth. Here is no resting idly on the credit of old greatness, but a resolute policy of expansion, which has already wrought great things, and is daily adding to their number so speedily that ere many years have passed we shall surely see this noble harbour filled to overflowing, and that supremacy in trade which is the lost inheritance of the West

once more returning thither. Then it may be that the other
ancient seaports will begin to stir, and the West resume its old
prosperity.

But let this be enough of dreams, especially of dreams with
which half of those who read this book will fail to sympathise.
It is time to go forth and look on Plymouth as she is; and
since the greatness of the town is on its seafront, and one
cares but little for the streets, one makes at once for the Armada
statue, where a Britannia stands looking seawards, as she
should, holding back her lion by a leash, while beneath, with
an honest recognition of the fact that it was not her sword
alone that saved England in those days of peril, are inscribed
the words, " He blew with His winds and they were scattered."

The Sound lies veiled in a thin blue mist, behind which a
hot sun beats, scattering it gradually with the aid of a stiff
breeze off the land. But it hangs around Mount Edgecumbe
on the right, where the grey towers of the mansion stand in
shadow among dark woods, while on the summit of the hill
above the green fields catch the sunlight. A little lower,
Drake's Island lies impalpable and dim amid the mist which
sweeps so softly round the forts and the green grassy slopes as
to touch it all with mystery one moment, while the next it is
bright again with sunlight, sparkling amid the dazzling sea.
Within the breakwater the sea is alive with craft : fishing boats
and little schooners beating out from Catwater ; great three-
masted ships lying idly at their anchors ; while from Hamoaze
upon the right, puffing volumes of black smoke from her three
short funnels, a torpedo-boat catcher shoots out swiftly, flying
the white ensign, and goes out to sea at the rate of fifteen knots,
ploughing through the water with a force which seems to leave
the throbbing of her engines still humming in the air long
after the low black hull has vanished in the creeping mist.

An Italian traveller in the middle of the last century, one
Baretti, compiler of a dictionary, and a lively and agreeable
writer, tells us that he " walked a while on the key of the

harbour and saw nothing but two bay mules." It is true that
before he left Plymouth he had convinced himself that bay
mules were not the only lions that the old town had to show :
but with the quick and ready interest which he displayed in all
around him, it is odd that he did not discover the sea front of
Plymouth to be what in fact it is, the most interesting spot
within the British Empire, if not also the most beautiful. It is
a large claim, but who can deny it ? Leave aside the beauty,
which speaks loudly enough for every one to hear. Where else
can one see a spot trodden like the Hoe by so many generations of the greatest men our country ever saw, and retaining
still almost the same aspect as it bore when their eyes looked
back upon it from the decks of the departing ships which
were bearing them to seas unsailed before, and by coasts which
were never mapped nor charted, through those far regions of
the West whose very peril was their great attraction. For it
was on this open ground that the townsmen used to meet to
watch the sailing of those expeditions in which many of them
had a venture, and all had the interest coming of a sympathy
with valour and a high delight in the deeds of their fellow men
of Devon ; and so they used to flock out upon the Hoe in crowds
to witness the departure and speed their friends upon their
way. "When I left," says Sir Richard Hawkins, writing of
that voyage in which he was unfortunately captured after a
heroic fight—" when I left, the most part of the inhabitants
were gathered together upon the Howe to shew their grateful
correspondency to the love and zeal which I, my father and
predecessors, have ever born to that place as to our natural
and mother-town ; and first with my noyse of trumpets, after
with my waytes and then with my other musicke, and lastly
with the artillery of my shippes, I made the best signification I
could of a kind farewell. This they answered with the waytes
of the town and the ordnance on the shore and with shouting
of voices ; which with the fayre evening and silence of the
night were heard a great distance off." And so, whilst there

Plymouth.

K

rang in his ears the sound of distant cheers and music and the
thunder of saluting cannon, Sir Richard sailed away, like many
a brave captain before him, carrying in his heart, we cannot
doubt, through many a day of storm and peril, the sight of
Plymouth Hoe as he saw it on " the fayre evening " crowded
with his friends.   Such scenes and such enthusiasm were
common in those days when there was so much to rouse them.
Thither came the townsmen rushing out of church on that
Sunday in August, 1573, when word was brought that Francis
Drake was home from Nombre de Dios, and " there remained
few or no people with the preacher, all running out to observe
the blessing of God on the dangerous adventures of the
captain." Perhaps they were right and there was more to be
learnt from the practice of the captain than from the precept
of the preacher ; for those were days in which the roughest
sailors made quite sincerely professions of religion which
would sound strangely in the mouths of modern tars. " Serve
God daily," wrote John Hawkins in the sailing orders which he
issued when he went a-slaving on the Guinea coast, and had
he found any member of his crew backward in serving God by
harrying black villages he would have made short work of him.
" Serve God daily, love one another, preserve your victuals,
beware of fire, and keepe good companie." It was a short
code, but it summed up a good deal of Christianity as understood in those rough days ; and it may be that something
more of the essential virtues, such as common sense and sturdy
comradeship, lay in those brief rules than in many others
drawn up since the world learnt to profess a liking for more
pretentious Christianity.   And since we have named Hawkins,
let us add to the memories we are recalling that proud deed
which he wrought on a Spanish admiral just beneath these
heights, for it is instinct with a haughty sense of mastery and
contempt of what other men could do, which tell us with a
sudden flash of understanding why these men served England
so well and what the model is which those must follow who

wish to emulate them.   There are no better words in which
to tell the tale than those which Richard Hawkins used and
no fairer testimony than that given by a son to the greatness of
his father.   This is how it happened : "There came a fleet
of Spaniards of above fifty saile of shippes, bound for
Flanders, to fetch the Queen Donna Anna de Austria . . .
which entered betwixt the island and the maine without vayling
their topsayles or taking in of their flags ; which my father, Sir
John Hawkins, admirall of a fleet of Her Majesty's shippes then
riding in Catwater, perceiving, commanded his gunner to shoot
at the flag of the admirall that they might thereby see their
error."   Strangely enough this gentle way of hinting a mistake
was not immediately successful ; for "they persevered arrogantly to keepe the flag displayed, whereupon the gunner at
the next shot lact the admirall through and through, whereby
the Spaniards, finding that the matter began to grow earnest,
took in their flags and topsayles and so ran to an anchor."

Earnest it was indeed, and had the Spaniards been aware
that Hawkins was in command they would have known themselves to be dealing with a man who never spoke save in
very deadly earnest.   They sent a boat with an officer of rank
charged to demand an explanation ; but Hawkins would not
hold any parley with him, nor even let him come on board,
sending word to the Spanish admiral that " inasmuch as in the
Queene's port and chamber he had neglected to do the ac-
knowledgment and reverence which all owe another majesty
. . . he therefore required him that within twelve hours he
should depart the port, upon pain to be held as a common
enemy, and to proceed against him with force."

How often in English history has a high claim been so
greatly voiced ?   Here was a man indeed, direct and terrible,
one who in his great and simple heart cared not one jot for
consequences, but meant one thing, and that a thing worth life
or death, namely that the prestige of England on the sea
should stand, and more than that, should be recognised and

bowed to by all comers, be they admirals of great princes or humble traders. Heaven send this country such a man again ; and till he come, teach us to fill our minds with what he should be by remembering John Hawkins.

The fame of Hawkins has been a little obscured by that of Drake, which, justly or unjustly, has caught the popular fancy more. Yet Hawkins was Drake's master, and neither in courage nor in seamanship did his pupil rise above him. At that great fight at San Juan de Ulloa, when the English ships were treacherously surprised by Spaniards, who had guaranteed their safety, it was Hawkins who was in command, and to his perfect coolness and cheerful courage in that desperate emergency, when the English ships had to warp out of the harbour, while actually fighting at odds of ten to one, it was chiefly due that any lives were saved. "When the *Minion* stood off," says Hortop, who wrote the tale on his return to England, "our generall courageously cheered up his soldiers and gunners, and called to Samuel his page for a cup of beer, who brought it to him in a silver cup. And he, drinking to all the men, willed the gunners to stand to their ordnance lustily like men. He had no sooner set the cup out of his hand, but a demi-culverin shot struck away the cup and a cooper's plane that stood by the mainmast and ran out on the other side of the ship, which nothing dismayed our generall, for he ceased not to encourage us saying, ' Fear nothing ! for God who hath preserved me from this shot will also deliver us from these traitors and villains."

Here was a man indeed ! Fear he never knew, but anger, disappointment, surprise, the overweight of numbers in the enemy, all those passions and emotions which deprive weaker men of their best fighting powers, did but render Hawkins cooler, deadlier, more terrible and cheerful, hardening his nerves to steel and his heart to stone. He had just seen his fortune wrecked and lost. He had seen his friends most basely and treacherously murdered. He was himself still in the very gates of death, a mark conspicuous and gallant in view of the

Spanish musketeers and gunners. There is not in all our
history a nobler picture than that of the great captain calling
at this supreme moment for Samuel his page, and quaffing a
cup of beer to the health of his crew. Here is a lesson for all
time on the use of bravado, the crowning grace of every leader
who does not seek it at the cost of better things.

Such was Hawkins when he was at sea. And what was he
in port? Why, the best answer to that is that he, more than
any other man, more than Drake, or Howard, or Seymour, or
Winter, or Frobisher, more than all these singly or in united
council, drove back the great Armada, and saved England from
the nearest peril she has ever stood in. For what could all
these warriors and sailors have done against the Spaniards, had
their spars and cordage been defective? The Armada came up
Channel in wild weather. It was strangely stormy and tempestu-
ous.   Not the oldest fisherman on the Devon coast could
remember such a season. The English ships were perpetually
wearing and manœuvring throughout the battles, and the strain
on their spars must have been enormous. Had the work been
left in the hands of contractors, who knows what the end might
have been; but Hawkins had seen to it himself, and no work
that he ever touched was negligently done.

And so no fleet was ever more finely fitted than that which was
warped out under the shelter of Mount Edgcumbe to wait the
coming of the Spaniards. It was early morning when they were
in position, and the Hoe must have been crowded, for the whole
of England was awake, and the beacon fires running through
the country had left no appetite for work or play. In Plymouth
least of all on that morning, could man, woman, or child do
aught but watch. "The day wore on," says Mr. Froude in his
prose epic. "Noon passed and nothing had been seen. At
length, towards three in the afternoon, the look-out men on the
hill reported a line of sails on the western horizon, the two
wings being first visible, which were gradually seen to unite as
the centre rose over the rim of the sea. On they swept in a

broad crescent . . . a hundred and fifty, large and small, were counted and reported to Lord Howard."

What was the conduct of the crowd upon the Hoe who were privileged to witness this tremendous crisis ? No one has told us ! but on the fleet at any rate there could be nothing but cheerful confidence when Hawkins and Drake were in command. There was no fighting that day, for the English ships lay waiting and the Spaniards were not off the port till night was falling. And so darkness descended, and the strangest night came on that Plymouth has ever witnessed. Was the Hoe crowded until dawn ? Did any one sleep that night in Plymouth ? At any rate whatever uneasy slumber fell upon the town must have been broken once for all when, early in the morning, the sound of cannon rattled through the streets, and the women heard for the first time that sound of Spanish guns, which their husbands had sought eagerly for years past, with fierce ardour to slaughter the enemies of their faith, and, as they conceived it, of God Himself.

Then those who hastened to the heights ;—and who could have stayed behind ?—saw the *Ark Raleigh* carrying Lord Howard's flag, sail with three other ships right along the Spanish line, firing into each galleon they passed, and then sail back again firing as before ; and from this glorious beginning a great and general action sprang ; and at length the whole pageant, wrapped in smoke like a great thundercloud drifting low along the deep, passed onwards up the coast and out of sight, leaving to the Plymouth people no part in it but prayer.

Since the waters under heaven were gathered into one place and the dry land appeared there has been no sight which one would rather call back from the mists of history than this. It is a tale which when told a hundred times is new as if never told, one which will be told with emotion on this spot in days when English rule as we know it has faded into the limbo of dead empires, and that wide federation which already is being knit across the sea into a world power which no other nation will dare to threaten, looks back on Plymouth as the fertile soil where the seeds were sown and watered which have germinated into so great a harvest.

When one begins to stir the memories of Plymouth, so thick a host of dead triumphs rises into the air that one is perplexed and baffled in the effort to select even one or two for special comment ; and that perhaps is why so few of those who look seawards over this exquisite expanse of haven see it peopled with any but the most passing incidents of modern life. Plymouth has too many heroes ; in the crowd the faces of all but one or two are blurred.   But before abandoning the effort, it will be well to remember, now that the whole of England is imperialist, and all parties vie together to maintain the bond which unites the mother country with the colonies, how great was the part of Plymouth in the creation of those ties.

> We were dreamers, dreaming greatly, in the man-stifled town.
> We yearned towards the skyline where the strange roads go down.

So sings our great imperial poet—there is but one who can put into his lines so intense a throb ; there is no need to name him.   And so his " Song of the Dead " runs on :

> Came the whisper, came the vision, came the Power with the Need,
> Till the soul that is not man's soul was lent us to lead.

That is the great and final expression of the spirit of the old Plymouth navigators ; and by any who would emulate them, the soul that is not man's soul must first be sought and found.

Many of the achievements of Plymouth men both in the days of Drake and Hawkins, and yet more in those which followed, are lost to us for want of chroniclers.   But in the most unlikely places we find them lingering ; and so in the garrulous pages of that windbag, John Taylor, the water poet, are set down quaintly enough the details of one which serves

as well as any to show in what way men of Plymouth upheld
the great tradition which had been handed on to them.

"On 17th June last, 1640," says the patriotic water poet, "a
ship of the port of Plymouth of two hundred in burden . . .
about two of the clock in the morning within two leagues near
to the Lizard, was assaulted furiously by three Turkish pirates,
when there was a most bloody and cruel bickering. The
accursed Mahometans having gotten the wind of the
Elizabeth . . . their Admirall being in burden two hundred and
thirty tuns with twenty two pieces of ordnance, the Vice
Admirall was of a greater burden and with twenty six pieces of
ordnance; the Reare Admirall two hundred tunnes and had but
eight pieces in her; so the Turks had in their three ships fifty
six pieces of artillerie: the number of their men is unknown.
The Elizabeth had but thirty men and ten pieces of ordnance
and of those they could make use of or plye but five gunnes,
the ship was so pestered with packes and other carriage betweene
the decks. The master of the ship's name was Doves, who
dwelt in Plimmouth, a man of an excellent and invincible
spirit, as the sequel of the fight and his worthy life and most
unfortunate death will shew. The fight continued about the
time between seven and eight hours; and though the English
ship had but five guns that could be used, yet, by God's
assistance, the master gunner being a skilful, valiant and
experienced man he so plyed and played upon the miscreants
that by God's assistance he killed many of them.

"The gunner of the ship's name is John Whidon, and all the
while that the master of the ship most manfully and courageously did labour and bestir himself, and by his valorous
example gave encouragement to all the rest of his companie
that were in the ship, amongst whom the three passengers did
most worthie deserving service . . . being so long a time
furiously assaulted with many ordnance and about 500
enemies, and also three times boarded and entered by the
Turks, who were three times beaten out again; their ship

being fired and their round house burnt, their mainsail was likewise consumed in the flames, and their rigging and cordage cut down and spoiled. At last the master was slain, ending his days nobly, likewise the master's mate and the pilot and the quartermaster were killed outright, and kept Master Doves company both in life and death and heavenly happiness.

" In this terrible turmoyle there were two of the Turks had got themselves into the top, and one of the three passengers shot at them and killed them both. One of those slain pirats was a man of an extraordinary great stature, and for his corpulence not to be equalled amongst them all. He being killed the English did cleave his head and then they divided it from his carcase, and shewed the head and corpse to the Turks, and with renewed courage and unwearied valour they hailed the enemy and in braving manner said: 'Come aboard, you dogges, if you dare, and fetch your countryman.' But the Turks finding the business so hot, and the men so resolute that their damnable courages were quelled that they had no more mind to assault the English ship any more."

Plymouth has always been renowned for its addiction to the gentle craft of privateering. In the difficult years which preceded the coming of the Armada, whole fleets of Plymouth vessels bore the Prince of Condé's commission, and proved their sturdy Protestantism by plundering and burning up and down the Channel any ships of Roman Catholic powers which were not too strong for them. For many generations afterwards war was so frequent that all kinds of pleasant pastime were to be had upon the sea; but in the last French war the people played so busily that they forgot how to work, and when peace was declared, and other people's money could not be taken from them honestly, the good men of Plymouth woke up to the fact that their commerce had gone to the deuce, and it cost them much time and labour to recover it.

However, these distresses find their proper record in the

local histories. We have mooned about the Hoe till we have grown chilly. It is high time to move on ; and as enough has been said about the port, while the streets are rather common-place, we will strike off at once towards the river, which, as already hinted, is of great interest and beauty.

"The navigable river Tamar," says our old friend Prince,— and as we shall have soon to trudge a great way onwards without his company we may pay the more attention to this remark,—"Tamar is a meer or bound, some few hamlets excepted, between Devon and Cornwall, both which shires she amorously smiles upon as she glides along to her desired ocean, into whose embraces she falls at Plymouth." It is charmingly put, and is all quite true moreover, except that Cornwall is not a shire, and Prince might have known better than to call it one. Indeed if the good vicar of Berry Pomeroy had been at the pains to travel in that sister land of which he never speaks so civilly as when he is about to steal one or more of her worthies, he would have known that the acute intelligence of the Cornish peasant gauges so accurately the importance of his native duchy that he regards the whole of England as consisting of two portions, Cornwall and "the shires." If a person is not in Cornwall, he is in the shires, unless of course he is out of England altogether, which could scarcely be a worse misfortune, and indeed is very much the same thing, all people born outside Cornwall being equally "foreigners," whether Scotch, Welsh, or natives of New Guinea.

Cornwall therefore forms no portion of the region of the shires. It is a duchy, and has no wish to be confounded in one common designation with the rest of England ; but with this deduction Prince's little effort may very well pass muster ; and as the smiling of the river Tamar is particularly amorous towards the time of high spring tides it will be as well to select that season for visiting the river.

There is but one way of seeing it, and that way is by boat. No road gives more than the feeblest appreciation of the

beauties of the finest river in the west. The journey must be
made by water, and equally of necessity the start must be
from the Hoe, in order that the approach to the scenery of the
upper river may lie along that great imperial waterway of the
Hamoaze whose portal is Mount Edgecombe, and in which
there lie from day to day a fleet of battleships and cruisers
and venomous torpedo boats such as might well strengthen
the nerves of any one of those who hold that the voice of
England must be low when others speak arrogantly and
yielding when they threaten war. Indeed it is a very noble
sight which greets us as we steam round from the Hoe between
the woods upon the left and the huge buildings of the dockyard
and its contiguous establishments on the right. Low hills
flank a winding estuary of great width ; and on its smooth
green waters lie at anchor some forty warships of every type,
from the somewhat antiquated turret ship, which has had few
friends since the *Captain* turned turtle in the Bay of Biscay,
to the newest pattern of torpedo boat-catcher darting out to
sea at the rate of thirty knots, while the vibration of her
engines sends the crew bobbing up and down upon her deck
like corks, and one learns to look upon the men who are
ready to take such a craft into action through a stormy sea as
setting their lives upon a cast somewhat more hazardous
than those who tied the white tape on their arms in the
breaches of Ciudad Rodrigo. Already the prophecy is being
falsified that the growing size and weight of armaments was
quickly rendering all combatants more equal, and stripping
dash and courage of their pre-eminence in sea-fights. The
pendulum has swung. The huge ships are no longer all.
Men's thoughts turn more and more to smaller craft of great
mobility : and in the next war there will be great chances for
young officers. " Keep then the sea that is the wall of England." It is here at Plymouth that the full force is felt of that
great cry of a voice silenced four centuries ago and more, here
where the strength and might of England are epitomised, and

where one knows and understands without instruction that come what may the sea will be kept in the coming time as in the past, and that England will never see that day when her town wall shall be stormed and captured by her enemies.

One of the regular mail coach routes into Cornwall crossed the estuary from the dockyard to Torpoint upon the Cornish shore ; and there is a curious half-forgotten story of a clergyman who was roused from his bed by some constraint which he could neither explain nor resist, and under the influence of which he dressed himself and went down stairs, still not knowing with what object, where he found his groom, who under a similar constraint had risen and saddled his master's horse, with another for himself in attendance ; and so the two men, led by some mysterious guidance, rode on through the dark to this ferry of Torpoint, where they found the ferryman roused and lying waiting in his boat to punt across he knew not whom. And so, led at every turn by an unseen hand, the clergyman reached Bodmin, where in the court-house a man was on the point of being condemned to death for want of that evidence which only he could give who had been so strangely roused and guided thither.

By this route, for the most part, travellers used to go who were bound for Falmouth to embark upon those Post-office packets which during the whole of the last century and some part of this were the regular vehicle of communication between America and England. It was for the majority of travellers a long and tedious journey ; but Baretti, whom we mentioned some way back, appears to have found it rarely pleasant, bringing to his three days of confinement a cheerful disposition and an incurable trick of gaiety. He travelled with an elderly lady and two nieces, who were so accommodating that they beguiled the way with songs, and very probably Baretti sang too, though he modestly conceals the fact. At any rate they all got on so well that when the girls and their aunt got out and left the poor Italian to continue his journey without their aid, "we kissed and parted with eyes not perfectly dry."

"Did I say kiss?" Baretti continues, evidently feeling that something more is needed in defence of his conduct. "Yes, upon my word. But you Italians make so much of a kiss that there is no enduring you. Here we make nothing of it, especially on such occasions ; nor is there any harm in it whatever you may think. What have you to say, you people on the other side of that huge mountain? I am sure I shall not abide your silly fashions now I am used to those of England. The English have twenty times more wit than you . . . In that coach none of us could receive any pleasure but what was got from one of the other five. The whole world was without the coach, and within there was nothing but ourselves. Therefore having nothing else to love we loved each other very fast."

It is really very nice to know on such good authority that the customs of England were so pleasant no longer ago than the year 1760. Perhaps some admirers of antiquity will attempt to recover the ground lost since then, and on their next journey try to love somebody very fast. If so, any statements of results which may be communicated to the present writer under seal of secrecy will be read with interest.

It will not do to stay here gossiping about Italian travellers, or we shall lose the tide, which is more important to the accomplishment of a voyage up the Tamar than any one might think who surveys the noble sheet of water which extends upwards from Saltash, an ancient town remarkable for nothing in particular, unless it be for the possession of a well, which, as the historian Carew tells us, possessed this peculiar and exasperating property that it would "never boil peas to any seasonable softness." Let no one think that housewifely troubles are beneath the dignity of history ; but if any one does propound that lofty view, let him hurry on to Landulph, not so very much above Saltash, where he will find himself in the society of emperors, albeit long since dead. For so strangely has chance, or some other force, drifted about the dead leaves of former days, that one cannot stroll round this quiet church of Landulph, filled as it is with monuments of men whose lives contained no incident, without being arrested by one small metal tablet, which suddenly opens all the gates of history, and carries one back to that great act of cowardice and shame which the Christian powers of Europe committed when they left Constantinople to be conquered by the Turks, thereby preparing for themselves a punishment of woe and bloodshed of which no man even yet, after four centuries and a half, can see the end. It is Theodore Paleologus who lies buried here, fourth in descent from Thomas, brother of that Constantine who fell gloriously in the breaches of his city; and if there had been in Europe any true sense either of policy or religion, Theodore or his fathers would have reigned in the city of Constantine. As it is, this little tablet marks a wasted chance such as does not return in the history of empires.

"Some twenty years ago," Cyrus Redding tells us, writing in 1842, "the vault in which Paleologus was interred was accidentally opened; and curiosity prompted the lifting of the lid. The coffin was entire, made of oak, and was sufficiently perfect to show that the dead man exceeded the common stature. The head was a long oval, and the nose believed to have been aquiline. A long white beard reached low down the breast."

Above Landulph the river quickly closes in. The stream takes a narrower channel, and its course lies between banks which rapidly increase in interest and beauty. The boat is no longer travelling on a wide sea flood, but threading the windings of an inland water to which the woods drop down with infinite sweetness, opening constantly into very fertile valleys, whose orchards gleam with luxuriance of pink blossom among the darker foliage. The ground rises steadily, and the trees grow thicker on it till, just where the hillside takes its

most gorgeous spring colouring of bronze and golden green
from the mingled growth of oaks and beeches, the towers of a
great gray castellated mansion rise flashing in the sunlight, and
we have reached Pentillie.

I do not know if there is on any other river in this country
a house placed so finely as this, but I do know there is none
in all the West. The sudden impression left by the aspect of
the house is very memorable. One moment the view is over
the brown woodland, a solitude of verdure, in the next the
trees have dropped down steeply to a valley, have risen again
as swiftly on the further side, while bursting out, still half
hidden by the foliage, comes this stately vision of terraces and
towers, and is gone again while still half seen, too swiftly passing
for any recollection save one of beauty, so fleeting that it
hardly seems more substantial than some fairy spectacle seen
in the quick illusions of a dream.

There are one or two thrice-told tales about Pentillie; but
they are rudely out of keeping with the frame of mind induced
by following the course of this lovely river. We will not
break the tune by any dissonance, but sit gazing idly as the
banks glide by, and woodlands on each side make the whole
tideway dark and cool. Over the brown water the slow
steamer ploughs its way until one sees ahead a little bluff,
wooded to the water's edge, and in another moment the gray
walls of a tiny chapel glimmer through the trees. We must
pause here, for the place is one of some interest, and the
history of the chapel carries us back as far as the wars of
Lancaster and York. Cotehele, the house which stands above
this cliff, scarce seen from the river, was the residence of Sir
Richard Edgcumbe, who, during the reign of the Yorkist,
Richard Crookback, fell under suspicion of holding communications with the exiled house of Lancaster, to which indeed
the greater part of the west country, with its passionate attachment to lost causes, had long since devoted its love and
energies. The accusation was not one to be disproved; and

Sir Richard resolved to flee while there was yet time. But the King was not one who let the grass grow while he was deliberating; and his men-at-arms were at Cotehele, charged to arrest its master, before any plans of escape were settled. A timely warning saved Edgcumbe from being taken in the house : but the soldiers were hard upon his heels as he fled through the woods which skirt the river; and at length, seizing his last chance, he caught up a huge stone, flung it into the water with a resounding splash, and sent his cap flying after it, while at the same moment he doubled back into the cover of the woods. The Yorkist soldiers hearing the sound, and seeing the floating cap, concluded that Edgcumbe had leapt into the water, and having watched for some time without seeing him rise, went back to those who sent them, and reported that Edgcumbe had been swept away by some strong current, and would trouble the house of York no more. Meantime Sir Richard, lurking safely in his covert, watched his pursuers go by, and doubtless laughed slyly at his own sagacity, as did Jack Rattenbury three centuries later in similar circumstances upon Hope's Nose. He was far, however, from ascribing all the credit of his escape to his own mother wit ; and years after when the wrongs of Lancaster had long since been avenged on Bosworth Field, and Sir Richard had risen to high office in the household of the Tudor Prince, he built this chapel as a lasting memorial of gratitude to heaven for the help sent him in an hour of great peril.

Here at Cotehele, early in the last century, a lady of the house of Edgcumbe fell ill, was pronounced to have died, and was laid in the family vault. That night the greedy sexton who knew she had been buried with rings of great value on her hands, went alone into the vault, opened the coffin, drew back the shroud, disengaged the hands and began with trembling, frightened fingers to tear off the rings. Perhaps he was handling the cold flesh rather roughly, for no man can rob the dead with steady nerves ; when at this moment the lady sighed and stirred

a little in her coffin. That slight movement was enough. The
guilty sexton fled in wild terror. His lantern was left behind.

Valley of the Tamar.

The lady recovered consciousness, and in a little while was able
to return home.

The house of Cotehele is rarely beautiful and interesting, a fine specimen of ancient domestic architecture, preserved with scrupulous care in the very state it bore when Tudor princes occupied the throne. There is no house in Cornwall better worth a close inspection ; but we may not linger there, for the distance up the stream is long, and the spring tides wait for no man.

Few rivers wind so strangely as the Tamar. Not far above Cotehele one passes on the left hand the little town of Calstock, famed for strawberries, a straggling hillside village of no great picturesqueness, but possessing a fine church on the summit of the ridge at a sufficient distance from the town to allow full opportunity for that sense of virtuous toil in going thither which has been claimed as one of the advantages of the inconvenient situation of so many Cornish churches. Now this church, as the steamer ploughs up stream, is left behind standing out nobly on the hill ; but half an hour afterwards, when it has passed completely out of mind, is seen again directly ahead of the steamer at a considerable distance. How it got there is a marvel unexplained ; but there is no time to wonder, for the scenery around has grown so singularly grand and lovely as to claim one's whole attention.

A few mines which deface and scar the river's bank a little way above Calstock do but increase the glow and colour of the forest by its contrast with their grimy galleries and black heaps of poisonous arsenic dust. They stand upon the shoulder of the hill ; and beyond their ugly prosperous smoke and dirtiness the trees stretch far away along the ridge, dense and close down to the water's edge, a mountain of gold and sunny green, broken in the midst by a high crag which stands up sheer and gray amid the mass of gorgeous colour.

This is the first peak of a great range of limestone cliffs, which for the most part, as the hill sweeps round above the village of Morwellham, are hidden in the woods. But when that tiny cluster of cottages and wharves is left behind, the stream creeps closer to the hill, and it is as if the buried rock stirred and flung the coppice off its shoulders, for the limestone precipices rise vertically out of the water to a vast height. The summits are weathered into most fantastic shapes, pinnacles and towers break the skyline, and wherever a crevice in the rock has allowed the lodging of a little earth, some oak tree roots itself, or a wild tangle of greenery drops down the scarred surface of the cliff.

Language exhausts itself quickly upon the beauty of this gorge. It is one which leaves an indelible impression on the mind; and of itself, if the Tamar had no other beauty, is enough to rank it at the head of all the rivers of the west.

On Dartmoor, near Princetown.

CHAPTER IX

THERE are few roads in all Devon so pleasant for travellers
of every kind as that which runs from Plymouth to Tavistock.
The first three miles are long and toilsome ; but when the
town and its dull suburbs are once left behind, the moors are
quickly reached ; and the road runs for many a mile undulating
gently over a lofty ridge of downs, having on the right hand at
a little distance a higher chain of rugged hills, across which
the cloud shadows sweep with amazing suddenness and beauty,
leaving those slopes in dark obscurity one moment which the
next are radiant with sunlight to their very summits, while the
tall granite church towers in the hollows change from dark
gray blocks hardly distinguishable from the gloomy hillside, to
living palpitating things, so brightly do they gleam and sparkle
in the sudden glow of warm light. It is a lonely rugged

country of infinite beauty, sterner and less wooded than the
fringes of the moor around Ashburton, offering vistas indeed
across the higher slopes which are so obviously seldom trodden
by any other feet than those of forest ponies that it is easy to
believe the story told of how a shepherd, wandering not so very
far away from his customary pastures in quest of some strayed
sheep, found the body of a sailor lying in a little hollow fully
clothed, his head upon the bundle which he had been carrying and the whole attitude that of a man who had lain
down to sleep in that desolate place for very weariness. At
his feet lay curled up his little dog ; but both dog and man
were skeletons ; and must have been resting there together for
many weeks.

There are numerous points along this road which are the
approaches to valleys of such interest and beauty that it is a
constant temptation to diverge. There is Horrabridge, most
lovely of moorland scenes, whence one looks up the Walkham
valley, lying exquisitely among a group of tors of singular
grandeur, Staple Tor, Mis Tor, Sheep's Tor ; and not far away
is that grand rock called the Dewerstone, which is the common
haunt or meet of the yeth-hounds that hunt across the moor
with phantom riders from Buckfastleigh to Tavistock along
the old track road called the "Abbot's Way." Bickleigh too,
where the great family of Slanning was seated, whose name
will never be forgotten in the west ; Buckland Abbey, where Sir
Francis Drake established himself; Princetown, on which we
look down from this high elevation, a drear and barren
monument of human suffering and crime,—there is no end to
the digressions which might be made, if there were time to
think of them, in this most interesting district. But Tavistock
has greater claims upon our space. Already one sees it lying
in a hollow on the right ; and a rapid descent brings the road
out on the brink of a swift stream, across an ivied bridge, and
by a grand stone gateway, which is one of the sights of
Tavistock, both for its handsome architecture, and for the

wealth of legend and tradition with which the fine imaginations
of the townsmen have endowed it.

Indeed this old gateway of Fitzford is a very ghostly spot :
but the present moment, with its bright midday sunshine, is
not the most suitable for speaking of its wild traditions.   It
will be better to stroll out here again in the evening, when the
growing dusk has induced a fitting attitude of mind to receive
the tales of Lady Howard and her coach of bones : and in the
meantime to spend the incredulous hours of sunlight in
following up those lions of Tavistock which have no connection
with the other world.   This will not be a very simple matter ;
for the mere truth is that this borderland of Tavistock is
steeped and drowned in old-time memories which in the act of
passing through the fertile western imaginations run back
quickly into that twilight country which lies at the rear of all
men's minds, however little they admit it, in this land of
ancient superstition ;   and so emerge touched with little
uncanny gleams, and sticking perhaps to some older recollection
with which they had nought to do originally, but with which
they blend quite charmingly ; and so the stories grow and a
striking legend is manufactured quite unconsciously out of next
to nothing.

Tavistock is certainly a very lovely town.   It is set in a deep
valley of rich pastureland around the banks of the River
Tavy, sheltered by dense woodlands over which the hills rise
bare and rugged, cutting off the winter storms from every
quarter.   Turn where you will in the old town streets, you
will see the wild downs rising over these lovely woods and hear
the noisy river singing over stones and boulders of all the
wonders it has seen upon the moor.   This sound of rushing
water fills the town.   You lose it for a moment as a heavy
waggon passes ; and then as the horses strain away with the
lumbering thing, once more the steady singing fills the air,
occupying one's mind with fancies, and drawing one's steps
towards the abbey bridge.

Here idleness is a virtue.

[To face p. 151.

This bridge is the true centre of the town of Tavistock, a wondrous place for reflection and romance. It was long since pointed out by qualified observers that a bridge across a running stream conduces to idleness. Yes, but much comes of idleness in such a spot as this. Here idleness is a virtue ; and he is the bad man who hastens by with no more than a passing thought for the brown water foaming under the old bridge, the dark pools round which it swirls, the trailing ivy which hangs in the cool shadow of the arches, the weir over which the river boils a few yards further on, the salmon ladder by its side, and the leaping of the fish in the still pool beyond, where the rush and turmoil of the fall is carried under water by its own weight and the foam and bubbles may be seen glistening below the unrippled surface. Black and broken by white rapids, the river hastens on, flashing over boulders beneath an avenue of high elm trees, through which the hot sunshine falls in dapples on the water ; and so sweeping sidewards is lost among the meadows where, until the floods of two winters since, there stood a hollow oak tree known as " Lady Howard's Oak." For here, too, the stories of that grim old woman intrude themselves ; and it needs an effort to cast them all aside a while, and follow the course of the abbey walls, which from this side only retain their ancient aspect.

Two of the celebrities of Tavistock dwelt behind the battlements of that long stone wall that skirts the river, standing still as strong as it did five centuries ago. Of one we know no more than that his name was John, a monk of the great abbey, and that he carried round the country an appeal, dated " Friday before St. Bartholomew the Apostele, 1370," asking alms from the faithful to be spent in repairing " the great stone bridge adjoining the town of Tavystoke, over the great water called the Tavy, which runs down violently from the moor (*de mora violenter currens*), where there is no good ford, and which cannot be maintained without the gifts of the faithful." So John, "collector for this purpose," was recommended to the good offices of all to whom the letter came ; and many a weary mile he must have trudged before he came back to his quiet cell beside the noisy river. One wonders even whether he came back at all, for the roads were very perilous, even for monks when they carried moneybags ; and apart from the natural dislike to collectors of all sorts, which in those happy days was more easily gratified than it is now, there was, and is, an ancient prejudice against men of Tavistock, which may have operated to make John's way the stonier. Heaven knows what this feeling springs from. In Tavistock it is ascribed to jealousy. Outside Tavistock they do not attempt to explain ; but act upon it with the promptness of three Okehampton men who, seeing a pedlar struggling in a flooded brook which was washing him away, were about to help him out, when one said, " Augh, tes aunly a Tavistock man. Let 'n goo," which they accordingly did without remorse.

The other famous person connected with the abbey is Betsey Grimbal, and she is famous in proportion as nothing is known about her. Of course one wonders what she or any other Betsey had to do with an abbey full of holy men ; but this is a question which cannot now be solved, and we need not be in any hurry to cry "*pro pudor*." At any rate there is her tower, Betsey Grimbal's tower, still standing when nearly all the rest of the vast fabric has been destroyed. Legend says that Betsey was murdered there, having set her affections on some monk who thus requited them. It is not wise to lean too heavily on Tavistock legends, for they have all been written up. Still there was doubtless some bloody story connected with the tower ; and, indeed, another legend recognises this fact by charging Lady Howard with the murder of two of her children on this interesting spot. There is no evidence that Lady Howard ever murdered anybody, but let that pass. Tavistock has long since made up its mind that she was a bloody woman, and has thus no scruple in thrusting her in where Betsey Grimbal has the better right to reign.

This abbey was a pile of splendour and its abbot a man of huge estates, some of which were not too scrupulously acquired. There was one Child, a man of property at Plymstock, who, when hunting on the moor, got separated from his followers and overwhelmed by a sudden snowstorm. He thought to save his life by cutting open his horse, and crawling into the warm body ; but the cold was too intense, and he died, leaving behind him a doggerel scrawl to this effect :

> Who finds and brings me to my grave
> My lands at Plymstock he shall have.

Now the monks of Tavistock happened to find the frozen body. They perceived at once that they had gained a prize, and proceeded to make preparations for a funeral befitting both the consequence of the donor and the magnitude of his gift. Probably they were too pleased to hold their tongues till the man was safely buried ; for the monks of Plymstock heard of what had happened, and, enraged to find themselves ousted from the possession of the lands, they gathered all their forces and lay in wait for the monks of Tavistock at a ford which they must pass, resolved to take away the corpse by force. But the brethren of Tavistock were very cunning and had forestalled them by building a bridge far up the stream, which is called " Guile Bridge " to this day ; and across Guile Bridge they carried the body home in triumph, so that while the monks of Plymstock lay chilling themselves beside the river, there were high funeral mass and gorgeous obsequies in the abbey church, and much rejoicing over the added wealth which God had sent them.

What became of all this wealth at the dissolution is an open question. Some say that there runs a secret passage underneath the town from the abbey precinct to Fitzford House, which is filled with gold plate and countless treasures. Others have it that the gold was hidden in this passage when the Civil

War broke out ; but all agree that it is there and will be surely
found some day, and that the bulk of it at any rate is ecclesiastical wealth.   This may very well be true if the good
people of the town were as liberal to the monks as they
were to the excellent Puritan who watched over their salvation
during the Commonwealth.   His name was Larkham, and he
has left a record of the benefactions of his parishioners.

"1653, Nov. 30th.   The wife of Will Hodges brought me a
fat goose.   Lord, do them good !   Edward Cole sent by his
daughter a turkey ; Lord, accept it !   Dec. 2nd.   Sara Trowt
a dish of butter ; accept, Lord !   Dec. 6th.   Margaret Sitwell
would not be paid for 2½ lbs. of butter ; is she not a daughter
of Abraham?   Father, be pleased to pay her.   Walter Peek
sent me, Dec. 14, a partridge, and W. Webb the same day
pork and puddings ; Lord, forget not !   Mrs. Thomasin
Doidge—Lord, look on her in much mercy—Dec. 19th gave
me 5s. . . . Jan. 25th.   Mrs. Audry sent me a bushel of
barley malt for housekeeping.   Lord, smell a sweet savour !
Patrick Harris sent me a shoulder of pork,—he is a poor
ignorant man.   Lord, pity him !"

Such were the traditions of liberality in Tavistock, and such
they may be, for aught I know, even to the present day.   It
was perhaps this vicar, so lustily fortified with pork and
puddings, who did yeoman's service against a witch, as
Mrs. Bray tells us in *The Borders of the Tamar and the Tavy*.
It seems that an old woman in this neighbourhood, having
dealings with Satan, had acquired the power of changing
herself into a hare whenever she pleased ; and as often as she
found herself short of money she used to perform this metamorphosis, at the same time sending her imp of a grandson to
tell a certain keen sportsman who dwelt hard by that he had
seen a hare in a certain place.   The sportsman always gave
the boy a sixpence for bringing him such news.   The dogs
were got out.   The old woman gave them a sharp run, and
always managed to slip into her cottage in some surprising

way without being seen.   At last the trick was suspected ; and
the sportsman took counsel of the parson, who laid his plans
accordingly.   And so the hounds were kept in readiness ; and
when the boy next brought his news, they were slipt with such
celerity that the witch found them much closer on her heels
than she liked.   The parson too came toiling after the pack ;
so that the atmosphere was growing hot.   The witch ran her
hardest.   The pace became terrific.   The boy grew so
apprehensive for his grandmother's safety that he forgot his
caution and cried out, " Run, granny, run ! "   The huntsman
heard him, and cheered on his dogs the faster.   At last the hare
doubled and the hounds overran themselves.   The witch
slipped into her own cottage through a hole not big enough
to admit a human form.   The huntsman saw her enter, and
riding up battered fiercely on the door, while the hounds leapt
up baying round the lintel.   But the strange thing was that
though the door was only an ordinary cottage planking of no
solidity or strength, no force the huntsman could apply made
it stir until the parson came, when it yielded instantly and the
whole hunt rushed in.   They found the old woman in bed
in an upper room panting furiously and actually bleeding from
wounds which showed the plain marks of dogs' teeth.
Notwithstanding this damning evidence she denied stoutly that
she was a witch ; until at length the huntsman, losing patience,
cried, " Let us have the dogs up, and see what they say she
is ; " whereupon the old woman threw up her cards, admitted
she was a witch and sued for pardon, which was improperly
accorded to her, for she reverted to her evil practices, and had
to be burnt after all.

   There are plenty of witches to be found even yet ; some
have been mentioned in earlier pages of this veracious work,
and there will be even more to tell of when we enter Cornwall,
where they are perhaps more numerous than in Devon.   As
for fairies, of which also Mrs. Bray has much to say, the
traditions of them seem to be dying out much faster than

those of other spirits. There are few people to be met with nowadays who will claim to have seen the fairies dancing in the moonlight, or even to have heard them singing by the river; while any farmer who went home now with such a story as that he "heard with his own ears they bits of pisgies laughing and tacking their hands to see he lead astray and unable to find the right road, though he had travelled it scores of times," would hardly get off without a curtain lecture such as he would remember when next he loitered at "The Seven Stars" after the proper time for going home. And perhaps in this dearth of fairy lore, which was once so plentiful in Tavistock, it may not be uninteresting to append a story told me by one whom I shall describe no otherwise than as my friend the doctor, knowing well that, should he read these lines, that description will please him best which most recalls his great privilege of easing others' pain. The story is a Cornish one, but we are very near the border now.

"I think," the doctor said, "this county must be unusually prolific in old women of distinct character, or curious antecedents. One especially I call to mind who claimed to be the granddaughter of a fairy.

"It was undoubtedly true. Old Nancy told me the story several times; and I have in my possession the very granite bowl out of which her grandfather might have drawn health, wealth, or happiness, if he had not wasted his opportunities. It stands in my study to this day, but I do not tell my visitors what it is, for to do so might spoil its virtue, and I quite mean to draw wealth and health at least, to say nothing of happiness, out of it myself one day.

"It happened in this way. Old Nancy's grandfather lived at Trelawn, a little hamlet bordering on the downs. He must have been singularly unlike the young men who live at Trelawn in these days, for he reached the age of twenty-one without ever having courted a girl. Nancy, anxious for his credit, always assured me that he was lacking neither in personal beauty nor in tenderness of heart ; so the thing remains inexplicable.

"However, so it was : and his character drew the attention of a 'white witch,' who at once perceived that he had become qualified for great actions in her own particular line of business, and accordingly advised him to go and dig for treasure upon the downs at Hallowe'en. He must go at midnight and alone.

"The poor lad did not much like the undertaking. But treasure was no more plentiful then than now ; and having been assured by the witch that he was safe from the assaults of all spirits, and could not fail to dig up something of ex- ceeding value, such as would make a man of him for life, he plucked his courage up, borrowed his father's spade, and went.

"Of course he was to dig in a fairy ring. There were a good many on the downs, and he passed by several fine ones for no other reason than because he was afraid to begin. The further he went, the less his courage grew ; so at last, feeling that if he waited much longer there would be none left, he struck his spade into the very centre of a ring larger than any he had seen before, and began to dig.

"It was heavy work, and he kept on looking over his shoulder, just to make sure the way home was clear ; so he only got on slowly. He did not speak even to bless himself; for the witch had particularly enjoined him to keep silence. At last his spade struck against something hard. He thought it was a stone ; and so it was, but not the sort of stone he had in his mind ; for in a very few minutes he saw it was a round vessel shaped out of granite—Nancy always called it a kist.

"It lay bottom upwards, and so distinctly suggested to his mind something valuable inside that he forgot the witch's caution, gave a great shout, flung himself on his knees, and caught the kist in his two hands.

"Before he had time to raise it out of the pit, however, an extraordinary thing happened. He suddenly saw that he was

not alone.   What it was that stood before the hole he had dug he
could not at first tell, for it was vague, and seemed to have
scarcely more substance than a wreath of mist under the moon.
But it grew denser and more distinct, and changed and moved
till he saw it was a beautiful girl, with long red hair flowing
down her back, stretching out her hands to him across the
fairy vessel and the pit in which it lay, as truly flesh and blood
as any maiden in Trelawn, only fifty times more beautiful than
the best of them.

"The poor man threw himself on his face and screamed with
fear.   But she raised him and soothed his fright, and talked to
him sweetly, and told him she was a fairy, and the guardian of
the treasure lying at his feet, bound to watch over it till
released by a man who had never loved a woman, and now he
had set her free, and might choose between her and the fairy
gold, for both he could not have.

"Now Nancy's grandfather was not an emotional man, and
had perhaps his notions on propriety.   But reserve and decorum
fled from him when he found the fairy's arms about his neck,
and her long hair sweeping his face.   Something leapt in him
that had never stirred before ; he suddenly found that flesh and
blood were of more account than gold, and vowed he preferred
the fairy.

"The fairy herself appears to have been charmed with this
decision, and he and she returned to Trelawn together, taking
with them the kist, though of course the treasure had vanished
when the grandfather made his choice.   There were still
uses to which the kist could be put, however ; for as the fairy
explained, health, wealth, and happiness might be drawn out of
the empty bowl by those who were pure-minded and single-
hearted—two difficult conditions, which perhaps Nancy's grandfather never succeeded in fulfilling, for he certainly died poor.

"Still, there the kist was on Nancy's shelf ; and being very
pleased with me one day, she promised me I should have it
when she died, unless of course I died first, which was not so

very unlikely, seeing that she had promised it already to three people, every one of whom had been dead for some years. Perhaps I might think this unlucky, and be afraid to come into the succession ? but if not, I might as well know that the kist would reach me with all its fairy qualities unimpaired ; because, though given away, it was given by a daughter's daughter, who can alienate fairy gifts without breaking the charm.

" It was very nice to know this.   I was not afraid ; I did not die first ; and I now have the kist ready for the moment when I can qualify for drawing forth the magic gifts."

Such was the doctor's story, one of many curious pieces of folklore which his industry has collected among the Cornish cottages.

But to return to Tavistock, where ghosts and witches are so very common that one would be tempted to dilate still further on them were it not time to be talking of Lady Howard.   First, however, before moving from the bridge, under which such a quantity of water has run while we have stood gossiping about things human and superhuman, it will be necessary to say something of the lady's father, Sir John Fitze, whose history is remarkable, besides being more authentic than her own.   It can be read in Prince's *Worthies* ; but the best authority for the facts is a work entitled *The Bloudie Book*, a very apt title as the reader will presently admit.

It is said that when the hour of John Fitze's birth was approaching his father erected a scheme of nativity ; and finding the conjuncture of the heavenly bodies portended dismal ill-fortune to the infant, desired the midwife to use all her skill to delay its birth but one hour.   The woman could not do so ; and the child was born under aspects which were but too truly verified in the evil days of his life and death.   He seems to have been noted as a turbulent, dangerous man, very ready with his sword on all occasions.   " Meeting on a time," says *The Bloudie Book*, " at Tavistock at dinner, with many of his

neighbours . . . they outstript the noontide . . . amongst
other talk Sir John was vaunting his free tenure, boasting that
he held not a foot of any but the Queene in England. To
which Maister Slanning replied that though by courtesie it
were neglected, yet of dewe and common rights he was to pay
him so much by the year for some small lande held of him,
the rent being by reason of friendshippe a long time intermitted.
Upon which wordes Sir John told him with a great oath he lied,
and withall gave fuel to his rage and reines of spight in the
unjustnes of his anger, offering to stab him. But Maister
Slanning, who was known to be a man of no less courage and more
courtesie, with a great knife that he had warded the hazard
of such threatenings . . . " The brawl was composed by the
interference of friends, and Slanning seems to have thought the
whole matter at an end ; for he shortly left the company, and
started homewards with a single servant. " Long had he not
ridden, but commanding the man to walk down his horses in
the way, himself the while taking the greene fields for his more
contented walking, he might behold Sir John Fitze with four
more galloping amaine after him, which sight could not but
be a great amazement to Maister Slanning." There was worse
than amazement in store for poor gallant Slanning, who was
known throughout the county as a brave and upright gentleman ;
for Fitze, egged on in his heady passions by a servant of like
impulses with his own, was resolved to have the life of the
neighbour who had dared to contradict him, and assailed him
instantly with all his following. When he was thus attacked by
five swords at once, Slanning had, if the local tradition may be
trusted, reached the gate of Fitzford ; and it was beneath the
archway that he fought, having fallen back, perhaps, in
the effort to get some solid protection in his rear. But he
had scarce a chance of defending himself ; for receiving a blow
from behind, he staggered, and in that moment was run through
the body by Fitze and fell, as clearly murdered as the victim of
any brutal highway robbery.

No judgment in those times or in our own has attempted to palliate this act, or represent Slanning as slain in fair fight. Fitze fled to France, where he lay until his friends managed to obtain some sort of pardon for him. It could not have been a full acquittance, for when Slanning's children grew to manhood they sued him for compensation for their father's death ; and this summons he was called to London to answer. Now in the intervening years the guilt of blood seems to have weighed very heavily on Fitze. His friends shunned him. He bore about a stain from which none could cleanse him ; and the sense of aloofness which this bred drove him into wilder excesses, so that there were few men who did not fear him, and most of all he feared himself. This summons to account for the crime of years before disturbed him greatly. He rode on his way a prey to wild fears, so unnerved that his servants could do little with him ; and one night he rode into Kingston-on-Thames very late, and knocked up the people at the " Anchor " inn, who were at first most unwilling to receive him, but yielded to importunity and took him in. He lay all night crying out in his sleep so terribly that the woman of the inn became alarmed, and when her husband got up to go and mow in the very early morning, she refused to be left in the house with the strange gentleman. Perhaps the noise of their movements may have been heard by Fitze ; for he leapt up with the fancy that officers were coming to his chamber to arrest him. He rushed out with drawn sword in the dark, and finding a man actually on the threshold stabbed him, so that he died then and there. It was, however, no officer sent to arrest him, but a poor groom, whom Fitze had himself directed to call him early in the morning ; and the miserable man no sooner saw this second victim lying at his feet than he turned his sword against himself and died.

Such was the very tragic ending of John Fitze ; and if his ghost had haunted Tavistock, it would have been small wonder. But oddly enough this, which one might have thought the very story for supernatural moss to grow upon, has bred none at all.

M

while the career of his daughter, Lady Howard, has swept the
countryside of its traditions and gathered them about herself.
As far as history tells us, she was simply a woman of great force
of character, who managed her estates admirably, and was
tenacious of her rights against a greedy husband. But
Tavistock will not hear of this view, preferring to represent her
as an atrocious monster, who had four husbands, which is true,
and murdered them all, which is not true, in addition to several
other persons who are not named with such precision as to
enable the charge concerning them to be very clearly met. And
the proof that she did all this is ready to the hand of any one
who will hang about the gate of Fitzford towards the hour of
midnight. For as the clock strikes twelve, whatever be the
weather, fair or foul, Lady Howard drives out from the portal in
a coach of bones. They are the bones of her four murdered
husbands, and at each corner of the coach one of their four
grinning skulls appears by way of ornament. She drives up
West Street towards the moor, and before her runs a coal-black
hound all the way to Okehampton, which is her nightly journey,
imposed by way of penance for all the woe she wrought in life ;
and the hound's part is to pluck a single blade of grass at
Okehampton, which he carries back in his mouth and lays on a
stone which stood in the courtyard of old Fitzford House.
When by these nightly journeys all the grass of Okehampton
shall have been brought to Tavistock, then the penance of
wicked Lady Howard shall cease.

There is an old ballad which still further adorns this grisly
story by representing Lady Howard as stooping forth from her
coach and inviting passers-by to ride with her.

> My ladye's coach hath nodding plumes,
> The driver hath no head ;
> My lady is an ashen white,
> Like one that is long dead.
>
> Now pray step in, my ladye saith,
> Now pray step in and ride.

I'd rather walk a hundred miles,
And run by night and day,
Than have that carriage halt for me,
And hear my ladye say,
Now pray step in and make no din,
Step in with me to ride,
There's room, I trow, by me for you
And all the world beside.

There are in Devon and Cornwall, and probably elsewhere
also, numberless tales of phantom coaches which from time to
time crop up to terrify the villagers ; but it is rare to meet with
one retaining such precise circumstances, so clear-cut and vivid
in these days which are fondly thought to be superior to
credulity. For many generations this tale has served to frighten
the good people of Tavistock home from their card parties in
reasonable time ; and many a farmer lingering in the town has
called for his horse in a terrible hurry on finding the time to be
at hand when the coach of bones would issue from Fitzford
Gateway. For when people say they do not fear Lady Howard
it is easier not to believe them. There are few among us who
would care to watch for her on winter evenings by the gloomy
gateway when the wind soughs long and heavily among the
trees, and the river running underneath them, swollen by rains,
surges tempestuously under the ancient bridge, filling the air
with sounds so strange that one knows not whence they come.
Even now, beneath the bright spring moon, there is something
weird and chilling about the spot, which makes me glad enough
to turn once more into the path beside the river, and wander
back towards the cheerful town. It is odd how Betsey Grimbal
keeps on coming into my mind : I ought not to think of
one so frail. The moon is rising over the hill, the river
flashes in the broken light, and here is a real Betsey Grimbal,
occupying with her lover the only seat whence one can watch
the water foaming over the salmon ladder. May she have a
better fate ! The lights are out in the little town. High up on

the hillside one or two are glimmering still. The stained glass windows of the church gleam red and purple, for a late service is in progress ; and above the dark tower a single star hangs in the western sky, where there still remains a fine opalescent brightness. A few people are in the streets, for there is no work to-morrow. Farewell, sweet Tavy, *"de mora violenter currens."* Long mayst thou run as swiftly ; and when the abbey bridge is sapped again, may Tavistock produce another John, who shall perambulate the country like him of old.

CHAPTER X

AH, exquisite Tavistock ! must we go before its beauties are half seen, or its neighbourhood at all explored ? All yesterday we loitered on the Abbey bridge, dreaming of the famous town and of its dead and gone inhabitants ; and yet forgot Sir Francis Drake, though he was the greatest of them all, and a mighty wizard too, if his fellow townsmen may be trusted in their recollections of him. For did he not bring water into Plymouth by compelling a Dartmoor spring to follow his horse as he galloped through Horrabridge towards the Sound, which spring refreshes the folk of the three towns unto this day ? Did he not offer to make Tavistock a seaport ? a feat as difficult, one might suppose, as the creation of a seaport in Bohemia, which raised so notable a difference of opinion between Uncle Toby and Corporal Trim during the progress of the latter's immortal story of the king of Bohemia and his seven castles. "There happening," said Trim, " throughout the whole kingdom of Bohemia to be no seaport town whatever . . . . " " How the deuce should there, Trim ? " cried my Uncle Toby ; "for Bohemia being totally inland, it could have happened no otherwise." " It might," said Trim, " if it had pleased God."

But uncle Toby was not convinced of that. " I believe not," he replied, after some pause, "for being inland, as I have said, . . . Bohemia could not have been propelled to the sea without ceasing to be Bohemia,—nor could the sea, on the other hand, have come up to Bohemia, without overflowing a great part of Germany and destroying millions of unfortunate inhabitants who could make no defence against it." " Scandalous," cried Trim,—" which would bespeak," added my Uncle Toby, mildly, "such a want of compassion in Him who is the author of it that I think, Trim, the thing could have happened no way."

The Corporal "made the bow of unfeigned conviction." Against reasoning at once so gentle and so cogent, there is no other course. Yet the man who destroyed the Armada by throwing chips of wood into the sea from Plymouth Hoe, which chips turned to fireships as they touched the water, might have done much, and may do it yet, for it is a mistake to think of Drake as bestowed safely in the shades out of the ken of living people. It needs only a roulade on his old drum to bring him back to the upper world, doubtless with all his magic powers unimpaired; and so it may some day happen that the boon rejected long ago by the men of Tavistock will be received more gratefully, that the sea will come lipping up the Abbey walk, and the ancient bridge with its rich growth of ferns and moss will be crusted over with oarweed and sea shells.

However, it is, as Yorick says, a singular blessing that nature has formed the mind of man with a " happy backwardness and renitency against conviction." And this choice gift of Providence will save most of us from any serious anxiety on the score of the impending advance of the ocean to Tavistock. Who could wish it changed? We look back on it as we ride out upon the Lydford road; there is a singular clearness in the fresh morning air, and a gusty wind drives the shadows hard across the hills and hollows. Every gable and house front in the old town stands clearcut in the keen air, scintillating slightly; and lastly, as the road turns away the church tower appears, gray and solemn, under a dark mass of cloud. It is such a day as shows this country to perfection. For in dull weather the moors look very sombre; and under an unbroken blue sky—

though to tell the truth that is a sight not often seen upon
Dartmoor - the Tors lack something, colour, mobility, I know
not what, of their utmost grandeur.   But now, while the light
is changing every moment, the outlook over the great grassy
downs is really glorious.   Up their long slopes the shadow
marches slowly, enveloping first one ridge and then a higher,
till even the ragged peaks of granite cropping out upon the
summit are obscured and hidden in the blackness.   And so it
lies, mysterious and gloomy, till at some sudden signal a blaze
breaks out among the crags and runs around them till the
whole peak is bathed and gleaming in warm, sunny light, and
then, having won the summit, the spreading glory hunts the
shadows down the hill, chasing them more swiftly than the eye
can follow over rock and bog and short sweet pasture, and
across the plains, till the hosts of light and darkness sweep
away together through the hills, and on the summits the battle
is already waged again.

Such are the sights of a whole day upon the moors, sights
so beautiful that they sink very deep into the memory, and
come back upon the mind even in the dull city streets, when
the heavy shadows are racing over housetops.   But we do not
come this way merely to store up lovely memories for dull days
in future.   We are moving on Lydford, a place which, though
now no better than a paltry village, is yet of immense antiquity,
and has some right to be considered the capital of the moor,
the whole of which vast area was formerly in its parish
bounds.

From a distance one gazes upon Lydford, seeing only a large
church with the fine squared tower so common on the moor,
the keep of an old Norman castle, and a mere handful of
cottages and houses, having evidently no mission to fulfil in
the desolate spot where they find themselves.   It is hard to
believe that such a shadow of a town once rivalled Exeter ; yet
this is almost if not quite true ; and comparisons apart, Lydford
was an important place in Saxon days.   It possessed a mint ;

and beyond doubt its townsmen, of whom we know so little, did find aims and objects worth pursuing on this bleak moor, where their modern descendant scrapes a bare subsistence, chiefly from the tourists. A walled town does not grow where life stagnates ; and even in old unsettled days, when a remote situation was the only safeguard from plunder, men did not so far consult the safety of their skins or goods as to bestow them where the difficulties of trade were unusually great. It is clear therefore that Lydford once lay on the bank of some stream of commerce ; and more than that, one might almost infer that when the town was in its youth, Dartmoor was less barren, and the tracks more easily passable than in these days. For streams of commerce do not choose the worst or most exposed roads in preference to the comparatively good and sheltered ones, nor march over quaking bog when they might tread across firm ground. Moreover, it is quite possible to cross Devonshire without penetrating Dartmoor.

However, in this work we are more concerned with facts than with speculations ; and whatever may have been the facilities for trade around this spot in ancient days, it is quite clear there are none now. Still there was a very busy active life upon Dartmoor from days more ancient than any one can trace, and a considerable population engaged in tin-works. It is a curious fact that when these tinners first emerge into the light of history, one finds them already organised into a cor-poration, having fixed laws which they were strong enough to execute, and meeting by primæval custom in the open air to regulate their common affairs. In the earliest days of which records have come down to us the tinners of Devon formed one body with those of Cornwall, and their meeting place was on Hingston Down. But so early as the first years of the four-teenth century there were signs of those differences of tem-perament which lead Devon, and what Prince calls " her deare neighbour," to disagree on most subjects that present them-selves, except of course the superiority of the whole west to the

unfortunate eastern counties ; and the result was that the Devon
men met separately thenceforth upon Crockern Tor, a wild
peak near Postbridge, where they continued to hold their open
air parliament, a picturesque and striking relic of primæval
custom, till the days came when men valued old tradition and
the habits of long ancestry less than they feared coughs and
colds and rheumatism. When these degenerate sons of hardy
ancestors once began to wonder whether granite seats among
the ferns and moss were as comfortable as oak settles in an inn
parlour, with a smoking roast upon the spit below stairs, the
game was up, and Crockern Tor was abandoned to the winds
of heaven.

Long before this happened, the Stannary Courts had ceased
to be much feared. But in older days they ruled with a strong
and heavy hand. They were concerned with maintaining the
purity of standard of the tin, which was tested by cutting off a
coin, or corner, and stamping the fresh surface thus exposed,
whence the towns privileged to perform this operation and to
collect the dues payable to the Crown, or in later years to the
Duchy of Cornwall, to which the whole of Dartmoor belongs,
were called coinage towns. But of more consequence to the
Stannary Courts than other persons' rights was the maintenance
of their own privileges, and their rather savage laws, such as
that which compelled any adulterator of tin to swallow so many
spoonfuls of the molten metal. In Devon, too, they were entitled to dig for tin on any person's land, without tribute or
satisfaction, and it may be conceived that such a privilege could
hardly be exercised even by men of gentle dispositions, which
as a rule the tinners did not possess, without giving rise to
lusty differences. To aid them in the settlement of such, a
stannary prison was maintained in the old keep of Lydford
Castle ; and round this prison there clings a tradition of such
barbarity as has made the very name of Lydford law hateful
through all the centuries until to-day.

Mr. Worth, whose fine insight into moot points of local

history makes his judgment of the first importance, thought that the origin of the peculiar odium attaching to " Lydford law " must be sought less in the practice of the Stannary Courts than in that of the older body which administered the terrible forest laws of ancient days ; and it does seem true that in years when the tinners' jurisdiction was too new at Lydford to have grown widely terrible the ill fame of the place was as notorious as ever. But whatever may be the truth of this, there is no doubt that a reputation so wide and so persistent could not have sprung up without some deep root in acts of terrible barbarity. Moreover if the practice of the Stannary Courts had been mild or merciful, the old tradition would long since have perished ; and it is thus fair enough that the more modern body should bear its full share of the odium.

Perhaps as much as it is necessary to say of Lydford now is contained in the subjoined lines by William Browne, author of " Britannia's Pastorals," a native of Tavistock, and thus not likely to be a prejudiced witness against a place which was so near his native ground.

I oft have heard of Lydford law
How in the morn they hang and draw
    And sit in judgment after.
At first I wondered at it much,
But since I find the reason such
    As it deserves no laughter.

They have a castle on a hill,
I took it for an old windmill,
    The vanes blown off by weather ;
To lie therein one night 'tis guessed
'Twere better to be stone and pressed
    Or hanged. Now choose you whether.

When I beheld it, Lord, thought I
What justice or what clemency
    Hath Lydford when I saw all ?
I know none gladly would there stay
But rather hang out of the way
    Than tarry for a trial.

The Prince an hundred pounds hath sent,
To mend the leads and planchens wrent
    Within this living tomb:
Some forty-five pounds more had paid
The debts of all that shall be laid
    There till the day of doom.

One lies there for a seam of malt,
Another for a peck of salt,
    Two sureties for a noble.
If this be true or else false news
You may go ask of Master Crews,
    John Vaughan or John Doble.

Now to these men that lie in lurch
Here is a bridge, there is a church,
    Seven ashes and one oak.
Three houses standing and one down.
They say the parson hath a gown,
    But I saw ne'er a cloak.

One told me in King Cæsar's time
The town was built with stone and lime,
    But sure the walls were clay.
And they are fall'n for aught I see,
And since the houses are got free
    The town is run away.

Oh, Cæsar, if thou there didst reign,
While one house stands come there again,
    Come quickly, while there is one;
If thou stay but a little fit,
But five years more, they will commit
    The whole town to a prison.

To see it thus much grieved was I,
The proverb saith, Sorrows are dry,
    So was I at the matter:
Now by good luck, I know not how,
There thither came a strange stray cow,
    And we had milk and water.

At six o'clock I came away,
And prayed for those that were to stay
    Within a place so arrant.
Wide and ope the winds do roar,
By God's grace, I'll come there no more,
    Except on some tyn warrant.

There is a fine healthy full-blooded sense of discontent and grumbling about these lines which makes them pleasant reading, and sets us wondering whether anything was the matter with Browne's digestion at the time. The place is little changed. The winds still roar " wide and ope," but for all that the place is well worth visiting, not only for the sake of its church and castle and historical associations, but even more for the beauty of the ravine over which that bridge is thrown on which we have been standing while making this distant survey of the town.

There are few scenes in Devonshire so remarkable as this. One comes along an ordinary country lane, for here the soil is not waste, but cultivated, and dropping down a little hill the bridge lies straight in front, looking in no wise different from any ordinary piece of stonework that carries a country road across a rustic brook, until one stands upon it. Then it is seen that the valley below is not only exceptionally deep, but that in the bottom of its richly wooded slope the stream has cut down straight and sheer a deep black gorge through the solid rocks, where it thunders on in shadow, far beyond the reach of sunlight, a gloomy torrent in whose sound the steady singing of the moorland streams is deepened into a harsh threatening roar. When rain has sent the water boiling furiously down this gorge, there is a distinct note of terror in the sound ; and even when the water is low, it runs along with none of that soft splashing which tempts one to linger on the bridge at Tavistock, but has a sulky murmur mingled with an occasional deep sucking noise as if the water had swirled into some deep hole and torn itself out again by sheer impetuosity and force. The gorge is deep

enough to be majestic. Here and there a tree lies prostrate
over it.

Once long ago a traveller was riding by night from Tavistock
to Lydford. There was a wild storm ; the floods were out in
the valleys ; the wind blew as it seldom does except on Dartmoor ; and the traveller kept his horse at a steady gallop, as
far as the roughness of the roads permitted, being anxious at
finding himself overtaken by darkness in a country with which
he was unacquainted. Those who know the ground will understand that he must have been a bold rider to go at any but a
handpace in so violent a storm, but he persevered, and at length
his horse gave a tremendous spring which made him think he
must have leapt a hedge, and darted panting up towards the
lights of Lydford, which at that moment came in sight upon
the hill. In five minutes more the tired traveller was dismounting, and answering as patiently as possible the ordinary
questions as to where he had come from. " From Tavistock,"
he said. " But the bridge is down ! " they replied incredu-
lously ; and when morning came they led him back and
showed him a broken arch spanning half way across the awful
chasm, and the swollen torrent roaring far below among the
mass of broken stonework, on which both he and his horse
would have been dashed to pieces had they failed in a leap
which no man would have dared to attempt in daylight.

There is another and a grimmer story of an Exeter man
intending suicide, into whose mind the recollection of this spot
came so persistently that he rode hither all the way from the
ever faithful city, with no other object than to leap his horse
over the parapet of the bridge, down into the depths of the
ravine. Once or twice the poor brute swerved away ; but the
third time the desperate man spurred him with such fury
that he cleared the parapet at a bound, and horse and rider fell
together to the bottom. It is a grisly tale : and we turned away
gladly from the spot towards the waterfall at a lower point in
the valley.

There is nothing grand about this waterfall, but it is exquisitely lovely. Imagine a rapid slender moorland stream, hurrying over a black and stony bed between high banks of primroses, swirling round boulders and tossed into constant jets of foam, cast suddenly down a precipice a hundred feet high in a single leap, through light and graceful birchwoods, to join a larger stream in the valley below. The wet black rock, which is the bed of the slide, shines in the morning light, the milkwhite foaming stream pours down with a merry splashing—it is not large enough to thunder. And now the sun bursts out full upon it, lights up the moss and liverwort beside the slide with the sweetest sunny radiance, makes the black rock sparkle, and sets the whole fall gleaming with quick lights and flashes.

A single holiday does not admit of seeing everything ; and the traveller who is going on into Cornwall will find moors enough before his distant journey is completed. We pass by, therefore, all the tempting routes which might be followed from Lydford, and return towards Tavistock, whence we shall make for Launceston, and so leave this lovely county which has surely not its equal either in beauty or in memories of famous men. But before we go it will be right to say something very briefly of those ancient stone monuments, the circles, and the avenues of winding stones, which must have stirred a temporary interest in the most careless traveller while to the enthusiast they offer a problem, knotty enough to occupy his utmost faculties during something more than the brief span vouchsafed by Providence for life on earth.

Here and there, in lonely places on the hillside, there are circles traced upon the grass—let us call them cromlechs, as the archæologists do, or ought, for they are not always of the same mind about their terms—the enclosure being formed by large upright stones placed at even intervals, the blocks for the most part of regular size, and tracing such a perfect circle as to prove that those who built them were not ignorant of science. In the days when these stones were set up—we know no more

than that they were immensely distant from our own—vast
labour must have been expended in moving them without
cranes or pulleys ; and as men do not take great pains save in
the pursuit of some great object, it is clear that these cromlechs
stood in some close relation to the inmost life of a long vanished
people, and that if we could know certainly to what use they
were put, we should have sent a strong and vivid ray of light
through that black darkness of the past, which has so many
secrets yet to yield.

There are many parts of Great Britain, and also many other
countries, France, Moab, India, in which these cromlechs still stand
as if to taunt us with our dulness ; but on Dartmoor they possess
one feature which is almost peculiar to that district. Wandering
away from many of the cromlechs, there radiate rows of little
stones, sometimes single, sometimes double, continued for great
distances, in one case for as much as two miles, and ending so
commonly in a menhir, or tall single stone, as to give colour to
the idea that this was the regular plan, and that those rows are
ruined or imperfect, which do not end in this way. Sometimes the
cromlech is built around a barrow— that is, a mound over what
is certainly a grave—or at least encloses one ; and so mound,
circle, avenue, and distant menhir, constitute a relic of old
days, which can hardly be looked upon without a throb of
curiosity to know what it meant, and in what age the people
lived who held those faiths or fancies which are worked out in
stone at the cost of such toil and labour.

We are here in presence of an antiquity so remote, that the age
of those which we call ancient things, is as nothing when beside
them. Rome was not built, Troy perhaps was not yet burnt,
when the oldest of these stones was set up on the Devon hillside ; and it may be that in ages far earlier than those, the rites
were practised for which these hoary enclosures were designed.
It is strange that even in Devonshire and Cornwall, where the
legends are so very plentiful and ancient, bringing down to our
own day, however mutilated, many a fragment of forgotten truth,

there is not one which sheds even the faintest ray of light on
the origin of these monuments ; and that these very conspicuous objects should be left practically untouched by a cycle of
traditions which records in its dim way so many very ancient
things, gives them a strange aspect of detachment from all we
read or learn and from all the peoples, Saxon, Briton, Keltic,
whose blood we know to mingle in our own.   Of almost all
things else when we question the past some whisper comes in
answer, some faint voice which can be heard by straining ears.
On these things there is deep silence.   Their use is forgotten,
even by legend which forgets so slowly, and she can no more
divulge their origin, than she can tell how the granite tors were
fashioned out of molten rock, or the river valleys cut down
deep and hollow by the running water.

Of course there are in existence names given to the cromlechs in ages possibly very distant, and even stories which relate to them ; but they betray at once their origin in the brains
or fancies of a people who knew no more of the true use of the
stones than we ourselves.   The cromlechs are dubbed " Grey
Wethers " or " Hurlers," or " Nine Maidens " ; and the rustics
tell you they represent people who danced or played the
ancient game of hurling on a Sunday, and were turned into
stone as a punishment.   Similarly the dolmens, or chambered
tombs built above ground, so much more plentiful in Cornwall
than in Devon, are " Giants' Quoits," and there is generally
some tale explaining how the local giant, Bolster, Cormoran
or another, hurled the huge flat capstone from some incon-
ceivable distance.   So that the riddle was already a good deal
perplexed by obviously modern nonsense when certain very
learned persons in the middle of the last century perplexed it
infinitely further, and sent several generations of honest inquirers off upon a wildgoose chase by declaring that all the
old stone monuments were the work of Druids.

Never did an utterly baseless notion obtain wider currency.
Druid judgment-seats and places of assembly were discovered

in wild profusion throughout the West. Druid groves were recognised where no one previously had suspected anything more remarkable than a simple oak wood. Countless pages of eloquent description were written upon the rites of this long vanished priesthood. The very children took the new ideas up ; and to this day, if you question a West Country peasant concerning any one of these remains you will probably receive an answer in which the Druids figure largely.

So men amused themselves for the best part of a century ; when, having succeeded in driving into the mind of the general public the idea that Druids built the cromlechs and the menhirs, they at last set themselves to inquire what the evidence was for any such belief. The moment this question was asked, the whole fabric of imagination tumbled down. It had absolutely no foundation. It served no other purpose than to hide the truth ; its *débris* embarrass more sober reasoners to this hour ; and it need only be added that scientific inquiry into this perplexing subject is hardly older than the present generation.

Recent as this inquiry is, it has already rendered some results of the very highest interest ; such as tempt me sorely to dilate on them. But prehistoric archæology is still a battle, in which he who engages must be prepared to join the fray, and use his hands, well armed with scientific bludgeons to keep his head, which is else like to be broken. There is no place on that field for peaceful tourists. We shall do better to keep the ring ; and catch what plain words we may hear emerging from the strife of tongues. Some day all will become clear. Archæologists will be patient of each other's views, and agree at least upon some small details. But till that happy time shall come, I know of no conclusion more deserving of attention than that put forward by Mr. Worth, not solely as his own, but as resulting from the work of a group of very able men whose toil he shared. "Devon," wrote this careful inquirer, "shows us that we are more likely to err in bringing

down the date of these memorials than in carrying it back."
And he proceeds to say that on Dartmoor the cromlechs are
clearly of the same age as the old hut dwellings which are
found here and there upon the moor. If, then, the age of the
huts can be determined, a real step will have been gained.

Now the huts have been very carefully dug out and the discoveries made therein prove them to have been the dwellings
of a people who did not know the use of metal, but fashioned
their arms and implements of stone. From this it follows
that the cromlechs have stood where we see them now not
only through the nineteen centuries or so which our English
history runs, but also during the whole of that period known
roughly as "the Bronze Age," because there is no better
measure to apply to it. And how long was that? Why, Mr.
Borlase puts its best period at about ten or twelve centuries
before Christ, and its commencement of course some centuries
further back; while Mr. Worth, reasoning on certain facts
connected with ancient stream works in Cornwall, suggests a
mode of calculation which throws back the commencement of
the Bronze Age at least fifteen hundred years before our era.

Before so great antiquity one hesitates and fears to take the
figures. It is very strange to find ourselves confronting monuments which looked just as they do now when Homer lived, and
were already ancient when the first walls rose on the seven hills
of Rome. We think of these islands as peopled in those days by
mere barbarians. We must learn to understand that civilisation of a sort is immensely ancient, and that our small faculties
have no right to set up limits of what was possible in the early
ages of the world. Many dynasties and races have looked at
these stones with wonder and passed on into the night of time.
Is ours the last of all that long procession?

There are such numerous remains of this nature in Cornwall,
whither we are going, that it will not be possible to avoid speaking further of them; and therefore I shall leave the subject for
the present, merely remarking that it is not to be supposed

that every old stone monument bears the vast burden of
centuries which is ascribed to the cromlechs and the rows.
The dolmens are in many cases much more modern, extending
far down into the Bronze Age; and of the barrows there are
some which are not earlier than the first years of the Christian
era.

If this long prehistoric disquisition has done no other good,
it has at least drawn off my attention from the jolts and bumping
of the moorland roads, and brought me back to Tavistock in
what would be good spirits were it possible to stay there and
spend another afternoon upon the Abbey Bridge.   But it is
really necessary to put a check on the discursive habits I am
falling into.   Devonshire has already spread itself into almost
half my book; though I set out with the firm resolve of showing
that Cornwall is a much better place, and of setting right at
last the injustice done to the duchy by its geographical
situation, which makes it impossible to walk or ride there
without passing through the unfriendly territory of Devon.
For whole centuries all Cornwall was believed by the generality
of Englishmen to be waste and barren.   Now when you find
so vast a misconception prevalent, do you not look to see by
what channel it was spread abroad?   Look then, and you will
find that information concerning Cornwall filtered through
Devonshire, which, recognising its own inferiority, must have
defiled the issue.   "Her deare neighbour" quoth complacent
Prince.   But was it neighbourly, I ask, to steal her cream and
call it "Devonshire," when all the world knows the trick was
caught from the Phœnicians who brought it into Cornwall?   Not
even the Devonshire Association has ventured to claim that the
ships of Tyre or Sidon brought their scald pans up the Tamar
or the Dart.   What said Mr. Treasurer Hawker at Dawlish in
1881, since when, as far as I can see, no mention of this
painful subject has been made in the reports of the Association.
" It is, I know, a vexed question whether Devon or Cornwall
ought to have the high honour of originating clotted cream."

It is, I take the liberty of saying, not a vexed question at all; and this complacent ranking of the receiver of stolen goods side by side with the rightful owner goes far to aggravate the theft. But let that pass. One might certainly have thought that a writer who was clearly upon trial would have brought forth some argument to palliate his county's guilt. But no! he waves the charge away with a jest about tradition; and adds gaily "for myself, I am content to rest upon old Fuller's maxim, *non ubi nascor sed ubi pascor;* and I take it that far more of the cream consumed is from Devon than from Cornwall." Was ever such a paltry argument on a grave question of right and wrong? It really amounts to an admission of guilt; and I should be very angry with Mr. Treasurer Hawker were it not that he disarms my just indignation by teaching me several verses of a charming poem, which, though somewhat defaced by the frequent occurence of the word "Devonshire" is happily not difficult to restore to the condition required by truth and historical accuracy. Thus purified, let me quote it—

> Nothing on earth or in poet's dream
> Is so rich and rare as your Cornish cream.
> Its orient tinge like spring-time morn,
> Or baby buttercups newly born;
> Its balmy perfume, delicate pulp,
> One longs to swallow it all at a gulp,
> Sure man had ne'er such gifts or theme
> As your melt-in-the-mouthy Cornish cream.

Who could be angry with even a worse reasoner who teaches one such lines as these?

But enough of county quarrels. We are running quickly out of Devon. Let us part good friends, remembering always that we have to come back through the territory of our "dear neighbours," and that it is never prudent to make enemies in one's line of retreat. We may cherish a conviction that the relation of Devonshire to Cornwall is that of the ante-room to the presence chamber, or the *hors d'œuvres* to the banquet ; but let us not express it. We shall soon be home in Cornwall, and can afford to think kindly of our neighbours. Already the high keep of Launceston Castle is in sight ; the highway drops, the Tamar is crossed and left behind, and in a little more we are climbing into the steep streets of Launceston.

CHAPTER XI

Now the strongest interest of this picturesque old town of Launceston lies in the fact that it was the scene of the very first encounter which took place in the West, between the forces of the King and Parliament during the great Civil War. And it is one of the humours of those sad years, that while swords were being whetted in every parish, and the village blacksmith had to turn his mind rather to pikes than ploughshares, this first skirmish occurred not on a bare hillside, but in a court of law ! Surely a wonderful mode of opening a civil war, and a testimony as strong as one need wish of the law-abiding character of the English. It happened thus.

In the autumn of 1642, Sir Ralph Hopton, with a hundred horse and fifty dragoons, passed into Cornwall, neglected by the Parliament commanders, who, having Devonshire on their side, thought that Cornwall must support them too. But it was not so, the Cornish had another mind ; and from this small nucleus of force sprang an enterprise so great and heroic that some brief record of it must be set at the beginning of what is here said of Cornwall.

"Nowhere," says Green, "was the Royal cause to take so brave or noble a form as among the Cornishmen." It is a true judgment ; for from the first moment when Hopton, dispirited by his march through hostile Devon, led his little troop across the Cornish border, there began to flock to his

standard those whose swords were worth more than rubies to
the King.

First, as he loved to be in all danger, came Sir Bevil Grenvile
from famous old Stowe, where he had so worthily kept up the
traditions of great Sir Richard, his grandfather, that there was
in all Cornwall no man able to influence so many others, or
draw after him so great a number of devoted followers of every
rank.   For Stowe in Sir Bevil's hands had become a school of
knightly training to which gentlemen sent their sons, to catch
if they could some tinge of his noble bearing.   So that when
word flew round Cornwall that Sir Bevil was out, and not only
he, but his giant body-servant, Anthony Payne, who had
trained all the lads of Stowe in manly exercises, there were
few manors in the county whence some one or two did not set
out to stand beside them in earnest as they had often stood in
play.

"Never a Grenvile wanted loyalty," so say the Cornish still,
for lessons taught by men such as Sir Bevil are remembered
from generation to generation.   Now the forces which Hopton
had led to Truro were increased from day to day by the
adhesion of many of the best names in Cornwall.   Thither from
Trerice came Sir John Arundel, who four years later held
Pendennis so stoutly for the King, and won the melancholy
glory of having commanded the very last loyal garrison in England, save Raglan only.   But these were days when King Charles's
star, though low, was in the ascendant; and many splendid
victories lay before the troops now gathering at Truro.   Thither
also came two friends, whose deeds were the wonder of the
whole Cornish army, and who met their death together in that
sad storm of Bristol where the King won victory at the cost of
so many noble lives : Sir Nicholas Slanning, of Bickleigh in
Devon, and Sir John Trevanion, of Carhayes hard by Mevagissey,
young gentlemen of great estate and greater promise, whose
names are very worthy to be remembered even by those who
held their judgment wrong.   There too, from the far West was

Sydney Godolphin, "a young gentleman," says Clarendon, "of incomparable parts," doomed like the rest, to quick death and long remembrance. These four, namely Grenvile, Godolphin, Slanning, and Trevanion, were "the four wheels of Charles's wain," of whom a melancholy distich yet runs about the county, rhyming "slain" with "wain." And there were Bassett of Tehidy, Trelawny of Trelawne, Kendall of Pelynt, and many less eminent by the accident of birth, but in conduct no less noble; and this party of gallant gentlemen was quickly growing formidable, when the Parliamentary leaders, Sir Alexander Carew and Sir Richard Buller, struck their first blow, by causing a presentment to be drawn in form of law at quarter sessions, then just assembled at Launceston, against "divers men unknown, who were lately come armed into that county *contra pacem*, &c."

Now in attempting to enlist the law against the Cavaliers, Carew and Buller were playing with fire; for Hopton, so far from being a disorderly person in any sense known to the law, held duly regular commissions from the King, the fount of all law, and from his appointed agents. And so, disdaining to misunderstand the insolent reference to "divers persons unknown," Sir Ralph repaired to Launceston, produced his commissions, and told the magistrate boldly that he was "sent to assist them in the defence of their liberties against all illegal taxes and impositions." Whereupon a great and notable change occurred in the aspect of affairs. For the jury, after a discussion as full and solemn as accorded with the gravity of the occasion, not only acquitted Sir Ralph Hopton and the gentlemen who acted with him of any offence against the peace of the country, but declared "that it was a great favour and justice of His Majesty to send down aid to them who were already marked out for destruction; and that they thought it the duty of every good subject, as well in loyalty to the King as in gratitude to those gentlemen, to join with them at any hazard of life and fortune."

In this measured declaration after full debate, the county of Cornwall ranged itself beside the King. It was a solemn and dignified occasion, a worthy prelude to the great events which followed, testifying eloquently to the reverence for law which, as Clarendon tells us, was conspicuous among the Cornish.

Having decided on their course, the magistrates lost no time in taking energetic measures; but straightway preferred an indictment against the leaders of the Parliament, and granted to the high sheriff an order of sessions for calling out the "posse comitatus."

Thus was the sword drawn finally in Cornwall; and such was the foundation of that "Cornish army" which wrought such wonders for the King that had they not been pitifully spent and wasted upon deeds which won them only barren glory, they might have broken through their enemies and set their monarch on his throne again in London. *Dis aliter visum.* Never were Englishmen more nobly valiant; but Heaven denied them wise leadership and for want of it they perished.

Backed as Hopton now was by a strong body of foot, it was an easy matter to drive the Parliament troops out of Launceston and Saltash; and if he could then have led his forces into Devon, much might have been done which proved impracticable later. But that very respect for the law which had impelled the Cornish thus far, proved an obstacle now; for the "posse comitatus" might not legally advance out of Cornwall; and "no man," says Clarendon, "durst presume so far upon the temper of that people as to object policy or necessity to their notions of law."

As soon as this difficulty was realised, the Cornish leaders, Grenvile, Slanning, Trevanion and Arundel, set themselves to raise voluntary regiments, which would be available for service anywhere; and their influence was such that they had quickly enrolled a body of 1,500 men, unproved as yet in military exercise, but so stout of heart and filled with so cheerful an enthusiasm for their leaders, even more than for their cause, that all men argued they would quit themselves well when the call came.

It was not long in coming, for the Parliament had not been blind to the danger growing in the west, and Ruthven, governor of Plymouth, was already advancing with all the forces he could gather not only out of Devon, but out of Dorset also.   By the bridge that crosses the Tamar above Weir Head, he was moving on Liskeard, with numbers far outstripping those of the Cornish, while the Earl of Stamford, with a strong party of horse and foot, was marching rapidly two days behind, hoping to effect a junction which, once for all, should crush the King's party out of Cornwall.

The moment was full of peril. Hopton fell back on Bodmin, once more called out the " posse comitatus " which responded nobly, and resolved to strike at Ruthven, before he could be joined by Stamford, who was by this time at Launceston, little more than twenty miles away.   Ruthven, with a rather childish vanity, also wished to fight, before Stamford came up to divide the glory of what he counted as a certain victory ; and Hopton's advance was no sooner reported to him than he drew out his whole army in a strong position on the east side of Bradock Down, between Boconnoc and Bodmin Road.   In these early days of the great Civil War, the strong religious feeling, which afterwards made so potently against the King, was more conspicuous on his side.   So at least it was in Cornwall ; and when Hopton had drawn his men out facing the enemy, he caused public prayers to be said at the head of every squadron, after which, observing that Ruthven's cannon were not yet in position—a piece of negligence which cost the Roundheads dear—he skilfully worked forward the two small drakes, which were all the artillery he possessed, masking them with parties of horse, until he had the main body of Parliament men within easy range.   A few shots from these small pieces, ploughing the dense mass, shook the enemy, who had not perceived the movement ; and Sir Bevil Grenville charging gallantly with his whole force exactly at the right moment, swept them off the ground.

Along the lanes and hedgerows into Liskeard, and far beyond, the Cornish drove their enemies in headlong rout, taking 1,250 prisoners, all their cannon and ammunition, and nearly all their arms. Yet here Clarendon notes that the Cornish "were always more sparing than is usually known in civil wars, shedding very little blood after resistance was given over, and having a very noble and Christian sense of the lives of their brethren ; insomuch as the common men, when they have been pressed by some fiercer officer to follow the execution, have answered that "they could not find it in their hearts to hurt men who had nothing in their hands."

"The messenger is paid," wrote Sir Bevil Grenvile on the outside of the letter which he sent off from the battlefield to "The Lady Grace Grenvile, at Stowe." "The messenger is paid, yet give him a shilling more." There is a very human gladness in the order ; and we may be sure there was no stinting towards the messenger who brought such joyful news to Lady Grace. Between these two there was the rarest love ; neither had any other wish than to live in peace at Stowe together ; and there are passages in their still existing letters which, to this day, one cannot read without a deep sense of pity for the sweet home life which both these lovers seem to understand is already lost for ever.

"My Dear Love," so the letter ran, "it hath pleased God to give us a happy victory on this present Thursday, being the 19th of January, for which pray join me in giving God thanks. I had the van, and so after solemn prayers at the head of every division I led my part away, who followed me with so great courage, both down the one hill and up the other, that it struck a terror in them, while the seconds came up gallantly after me, and the wings of horse charged on both sides. But their courage so failed as they stood not the first charge of foot, but fled in great disorder, and we chased them divers miles.

> "So I rest, yours ever,
>
>   "Bevill Grenvile."

So the Cornish stayed their hands from slaughter, while the soldiers of the Parliament fled along the lanes; and Ruthven himself, "with those few who could keep pace with him," fled to Saltash, where he threw up earthworks, planted "great stores of cannon," and moored a ship in such a position in the harbour that the path of an attacking force must be swept by her guns. Thus fortified, he felt confident of holding his ground; but he had not yet learnt how the Cornish fought. In three days Hopton, with a part only of his Cornish regiments, appeared before Saltash, stormed the breastworks, drove the enemy headlong through the town and over the steep bluff into the river, where many were drowned; captured all the cannon, the colours, and a goodly store of prisoners; while Ruthven saved himself, for the second time in three days, by an ignominious flight.

Courage is infectious like defeat; and the little campaign, which ended for the moment so gloriously on the ramparts of Saltash, had taught the Cornish their own strength. Yet as Hopton, on that January day, stood sword in hand upon the hill, looking across the narrow streets below him, where the slaughter was yet going on, over the noble harbour, to the grim town of Plymouth, so strong, so easily relieved by sea, and so constant a menace to Cornwall, even the thrill of victory must have been checked by a consciousness that it would serve the King but little unless a greater triumph could be won.

For the moment it was useless to think of this, short as the troops were of ammunition, which was indeed a very grievous perplexity to the commanders; so that in the impossibility of making any important movement at the time, the operations subsided into a series of skirmishes in Devon, in one of which Sidney Godolphin was unhappily killed — shot, according to tradition, in the porch of the Three Crowns Inn, at Chagford. This was the first gap made in that little band of noble and heroic gentlemen who led the Cornish. There was more glory reserved for Grenvile, Slanning, and Trevanion, in the few months before they followed him, yet none among them all has left a more fragrant memory than this fragile lad, whose counsel was valued by old and tried commanders, and whose courage carried him ever abreast of the foremost.

The course of hostilities was again interrupted by futile negotiations for peace, which were scarcely broken off when James Chudleigh, the Parliamentary General in Devon, made a dash at Launceston, and all but captured it, yet in the end was beaten back into Devon once more, where he lay while a greater effort was preparing. For early in May the Earl of Stamford had collected an army of nearly 7,000 horse and foot, more than double the number of the Cornish, with a good train of artillery, all perfectly equipped and victualled; and in the middle of the month he marched into Cornwall by the extreme north roads, resolved to crush the Cornish once for all, and having no feeling for them but one of contempt.

For this disdain of his enemy he was not without excuse; for the Cornish were not only far inferior in numbers, but were notoriously ill equipped, short of ammunition, as well as food, so that Stamford had no doubt of breaking them, and the only thing he feared was that the " posse comitatus," which had before served the King so well, might be called out again, and thus make Hopton's forces equal to his own. To prevent this, he detached a body of 1,200 horse to guard the county town of Bodmin, and entrenched himself on Stratton Hill, a lofty eminence which on all sides was easy of defence, and on one should have been impregnable.

Now the Royalists marched out of Launceston on Monday, May 15th, with a firm resolve to fight on any odds or disad-

vantage, being indeed unable to wait for choice of ground,
since their provisions were so short that for two days the
highest officers had but a single biscuit.   And so they marched
to Stratton from Launceston, twenty miles, and halted in the
spring evening, footsore and hungry, a mile from the base
of the high hill on which the enemy lay in overwhelming
strength.   Here, if not earlier, they learnt the absence of so
great a portion of the horse ; and resolved to attack at daybreak before the troopers could be recalled.

This was Sir Bevil Grenvile's country.   His own home of
Stowe lay only eight miles to the north ; and there his thoughts
must have travelled often through the short spring night, and
when the dawn lighted up the familiar fields and hedgerows,
over which he had hawked and hunted since he was a boy.
It was strange to lie out in the fields, cold, weary, and starving,
and in peril of his life, while home and wife and children were
so near ; and many a man around him, recruited from his own
estate, was in the like case : in which circumstance lies doubtless some part of the explanation of the great event that
followed, for no one who knows the passionate love of the
Cornish for their homes will easily believe that they could be
beaten when fighting in full sight of them.

Weary as they were, the men stood in their arms all night,
for the enemy were too near to make rest safe ; and with the
first light they divided their little army of 2,400 men into four
columns, assigning to each a different direction of attack, and
at five o'clock led them out upon the slopes.

Now any one who walks over Stratton Hill to-day may see
how dangerous it must have been for wearied men to storm
fresh troops well provided with artillery and lying behind
breastworks on such an eminence ; and it can be no matter of
surprise that the attack was repulsed again and again.   Hour
after hour the Cornish pressed on doggedly, yet no ground was
gained that was not lost again, and the chances of success grew
few as the strength of the men was lessened by fatigue.   Then

when the battle had lasted ten hours, one of those emergencies occurred which would have shattered any but the best troops—it was suddenly reported that the powder was almost spent.

Hopton called a hasty council; and it was agreed that no more powder should be used until the Cornish were on the summit of the hill, and at close quarters, so that every shot would tell. And with that resolve the four columns advanced together and in silence.

There was evidently something in the steady march of these four silent columns which struck the enemy behind their breastworks with a strange feeling of awe. It was out of their experience of war; it seemed scarcely human to fire on men who were making no reply. A sort of fascination seized them as they watched their enemies climbing nearer. Demoralisation was setting in. Chudleigh saw it, and headed a gallant charge upon the column led by Berkley and Sir Bevil, which for the moment drove the stormers back in some disorder. But it was too late; the column was re-formed, and advanced again; Chudleigh was taken prisoner, fighting valiantly. His bravest followers were killed; and the rest, fleeing back to the main body, increased the growing disorder. From this moment the long fight was lost and won. A few minutes later the leaders of the four columns met together on the very summit of the hill: none had failed, none was missing, and the glory of the great battle was unclouded.

In a few minutes more the Cornish soldiery were handling the cannon they had faced so well; and it needed but few discharges from these "thirteen brass field pieces and one mortar" to send the beaten soldiery fleeing in wild confusion. Stamford, with the little body of horse, at the head of which he had sat safe and idle all day long, was already pricking off the field. Chudleigh was a prisoner. There was none to re-form the scattered host, which straggled away across the fields, a desolate, humiliated mob, pursued only for a mile or two, but formidable to no one any longer.

"Dearest soule," wrote Francis Bassett to his wife, "oh, deare soule, prayse God everlastingly. Reade this enclosed; ring out the bells, rayse bonfires, publish these joyfull tydings. . . . Your dutyous prayers God has heard. Bless us accordingly, pray everlastingly, and Jane and Betty, and all you owne. . . . To my dearest, dearest friend, Mrs. Bassett att the Mount. Speede this, haste, haste."

Doubtless the bells did clash out joyfully and thankfully from many a church tower in Cornwall, and many a heart beat as high as Bassett's when the bonfires flared along the hilltops and the news was known that the Royal Duchy had cast out the rebels, and from end to end was won for the King.

The news of this great rout flew quickly to Bodmin, where Sir George Chudleigh, father of the captured Major-General, lay with his compact body of 1,200 horse; enough, one would have thought, to have attempted something, even then, for the benefit of the cause he had adopted. But the heart of a great leader was not in him; and this strong force crowded out of Bodmin in disorder as if they too had been beaten, taking the direction of Exeter, where they arrived sorely reduced in number, for the country people harried them in their retreat up to the very border of Cornwall.

Thus swiftly were the forces of the Parliament cast out of Cornwall; and as not much fighting occurred in Devon during the advance which followed, the remainder of the story of this Cornish army, which was so famed and dreaded in its day, lies somewhat beyond the scope of this little book. But those who would know the Cornish must know their memories; and there is no child in Cornwall who does not cherish the tale of Lansdown, where Sir Bevil fell, as much as that of Stratton, and who would not feel himself defrauded if he were told the bright opening of this story without its melancholy close.

The Cornish army, then, marched out of Cornwall uncertain whether to attack Plymouth or Exeter; and while still undecided they received news that the Parliament had

appointed Sir William Waller to march into the west with a
new army, and that the King on his part was sending them
more forces under Prince Maurice and the Marquis of Hert-
ford. This news settled the movements of the army; and
marching by Exeter, where Stamford with his beaten troops
lay watching their advance, but not daring to attack, they
joined Prince Maurice at Chard about the middle of May,
being in all a body of some 7,000 men, well provided with
artillery and ammunition, and all distinguished by a "handsome impatience" to meet the enemy.

There was no enemy to meet in Somerset; for though it was
a hostile county, Taunton, Bridgwater, and Dunster fell without a blow. And here Clarendon takes occasion to praise the
strict discipline of the Cornish soldiery, "whose commanders
had restrained them from all manner of licence, obliging them
to solemn and frequent acts of devotion, insomuch as the
fame of their religion and discipline was no less than that of
their courage." The time was at hand when both courage and
discipline were to be needed; for each day's march brought
the army nearer to Waller, who lay in great strength at Bath;
and nearer still the country was patrolled by the routed troops
from Stratton, who had gathered head, and associated themselves with other fugitives from Taunton and elsewhere.
Before reaching Wells the Royalists came in contact with these
forces, and fought their way onwards amid continual
skirmishes, among which one on the hills above Chewton in
the Mendips was almost of the dimensions of a cavalry battle,
and deserves to be remembered for the extraordinary gallantry
shown not only by Prince Maurice, but by the Earl of
Carnarvon, "who always charged home," and so the army
advanced fighting to Frome and Bradford, whence they could
see the heights of Bath, on or near which all men knew that a
great battle must be fought.

It was early in July when the Cornish army lay out in the
hayfields offering battle to Waller, who on his part as steadily

refused it until he could engage with the full advantage of position. Day by day the two armies skirmished fiercely up and down the midsummer meadows ; and in these scattered actions the King's cavalry for the first time met their match, not in the main body of Waller's horse, for which indeed they cared but little, but in a new regiment, recently arrived from London under the command of Sir Arthur Haslerig, in which the troopers were so fully armed that they could hardly be touched by swords, which for the most part were the only weapons carried by the Royalist horse, and so charged with a carelessness of opposition which the latter could hardly imitate. And in these constant skirmishes the waste of powder alone—which was none too plentiful in the Cornish army—was so great that at last the leaders resolved to spend no more time in offering battle, but to march onwards towards the King at Oxford, leaving Waller to follow if he chose.

Now it was quite certain that he would choose to follow, since his whole business in the west was to prevent the Cornish army from joining with the King; and therefore Hopton and Prince Maurice had nothing more to do than to draw him on until they reached a ground where they could turn on him with advantage. But the whole army was straining like a greyhound in the slips, lusting for a battle, confident of winning against any odds of numbers or position ; and so when Waller saw them moving, and sent after them Haslerig's regiment—"The Lobsters," as the Cornish called them—they faced round instantly in their tracks, too proud to think of prudence. Yet when they had routed this first attack of horse, and chased them to the hill whence they had come down, the King's troops saw a sight which gave them pause.

For Waller had entrenched himself on the brow of Lansdown Hill, and had thrown up earthworks on the edge of it, lining them with musketeers and cannon. On either side of the plain route up this hill grew thick woods, and in them Waller had planted strong parties of musketeers ; while his reserves lay

close behind him on a level ground, whence they could be
brought into action with the greatest ease, and at any moment.
The most careless of the Royalists must have seen the tremendous strength of the position, and they wisely resolved not
to break themselves upon it, and were actually turning to
resume their march when the whole body of Waller's horse
came thundering down the hill upon their rear and flank,
striking them with a crash which the Royalists could not with-
stand, and throwing them into disorder from which they could
not recover till Slanning came up with a party of 300 Cornish
musketeers, and with his aid the enemy were beaten off, and
chased back to the hill again.

Perhaps the strongest captain could hardly have turned his
men back on their line of march after this. The blood of the
whole army was beating hotly. The Cornish were crying out
aloud that they might, " have leave to fetch off those cannon,"
the troops as well as the officers were flushed and glowing with
success, and the order was given to attempt the hill with horse
and foot.

It was necessary first to clear the woods, into which accordingly a portion of the musketeers was sent, while the rest
advanced with the horse up the steep roadway by which the
crest of the hill was approached—only to be rolled back by a
charge of the enemy in overwhelming force. Then Sir Bevil
Grenvile took command of the attack, and chose his ground
somewhat differently, placing the horse on his right where the
ground was a trifle easier, the musketeers on his left, and himself leading the pikes up the hill in the centre. In this order
the Cornish moved forwards much as they had moved at
Stratton, slowly, doggedly, gaining point by point, unheeding
the storm of shot which greeted their approach, drawing together to resist the cavalry which Waller sent thundering down
the slope, only to recoil broken and disordered from the close
array of Cornish pikes which stood together so well and firmly.
Twice the Parliament horse were hurled backwards from the

pikes, and the Cornish were still moving up, when the troopers came crashing down in a third and final charge; and whether it was that the Cornish were growing weary, as well they might, or the enemy had become desperate, as was also reasonable, or whatever else the cause might be, the fact is that this last charge shook the pikemen. Sir Bevil's horse gave way, the cohesion of the pikes was broken, and instantly the enemy were in among them, hewing them down; the officers were falling fast, and Sir Bevil himself, sorely wounded and fighting valiantly, was struck out of his saddle by a poleaxe, of which hurt he died very shortly. Anthony Payne, his true-hearted giant retainer, caught his master's horse, and with a fine knightly impulse, set little John Grenvile, a lad of sixteen, who had followed his gallant father close, on the hacked and gory saddle, and led him to the head of his father's troops. There was no more giving way after this sight, and the Cornish followed the lad up the hill like men possessed. By this time too the musketry had practically routed the Parliament horse, which were already retreating; and so while Sir Bevil lay dead on the hillside, his own regiment, led by his giant servant and his little son, gained the top.

Spent and shaken to almost the last extremity the Cornish yet made good their footing on the ridge, while the enemy fell back sullenly behind a stone wall at a little distance, where they stood in good order threatening a further onslaught. But in truth the one army was no more fit than the other to renew the fight. Both were scattered and intensely weary. It was already night; and except for the occasional spit of fire from a cannon discharged on either side, the two hosts faced each other silently till near midnight, when the Parliament men gave indications of advance; but after the exchange of one or two volleys on either side, all was as silent as before. Still the Cornish lay under arms, until at last Prince Maurice sent a soldier to reconnoitre; and the man, working forward cautiously, came at last to the stone wall behind which the enemy

The Cornish followed the lad up the hill. [To face p. 196.

had retreated, and found lighted matches fixed in it, but no
troops near them ; and so returning, reported that Waller had
abandoned his position.   When daylight came, this report was
fully confirmed.   Waller had fallen back on Bath in so much
disorder as to leave a great store of arms and powder behind
him ; and thus the Cornish won their third great battle.

It was a mighty victory but a sad one ; for the loss of Sir
Bevil Grenvile was irreparable.   From the first gathering of
the King's troops in Cornwall, Sir Bevil had been the heart and
soul of the army.   There were other Captains as wise as he in
council.   There were many no less brave in action.   But there
was none among them all whose courage was so cheerful,
who was at all times so absolutely proof against depression,
or who could raise the spirits of the soldiery like he.   For to
them he was not only the chief of that great family of
Grenvile, to whom they owed obedience and service, nor only
the commander who had led them on to victory.   He was all
that and more ; for he possessed the rarest power of winning
love, and used it very nobly, so that to this day his memory
remains in Cornwall, where he is spoken of with a sort of
personal attachment which only some very rare quality or gift
could keep alive during two hundred and fifty years.   He was
a very brave and noble gentleman, one of those finely tempered
spirits, so numerous in the sad Civil Wars, whose motives were
absolutely pure and their action so unstained by selfishness
that even men who think them wrong may well afford to dismiss
their memories in the words of the noblest elegy yet penned
by mortal man, "Si quis piorum manibus locus, placide
quiescas "

CHAPTER XII

THE traveller who visits Launceston receives and bears away one impression that dominates all others ; and just as when he is strolling round the ancient town it is the castle whose dark and lofty keep towers at the head of every street, so he finds on trying to disentangle his recollections that they are inseparable from the castle, which does in fact give its character to the whole town. From whatever point one looks at Launceston, near or distant, the shell of the old keep rises high and sheer above the houses. The rich growth of ivy and other verdure which has crept up the disused walls does by no means rob them of their aspect of grim strength ; and even in these days, trained as we are to contemplate such ruins with no more dread than a case of stuffed lions in a museum, it is not hard to understand how great the impression must have been on the minds of those who saw that living which is long since dead, who had tasted the insolence of men-at-arms and the rough tyranny of the soldiery. But that is long ago. The old castle has been decaying any time these six centuries and more. There was no occasion in the west, so peaceful on the whole, so guarded by its remote situation from being forced into more than rare outbreaks of disorder, for a stronghold so great and powerful as this ; and thus when the castle ceased to be needed as the dwelling of a great Earl, it had no longer

any use, and passed quickly to the base purposes of a prison
and execution ground.

Still it is splendidly picturesque ; and so strongly does it
draw one's eyes, towering gaunt and dark far above the outer
buildings, a double concentric shell, that at first one is only
vaguely conscious of the old town clinging to the precipitous
sides of the hill, and straggling downwards into a deep valley,
where a river brawls along amid luxuriant foliage and rich
summer meadows.   On the opposite hill the fine square tower
of St. Stephen's catches the sun ; and beyond it to the eastward
the distant heights of Dartmoor bound a rich land of hill and
valley, well wooded and watered by many streams.

It will not do to linger at Launceston very long, for the road
we have chosen to Liskeard crosses country on which no wise
man is surprised by night, a bleak and comfortless region, yet
full of curious interest, and indicating, as well as any could,
how great the stride is which was taken when the Tamar was
crossed, and Devon was exchanged for Cornwall.   It is not in
speech that the difference is felt.   There is a district further west
in Cornwall where the language, and even more the intonation,
are as little like those of Devon as can be well conceived.   But
here, in the eastern portions of the county, one may listen long
and carefully and yet detect no sign that another language was
once spoken by the peasants.   The fusion of speech is almost
perfect, and it is by the witness of inanimate things that we
know we are moving in a land whose past life and inherited
ideas have not been similar to those of the folk who dwell
beyond the Tamar.

It is the main road from Launceston to Bodmin which we
are following, and for eight miles it runs pleasantly through fields
and pretty valleys which call for no remark.   Not far from the
eighth milestone is the village of Fivelanes, where the wise
man will pause and consider how far his strength and temper
may hold out unless he lay in a fresh supply of both at the
little inn.   For he will get but sorry fare at the Temperance

Hotel five miles further on ; and after that he need look for
none at all till much beyond the time he wants it. And so
let him take heed while he can.

But it was not merely to give friendly counsel that we paused
at this humble village.   Fivelanes is practically Altarnun ; that
is to say, the ancient church of that wide moorland parish is
but two fields away, and though it has no great outward beauty,
its interior is worth inspection, if only because it possesses
a fine oak screen—none too common an ornament in Cornish
churches—as well as some carved bench ends of remarkable
merit.   And near the church are the poor ruins of a holy
well, one of many which one finds by the waysides in Cornwall, or hidden on the moors and cliffs of that wild western
land.   These very ancient springs are not lightly spoken of as
holy.   They were so in very fact.   Almost invariably they were
associated with some saint, whose name they bore, and of whom
a legend often clings to the shattered stones.   This is St. Non's
Well, and it had a widespread reputation in old days for the
cure of lunacy.   The manner of the cure is left on record by
Carew, whose joy it was to gather up these scraps of curious
lore ; and as it is probably many years since any patient has
been treated in this way, it may be worth while to repeat what
the Squire of Antony details :—" In our forefathers' days when
devotion as much exceeded knowledge as knowledge now
cometh short of devotion, there were many bowsening places
for curing madmen ; and amongst the rest one at Alternunne,
called St. Nunne's Pool, which saint's altar it may be, *pars pro
toto*, gave name to the church.   And because the maner of
this bowsening is not so unpleasing to heare as it was uneasie
to feele, I wil deliver you the practice as I receyved it from the
beholder.

" The water running from St. Nunne's Well fell into a square
and close-walled plot, which mighte be filld at what depth they
listed.   Upon this wall was the frantick person set to a stand,
his backe towards the poole ; and from thence, with a sudden

blow in the brest, tumbled headlong into the pond, where a strong fellowe, provided for the nonce, tooke him and tossed him, and tossed him up and downe, alongst and athwart the water, until the patient, by forgoing his strength, had somewhat forgotten his fury. Then was hee conveyed to the church, and certaine masses sung over him ; upon which handling, if his right wits returned, St. Nunne had the thanks ; but if there appeared small amendment, he was bowsened againe and againe while there remayned in him any hope of life or recovery."

Such were the gentle remedies in vogue in Cornwall in old days, and such the virtues conferred on the water of this her well by St. Non, mother of Saint David, who, though she possessed another holy well near her son's Cathedral of St. David's in Wales, blessed this only with the singular powers that have been described. The spring is dry now, and the well has been almost destroyed. It is said, too, that "franticke persons" are more common in the west than formerly. It may be that St. Non, looking from the serene dwelling she inhabits down on the earth beneath, finds some amusement in the fact that the superior methods of the County Asylum have not after all produced a better result than the bowsening she taught the people so many centuries ago.

Wells such as this are very numerous in Cornwall, and though they are little seen by strangers, they constitute a group of antiquities as interesting as any in the Duchy. For in this remote land, accessible on one side only to the spread of new ideas, there are still traces of well-worship, scant, it is true, and quickly vanishing ; but enough to show how strong a reverence was felt in past days for the springs. There are still old people to be found in Cornwall who believe that mischief will fall on any one who damages a holy well or attempts to remove the shrine that often covers it. What is this but a lingering faith that the demon of the well is still potent enough to revenge an insult? It is a trace of Paganism which here crops out, a relic of the faiths which were current before the incoming saints took possession of the wells among other sacred places, and gave them their own names. Such also are the offerings of pins, and here and there of coins, which were left beside the well to propitiate the demon, quaint and simple practices which have perished fast along all the countryside since Board Schools, perhaps for our greater good, drove the picturesqueness out of life.

It is not long after leaving Altarnun before we feel the breath and odour of the moor. The road ascends and the hills rise fast, bare and uncultivated, swept by storms and having but little beauty of outline to compensate for their savage wildness. This ridge which we are mounting is the highest point of the great range of Cornish moors, the backbone of Cornwall, as the Apennines are of Italy ; and this bleak spot it is which has awed many travellers into the belief that all the duchy is waste and sterile. That is quite a false conclusion, as we shall see in time ; but for the present it need not be admitted that the moors are so unlovely. They are bare and lonely, it is true, but on a gusty day the play of light and shade on their slopes is glorious ; and in hot weather there are rich purples in the hollows which mount upwards as the sun sinks till they cover all the hills. There are fine outlines, too, when the highest point of the road is reached, and the great crag of Roughtor is seen breaking the skyline with its jagged crest, while beside it the sister peak of Brown Willie rears a summit which is rounded and less impressive, but equally associated in the wild traditions of the spot.

These two mountains are the most conspicuous in Cornwall. From far and near their twin peaks are visible bathed in brilliant sunlight or glowing in the evening with rose and purple. In a country of greater elevations they would hardly catch the eye ; but here no higher eminences draw off attention from them, and it is not difficult to understand how suitable the simple minds of early dwellers in the west thought their

rugged slopes both for their own hut dwellings and for those
sacred monuments which were spoken of at length in the last
chapter.   And so there are on the slopes of these two hills a
group of stone circles or cromlechs, which are as interesting as
any in the country, though they have not been much noticed
until recently ; and if I were bold enough to feel unconcerned
at the risk of drawing on myself those furious attacks with
which archæologists welcome rival theories, I should be dis
posed to dwell on what Mr. A. L. Lewis has written of this
group of cromlechs, of which his plans were the first published,
to give prominence to his discovery that both the diameters of
the circles and their distances from each other were planned
with a measure of an Egyptian or Royal Persian cubit, to lose
myself in wonder how such a measure got into Cornwall, to
follow him in his discussion of the position of the cromlechs
with regard to the midsummer sunrise, and generally to amuse
myself with speculations of the sort which antiquaries of the
opposite persuasion brush aside angrily with the obnoxious
word "orientation."   God forbid that I, who am so little able
to defend myself, should try to conjure with this word of dread ;
but I may be allowed humbly to point out that it does emerge,
really and soberly, from what Mr. Lewis tells us that Roughtor
was regarded as a sacred hill, which is exactly what, from its
appearance, we should have suspected.   This is surely safe,
and if any one belabours me for saying so, Mr. Lewis, who is a
doughty warrior, ought to come out and beat him off.

   Here then is a region which might be expected to be rich in
tradition, and that is exactly what it is.   At a little distance
away across the moors lies the only inland lake in Cornwall, a
lonely tarn on an elevated plateau among the hills, and insigni-
ficant as it may be, regarded as a lake, it is in association the
most famous ground in England, if there be any faith in Sir
Thomas Malory at all.   For this is doubtless that lake to which
Merlin and King Arthur rode, when the King had fought with
Pellinore, and been sore hurt and lost his sword ; and in the

midst of the lake " Arthur was ware of an arm clothed in white
samite, that held a fair sword in its hand.   'Lo,' said Merlin,
'yonder is that sword I spake of.'   So Sir Arthur and Merlin
alight, and tied their horses to two trees, and so they went into
the ship, and when they came to the sword that the hand held
Sir Arthur took it up by the handles, and took it with him, and
the arm and the hand went under the water."   Now if any one

Slaughter Bridge, where Arthur got his death wound.

object that this was near Caerleon, yet Dozmaré, as this tarn is
called, has certainly the greater scene.   For it is but a little
way across the mountains to the bridge near which Arthur
gathered his great host to face the army of Sir Mordred; and
when the fight was over and the King lay swooning of his
death wound in a chapel near the field of battle, while " in the
moonlight the pillers and robbers were come into the field to

pill and rob many a noble knight, then Arthur gave his
sword to Bedivere, saying "My time hieth fast. Therefore,
take thou Excalibur, my good sword, and go with it to yonder
water's side, and when thou comest there, I charge thee throw
my sword in that water, and come again and tell me what thou
there seest."

Now every child knows how Bedivere went down to the
water's edge, and fell to coveting the sword, and hid it ; and came
to the King, avowing he had seen nothing but "the waters
wap and the waters wan ;" and how he betrayed his King a
second time till, stung by his reproaches, he ran a third time
to the water, and took the sword up, and bound the girdle
about the hilts, "and then he threw the sword as far into the
water as he might, and there came an arm and an hand above
the water, and met it and caught it, and so shook it thrice and
brandished, and so vanished away."

"So Sir Bedivere came again to the king, and told him what
he saw.   'Alas,' said the King, 'help me hence, for I dread me
I have tarried over long.'   Then Sir Bedivere took the King
upon his back, and so went with him to that water's side.   And
when they were at the water side, even fast by the bank hoved
a little barge, with many fair ladies in it, and among them all
was a Queen, and all they had black hoods, and all they wept and
shrieked when they saw King Arthur.   'Now put me into the
barge,' said the King ; and so he did softly.   And there received
him three Queens with great mourning, and so they set him
down, and in one of their laps King Arthur laid his head, and
then that Queen said, 'Ah, dear brother, why have ye tarried so
long from me? alas, this wound on your head hath caught
overmuch cold.'   And so then they rowed from the land ; and
Sir Bedivere beheld all those ladies go from him.   Then
Sir Bedivere cried, 'Ah, my lord Arthur, what shall become of
me now ye go from me and leave me here alone among my
enemies.'   'Comfort thyself' said the King, 'and do as well as
thou mayest, for in me is no trust for to trust in.   For I will

go into the vale of Avilion, to heal me of my grievous wound :
and if thou hear never more of me, pray for my soul.' "

But it is not with the noble figure of the King, unto whom
was " none like nor pareil in all Christendom," that the interest
of Dozmaré Pool begins or ends ; and indeed the Cornish
folklore contains curiously few allusions to one who might have
been expected to dominate it all.   It is not of Arthur but of

Dozmaré Pool.

Tregeagle that the peasants talk when Dozmaré is mentioned ;
it is him they fear when the winter twilight darkens down
among the hills, and the storm wind runs wailing up the valleys.
For on such nights the moormen cowering in their
cottages hear a great voice above the whistle of the tempest
and the lashing of the rain upon their windows, a sound of
human pain and anguish, the bellowing of one in mortal fear ;
and as that terrifyng voice reverberates and spreads down into the

lower country, many a cottage door is barred more tightly, and
the mothers call their children to their side, for they know well
that the cries are uttered by Tregeagle, whose soul is lost for
ever if he pause in his penance of baling Dozmaré dry with a
single limpet shell, and that pierced by a hole through which
the water drips as often as he lifts it.   Day and night he toils
desperately at his task, as a man would who has tasted, as he
has done, the torments of hell, and fears no earthly penance
half so much.   And from time to time the devil pounces on
him, hoping that he may find the wretched sinner resting, and
hunts him round the margin of the pool, and across the downs,
while Tregeagle flees with loud cries of terror, and can find no
safety till he reaches the ruined chapel on Roche Rock, many
a mile away, and at last from the sanctuary of its shattered walls
bids defiance to the fiend.

But who was Tregeagle, and how did he escape from the
doom of sinners in the world to come ?   It is a long story,
but worth telling ; the more so as its central scene occurred at
St. Breward, a moorland parish just beyond these mountains,
so wild and barren that one feels no wonder on hearing that
strange things have happened there.   Now Tregeagle was of
an ancient Cornish family located in St. Breock, and in the
church of that parish the monuments of his race may still be
seen.   He himself was steward to Lord Robartes some two
centuries ago or more ; and earned a bitter reputation as a
hard and cruel man among the peasantry.   At last he died,
and when his books came to be inspected a dispute arose as to
the payment of rent by a certain small farmer in the neighbourhood.   The man maintained that he had paid Tregeagle,
but by some oversight had not obtained a receipt, and as he
had no proof of payment he was told that he must pay again,
or be sued as a common debtor.   In despair, the farmer
thought of consulting the parson of St. Breward, who was a
noted wizard.   The parson listened gravely to his story, and
when he had done asked him merely whether he had faith.

The question suggested strange fears to the poor farmer.   He could not say he had faith enough to face the other world, and so came sorrowfully away.   But in a little while, plucking up courage at the near approach of the day of trial, he returned to the lonely vicarage upon the moor, and professed his faith was strong enough to bear him through.   Whereupon the parson, to quote the words of a countryman who told the tale to a correspondent of Mr. Hunt, "draed a ring out on the floor ; and he caaled out dree times, ' Jahn Tergagle, Jahn Tergagle, Jahn Tergagle ! ' and—I've a heerd the ould men tell ut, sir—theess Jahn Tergagle stood before mun in the middle of the ring.   And he went vore wi' mun to the czaizes and gave az evidence, and tould how this man had a paid az rent ; and the lord he was cast."

That must have been a strange and unforgettable scene when this witness from another world was led into court and gave his evidence.   Outside the court-house fiends were gathering thick and frequent, on the watch to pounce upon their prisoner the instant he was abandoned by the holy spell which had drawn him from their torments for a time.   The spirit stood there motionless, and judge, jury, and counsel were alike appalled.   The frail barrier which the Church had cast up between that lost soul and the clamorous fiends without was easy to remove ; but it was not in the hearts of the churchmen to cast him who had once issued forth from hell back again into the torment.   There was long and anxious counsel, and at length it was resolved to set the spirit some impossible task, which might secure him from the assaults of the devil so long as he laboured at it constantly, but no longer.   Now Dozmaré Pool was believed to be bottomless, a thorn bush which had been cast into it not long before having been found floating in Falmouth Harbour ; and thus Tregeagle was set as his first penance to bale this tarn out dry.

Of course the story varies.   In one version the judges washed their hands of the ghostly witness, and told the trium-

phant suitor to get rid of him as best he might. "Tergagle
gave mun a brave deal of trouble," says the account already
quoted ; " he was knackin about the place, and wouldn't laive
mun alone at all. And they went vore to the minister and
asked he vor to lay un . . . . the minister got dree hunderd
pound for a layin of un again. And first a was bound to
the old epping-stock up to Churchtown ; and after that a was
bound to the old oven in Tevurder ; and after that a was
bound to Dozmaré Pool, and they do say that there he ez
now." Other accounts say that he is by no means there,
having on the contrary baled out Dozmaré with surprising
speed, and that he was then set other tasks of a similarly hopeless character at Padstow, Helston, and many other places on
the coast. Usually he is said to be spinning ropes of sea
sand ; and then again he is represented to have achieved that
task by the aid of a kindly frost, which stiffened the sand
grains into a coherent mass. We shall hear of the restless
spirit again as we go west, always labouring at some task which
is well-nigh impossible, always hunted by the devil, a terribly
pathetic figure, probably far older in reality than the wretched
man on whom some freak of mythology, always seeking to
localise its wildest tales, has fastened this burden of guilt and
awe.

It may be well to observe before moving onward from these
moors that the chance of meeting with Tregeagle is by no
means the only unpleasant incident which is likely to befall
unwary travellers of the kind who value their own judgment
above that of those who know the locality well. There are
bogs and sudden mists ; and of each an instructive story shall
be told, since experience teaches that warnings not driven
home by concrete instances of disaster are too often treated
with derision.

Not very many years ago a certain noble lord, who, having
run a distinguished career in the army, had accustomed himself to a greater degree of unquestioning obedience than is

P

always prudently demanded in private life, was hunting on these moors, and at one marshy spot was advised by his huntsman, a keen old moorman, to fall behind and follow him closely in the same narrow track. The worthy peer was better used to lead than follow, and though he accepted the advice and dropped behind, he grumbled so loudly and availed himself so freely of a certain vivid language which was more commonly used in his youth than in our own day that the huntsman grew tired of hearing him at last, and drawing his horse aside with a low bow, made way for his lordship to pass by. The fine old warrior went on at a trot, singing out that the path was as good as Bodmin turn——He did not finish the word ; for just as the letter P was shaping itself on his martial lips, his horse floundered in up to its girths. Then there was a sad commotion. French squadrons were less dangerous to charge than a Cornish bog. Ropes had to be brought from a neighbouring farm, peer and horse were hauled about with utter loss of dignity and some risk of loss of life, and when at last they stood dripping with black moorwater on the bank of the morass we may hope they had learnt the lesson which it is the object of these lines to impress.

And now about the fogs. There was once an excellent vicar of St. Breward, who set off with his wife in their little pony carriage to visit Bodmin, the nearest place at which they could enjoy the delight of shop gazing, albeit a long way off and of a humble kind when reached. Poor as the entertainment may have been, their uncritical taste, spoilt long since by the constant contemplation of moors and granite boulders, gloated on it so long that they started homeward a full hour later than was wise, and so found wreaths of light vapour sweeping silently around them before their stout pony had climbed half the distance to the eyrie where they lived. The fog grew thicker. The well-known land marks lost their shape, and assumed strange forms. The vicar grew perplexed. He was not certain whether he had taken the right turn. He got down and looked about him, but saw nothing he could recognise, and so got up again and drove on blindly till the old lady grew frightened, for it seemed to her that they had travelled twice the distance to the vicarage, and must be wandering away in quite a wrong direction. The vicar pulled up and shouted, but there was no reply ; and at length the two old people could see nothing for it but to remain quiet where they were till daylight. Fortunately they had some rugs, and they packed themselves up and dozed as well as possible till the pony got strangely restless, and the parson, fearing he might do some mischief, got down, unharnessed him, let him trot away, climbed back and slumbered soundly till his wife woke him up pointing out that it was day, that the fog had gone, and that the spot where they had passed the night in despair of getting home was no other than the gate of their own vicarage. It was little wonder that the sagacious pony could not be contented to spend the night in harness when his own stable was actually within smell ; and perhaps this story may serve not only to teach a certain fear of fogs, but also to reduce the contempt with which some people regard what they are pleased to call the lower animals.

It was not necessary to stand still upon the moors while we gave these friendly cautions ; and accordingly we have by this time got some way down the valley of the Fowey River, which cleaves the ridge at no great distance from Dozmaré Pool. There is a very fair road in this valley, and it runs for some four miles on the river's bank, pleasantly enough, for the stream is brown and rapid, but in no wise calling for remark. At Redgate, a tiny hamlet of no interest, the road turns eastwards, and in a very little way it passes a monument, half hidden by a high hedge upon the right, on which learned people have spent much time, and even ignoramuses, for whom this book is chiefly written by one of their own number, may very well stop and spend a little.

" Near Redgate," says Borlase, "are two monumental stones ; one seven feet six inches high, like the spill of a cross, and which, part of the shaft being lost, is called 'The Other Half Stone.'" The nomenclature is a thought confusing; one forgets which is "the other half." But the one which is not the other half bears an inscription read as follows, "Doniert rogavit pro anima." Now Doniert, or Dungerth, was a King of Cornwall and was drowned in or about the year 872. There is no reason to doubt that the cross is sepulchral and erected in his memory; and this is the first and not the least interesting of a group of antiquities of very different dates which are possessed by the village of St. Clear, and which, if this stone had not lain so directly in our way, it might have been more convenient to mention all together.

"St. Cleer parish, coasting Liskeard," says Carew, rather ill-temperedly, "brooketh his name by a more piercing than profitable air, which in those open wastes scoureth away thrift as well as sickness." This is a trifle severe on the people whom the master of Antony found in St. Clear when he made his classic journey something like three centuries ago; but as for the present ones, poor souls, if the piercing wind scours away thrift from their cottage doors, there is nothing left but to wait until he scours it in again. For this is the first reached of the Cornish mining districts, and not the least distressed. The grand hills which we are approaching are a mass of tin and copper, but it does not pay to work it. The subject is a sore one; and we may very well leave it to be spoken of when we reach a district where it cannot be thrust aside. Here on the fine moors above Liskeard, there is something of interest in every mile; and at this moment, when the hedgerow begins to fall away, and the moor itself comes cropping out on the road, are two shallow gullies meeting at a point and meandering away till they are lost to sight among the furze and heather of the moor. They are not very noticeable. A man might pass that way a dozen times and hardly stay to wonder what they are; yet if he did so, and was at the pains to follow one of them, marking how it runs mile after mile near the modern

road, sometimes straying away a little distance and suddenly
sweeping back again, sometimes disappearing and then cropping
up on the other side of the highway, he would see that he has
to do neither with an accidental depression nor a watercourse,
but with some very ancient trodden way.

It is indeed difficult to guess how old these overgrown,
neglected ways may be that stretch so silently across the moor.
They represent a state of manners which disappeared not
more than eighty or ninety years ago ; but during how many
centuries they may have been in use before the modern roads
were made is nothing more than mere matter of conjecture.
For these are the old packmen's tracks, and the hollow paths
are those which commerce trod out for itself when the face
of the whole country was trackless, and the beaten highways
were as few as they now are on an African veldt.   Now as it
is perfectly idle to speculate when the ancient inhabitants of
Britain began to hold regular communications with each other,
so it is futile to attempt to guess how many centuries ago that
stream of traffic began to flow along these ancient courses
which has only ceased in the memory of living men.   We can
but look at the old tracks with interest such as we feel for all
places which are soaked in bygone memories ; and indeed,
sometimes, amid the silence of the moor, these grassy winding
lanes, just wide enough for mules to pass along in single file,
strike us as a little ghostly.   We find ourselves at the fall of
evening following them with our eyes in the growing dusk, and
every moment we fancy we hear the crack of the packman's
whip, or the jangling of the bells, or round some corner see
the patient, plodding mules come snuffing with their cumbrous
saddles and their high-piled burdens, pricking their ears and
opening their wide eyes in wonder at the sight of a traveller
on the lonely moor.

Those are mere fancies ; but indeed there is something in
the illimitable outlooks over hill and valley which break upon
our sight at every turn of this lofty road which makes us quick

to doubt whether old things do indeed pass away. There is
so much that has not changed from age to age; not only in
the glorious natural outlines of the land, the steep slope
dropping to the lower country, the wide broken valley, the
towering hills on every side, and far away the great ridge of
Dartmoor heights, not only in this view, so glorious and
memorable that I shall not seek to plaster it with words, but
even in the objects of curious interest fashioned some by
Nature, some by the hand of men, which bring those wandering
out here who perhaps would never come for the scenery alone.

Of these objects I suppose the best known is the Cheesewring. It is futile to describe again that singular pile of
granite blocks, whose very name suggests its aspect, and
which is figured in every guide book till the thing has grown
a trifle stale. Nor shall I say much about "The Hurlers," as
the country people have always called the three stone circles
lying on the slope, except to remark how well the childish
tradition that these hoary megaliths are the bodies of men
turned into stone for playing the ancient game of hurling on a
Sunday illustrates the complete ignorance of legend as to what
they really are. Not a trace of intelligible tradition lingers
round any one of these monuments either here or elsewhere in
Cornwall; and this is doubly strange in a country where the
name of every hill and valley, every ancient house or farm, is
descriptive, and by no means given at random. But there is
one among the innumerable relics of primæval times strewn
about these hills that may be briefly mentioned; and that is the
singular discovery made in one of the barrows, or ancient
burial mounds, which dot the surface of the country.

A huge pile of stones, thirty yards in diameter, covered an
oblong cavity, in which lay a human skeleton stretched at
length. This of itself was worthy of note; since in Cornwall
the practice of cremation was so widespread in the very ancient
times to which the barrows must for the most part be assigned,
that it is rare in the extreme to find one of them containing a

skeleton. But what was more remarkable than the omission to
burn the body, was that near the breast there stood an earthen
pot, and in it a golden cup of a pattern unlike any other found
in Britain, formed of a number of concentric rings not very
different from those collapsible drinking cups which are used
by modern travellers. Objects of gold are rarely found in
barrows ; and it is curious that in the neighbourhood there was
a persistent story that in some former time a golden boat had
been dug out from a barrow near the Cheesewring. This tale of
a golden boat turns up at other places round the coast, notably
at Veryan, west of St. Austell, where it is believed that a king
lies buried on the beacon with his golden boat beside him, and
that some day he will rise up in his armour as he lived, and
sail away across the sea. Idle tales these are ! I almost fear
to set them down lest I should incur the passionate reproach
levelled at another foolish person who valued trifles even as I
myself appreciate them. "Yea, such," said the censorious
author—I shall not name him—"yea, such are the tales of
indistinctness, the anecdotes of confusion, the narratives of
ignorance that all travellers hear, that the injudicious receive
with the very stamp of folly on their brow, and that the
presumptuous publish." See how far one may go astray without
suspecting it ! I almost wish. . . but no matter. I will drop
this chapter full of trivialities, and try seriously to do better in
the next.

I turn away rather sadly from the moor, remembering as I
go a dozen things that I had meant to say and that were well
worth mentioning, if it were not that life is short, as I am
reminded from time to time by one of the numerous ravens
which frequent the moor, and which go flapping heavily a little
way above my head, croaking out "corp, corp, corpse," after
the disagreeably suggestive habit of their kind. Perhaps the
bird means well, and it was time to jog my wandering thoughts,
which were straying on as if I had forgotten all the miles that
lie before me, and cared nothing for the bays and headlands of

the West. Moreover the light warns me that the day is far
spent. *Sol ruit ;* and it is time to get down out of the
mountains, or else stay there for the night. I choose the
latter course ; and turning into the Cheesewring Hotel find a
kindly hostess, an excellent cut of moorland mutton, the best
of home-brewed cider, and a chamber fragrant with the
infinite sweet odours which are borne across the highlands by
every wind that blows.

CHAPTER XIII

IT is an easy and pleasant road which runs down out of the moors towards Liskeard; and there is nothing to delay the traveller by the way except the singular group of antiquities at St. Clear. One of these, namely The Other Half Stone, has been mentioned in the last chapter; and as it falls into its proper place as not the least interesting among the curiosities of this village, it may be referred to once more, if only to observe that the inscription carved on it is the solitary instance in Cornwall of any memorial being found carved on a cross. Numerous as these wayside calls to devotion are, lying half buried in the ferns and mosses of the hedgerows, or standing free and erect at the meeting of cross roads, their shafts and bases were never, save in this one instance, used to call back any human memories, or mingle the sorrows of mankind with those of Him who died upon the Tree. By whom, or in what age, the crosses were set up, is one of those questions which wise men do not dogmatise upon. Nor is it necessary to speculate widely where the introduction of Christianity supplies a limit backwards; while the date of The Other Half Stone helps us a little in the contrary direction. However, it is clear that wayside crosses were being set up in Cornwall much later than the year in which Doniert was drowned; for the will of one Dr. Reginald Mertherderwa, who died in 1447, directs that " new stone crosses are to be

put up of the usual kind in those parts of Cornwall from Kayar
Beslasek to Camborne Church, where dead bodies are rested
on their way to burial, that prayers may be made, and the
bearers take some rest," and in that extract from the good
man's will is contained as much as can or need be said about
the uses of these crosses.

St. Clear.

There is another cross in the village of St. Clear, but it is
less interesting, being of ordinary Latin form, while The Other
Half Stone is of Celtic modelling and ornament. This Latin
cross stands beside the holy well which like the well at
Altarnun is reputed to have been used for the drastic cure of
maniacs, but unlike its rival sanatorium possesses a beautiful

little chapel built over the clear spring. There is hardly space within the tiny building for the meeting of a congregation ; nor does any record commemorate the services which were held there. Yet the small chapel stands as an abiding witness to the reverence which the Cornish felt for springs—a feeling which, as has been said already, is doubtless much older than Christianity, and one indeed which is in some degree common to the hearts of all men, as any one may test who has ever on some burning day of midsummer come down from the highlands into a shady road, weary and hot, and having no means of slaking thirst for many a mile. Then if he find by the wayside, in the cool shadow of the hedge, a crystal well, covered over with a wooden planking, lest any ray of sunlight should heat it, or passing animals defile it, and quenches his thirst and cools his hands and forehead with the living water, it may be he will feel some emotion stirring in his heart which is not so very different from that which sanctified the wells long centuries ago.

Sometimes these wells beside the highway were used for a double purpose, being fitted with shelves in the sides above the water level on which butter was set to cool, and where it was kept safe from the hot sun, and in no danger from strolling larceny, which in old days did not exist in Cornwall, and is rare enough even now. There is such a well in a lane at no great distance from St. Clear.

Last among the lions of the village, and immensely more ancient than the rest, comes the Trethevy dolmen, the largest of its class in Cornwall. The guide book calls it a cromlech, but as we commenced by assigning that name to stone circles, we have no other left than dolmen, which really saves confusion, since those who take the other course use both names indifferently. It stands upon a rising ground, a rough chamber formed out of vast unhewn slabs of stone rising to a height of five or six feet, and roofed by a colossal capstone of such size and weight as would tax the skill of a modern engineer to poise on the support where it has rested for not less than twenty centuries. The purpose of the dolmen is evident. It was a grave ; just such another as one may see to-day standing in any churchyard and called an altar tomb. There is a singular feature about the capstone, which is pierced by a hole at one of its projecting corners. Great and notable battles have been fought by archæologists about this hole ; but as none among them have yet been able to explain it, we had better let it be, and pass on.

But we really must get away from this interesting village, where the relics of such different ages are shown us in so small space that one might study a good deal of Cornish history without travelling beyond the parish bounds. The Liskeard road crosses another fine range of downs, from which there is a glorious view westwards towards St. Austell where the China clay works gleam white in the far distance, and eastwards to Rame Head and the crest of exquisite Mount Edgecumbe dimly seen, and the Dartmoor hills beyond, and between us and them such miles and miles of rolling, swelling moor, gold in spring time, purple when the heather blooms, and always fresh and keen and bracing, so that weariness drops away from the shoulders of the man who walks across its springy turf, and middle age has the vigour and the strength of boyhood. Too soon the moors are crossed, the road falls steeply, and presently we are passing through the streets of old Liskeard.

Liskeard is not a very interesting town, or if it is, it keeps its charm for those who know it closely. It has but little for those who travel swiftly. We will pass it by ; and riding out beyond the station, set ourselves in the track for Looe.

There is an easy road running through the valley to that picturesque old town ; but those who are curious about the stone circle at Duloe or the yet more famous well of St. Keyne, must resign themselves to a rough and hilly wandering. Stone circles pall on almost everybody, and one well is some-

thing like another, while even the story attached to this one,
attributing to its water the power of giving mastery in marriage
to that one of the spousal pair who drinks it first after the
ceremony, is so threadbare that it cannot be necessary to dwell
on it. We will pass on therefore down the valley till we meet
the salt water flowing up the wooded estuary, a narrow winding
river bottom, so deep and shady that it might be more appro-
priately termed a gorge among the lofty hills that flank the
coast ; and when, after running for some mile or more beside
the marshes and the ebbing tide, the road turns and shows us
the first houses of the ancient town, the impression of a
mountainous country is but so much heightened. For on both
sides of the river the hills rise very steeply out of the water ;
and the gardens and orchards on their precipitous sides are
banked up on terraces and walls. Pink apple blossom glows
softly all along the hill. A little gusty wind strews its petals
thickly on the grass, and brings with it the bitter odour of the
sea, which the winding valley hides as yet, though already the
river has become a harbour, and the masts of half a dozen
coasting schooners rise over the stone bridge of many arches,
which unites East Looe with its western namesake.

For there are two Looes, and the river parts them. To one
who visits them to-day it scarcely seems that in this small seacleft there can at any time have been a life vigorous enough to
maintain two towns. Yet both were incorporated in the reign
of Queen Elizabeth, though their greatest history lies further
back than those days of Spanish warfare, extending indeed into
the period of piracy and ceaseless fighting with the Bretons, of
which we spoke at length when contemplating Dartmouth.
There are no existing records of those lusty days ; and the
historian of the Looes was obliged to make out his slender
volume with details of far less interest and value. We would
give many volumes of patient gleanings among old deeds for
one page reproducing that quick full-blooded life which the
Looe men lived when they went fighting up and down the

channel with whoever came their way, for a true account, however brief, of the experiences of some one among those sailors who manned the ships sent to the siege of Calais, or for the story of that fight in which the Looe ship *George*, heaven knows how many centuries ago, attacked and took three French galleys, whence, as Carew tells us, there has always been one vessel of that name sailing out of Looe to keep the glorious memory alive. These things are lost beyond recall; and it is only by carefully collating scattered details that we can build up shadowy outlines of the great achievements of the past.

Some traces there still are however of the mode of living in the Looes. There exists in one of the old boroughs, or did exist not many years ago, a cage for scolds, as well as a ducking stool, which two engines taken together may be presumed to have made the valley a very quiet peaceful spot. Cages are not very common, though there is said to be one at Penzance; and therefore it may be well to set down an authentic record of an occasion on which this one was used.

"At East Looe," says Mr. Bond, for it is a delicate subject, and he shall be responsible for his own story, "At East Looe, Hannah Whit and Bessy Niles, two women of fluent tongue, having exerted their oratory on each other, at last thought it prudent to leave the matter in dispute to be settled by the Mayor. Away they posted to his worship. The first who arrived had scarce begun her tale when the other bounced in in full rage, and began hers likewise, and abuse commenced with redoubled vigour. His worship, Mr. John Chubb, ordered the constable to be called, and each of the combatants thought her antagonist was going to be punished, and each thought right. When the constable arrived, his worship pronounced the following command to him, 'Take these two women to the cage, and there keep them till they have settled their dispute." They were immediately conveyed thither, and after a few hours confinement became as quiet and inoffensive beings as ever breathed, and were then liberated to beg Mr. Mayor's pardon.

Firmness and decision of character are qualities so little found in public life to-day that it gives me pleasure to record this anecdote of Mr. Chubb.   May his successors deliver judgment as courageously as he !   One dwells the more fondly on this story since it is indeed the single remaining memory which can be called great in Looe.   You may wander round the ancient boroughs, admiring the narrow streets with their irregular, antique houses clinging to both sides of the steep ravine, a strange, confused medley, built upon no settled plan, one house elbowing another out into the roadway ; you may marvel at the beauty of the hillside, where grey rocks jut out among the golden furze ; you may look seawards where the white gulls wheel and flash across the narrow channel at the entrance of the harbour, and see a little schooner running in, the poor relic of a trade which up to the beginning of the last century sent many a good ship up the Levant. But you will see nothing more considerable than these sights ; for the great days of Looe are over, and her chief reliance is on a fleet of some fifty fishing boats which fish a good deal off the coast of Ireland, a ground deserted by the larger fleets of Newlyn trawlers, for the Newlyn men, after their somewhat combative fashion, are at war with Ireland just at present.

There is but a narrow space of level ground in East Looe between the water and the hill, while in West Looe there is none at all.   So that when we cross the bridge and set our faces against the hill towards Polperro, there is a long and weary climb up a road which shirks no difficulty, but cuts straight upwards with a courage which might be called heroic. Unhappily, some of us are too shortwinded to play the part of heroes on a Cornish hill, and so catch every excuse for looking backwards over the lovely intersecting valleys, and the high shoulders of the wooded hills, each one blazing with gold and green as the alternating sunlight flashes down upon the fresh spring foliage.

There is nothing to be seen when the top of the ridge is attained. The two miles along the summit are uninteresting, and it is only when the road begins to drop as steeply as it rose that it becomes plain there is something in the ravine below which is well worth seeing.

Indeed it is a noble valley into which the hilly road conducts us. At the foot of the mountain lies the white village of Crumplehorn, half covered up in masses of blowing apple-blossom. Beside the houses a rushing stream sings down the valley between bluffs so lofty, and along a cleft so narrow that one marvels how the sunlight finds its way down upon the water on which it flashes so brightly. Just at first one sees nothing of the town, but all at once it bursts upon the sight as the road runs round a bend, a striking huddled group of houses, cast so strangely into a heap as to produce the impression that they must have been built originally upon the hillside at comfort-able distances apart ; and that by some slipping of the rock foundations the houses have slid and slid until they can slide no further, but are brought to a standstill in the very bottom of the hollow. The confusion of the town is immense. It is a labyrinth of winding alleys, often ending in a *cul-de-sac*. But the downward sweep of the headlands is superb ; and under the towering cliffs studded with bosses of golden furze lies a little pier and harbour with the sea foam flying sharply round the jutting peaks of rock before a stiff south-wester, while the gulls wheel shrieking overhead, and out at sea a schooner is labouring heavily.

" In the time of a storm," says Mr. Jonathan Couch, a native of Polperro, and author of the very pleasantest local history which it has been my good fortune to light upon, " in the time of a storm Polperro is a striking scene of bustle and excitement. The noise of the wind as it roars up the coomb, the hoarse rumbling of the angry sea, the shouts of the fishermen engaged in securing their boats, and the screams of the women and children carrying the tidings of the latest disaster, are a

Polperro.

Q

peculiarly melancholy assemblage of sounds, especially when heard at midnight. All who can render assistance are out of their beds, helping the sailors and fishermen ; lifting the boats out of reach of the sea, or taking the furniture of the ground floors to a place of safety. . . . When the first streak of morning light comes, bringing no cessation of the storm, but only serving to show the devastation it has made, the effect is still more dismal. The wild fury of the waves is a sight of no mean grandeur as it dashes over the peak and falls on its jagged summit, from whence it streams down the sides in a thousand waterfalls and foams at its base. The infuriated sea sweeps over the piers and striking against the rocks and houses on the warren side rebounds towards the strand, and washes fragments of houses and boats into the streets, where the receding tide leaves them strewn in sad confusion."

Such is the graphic record of a night of storm and terror, left us by Mr. Couch, who must have witnessed many such during the long years he dwelt in the townlet where he was born, finding in that narrow limit a sphere wide enough to occupy his keen and searching intellect a whole lifetime. None knew by more experience than he how pitiful is the terror which falls on Cornish fisher houses when the October storms rise along the coast, nor can any one who has witnessed it forget the sight when the people stand huddled together on the cliff in the driving rain and watch the boats trying vainly to make the harbour, while every time they are hidden by the trough of the mountainous waves, the women's shriek is heard above the barking of the storm, and the men stand silent waiting to count the number which emerge again. There is a trifling Cornish custom, which tells us more of the abiding fear that haunts every household all along the coast than could be taught in any other way. The children are always corrected if they bring a loaf to table resting on its cut side—they are told it looks so like a boat turned bottom upwards.

But to return to Mr. Couch, which I do with the greatest

pleasure, since his book is the very opposite of what is commonly understood by a local history ; that is to say, it is the work of a man who knew and loved his own people, cared for their small differences from others, set down their old customs, and in truth verified the old text reversed, which tells us that where a man's heart is, there will his treasure be also. And a very copious treasure the old naturalist dug out of Polperro, a rich store of life and character which makes fascinating reading. There were such strange survivals in Polperro.   As late as the end of the last century the society of the little town was adorned by no less a person than an alchemist, a kind of wildfowl long since grown very scarce in the more frequented parts of England ; while the commoner astrologer, no almanac maker like Zadkiel or old Moore, but the genuine searcher of the skies, with strange brass instruments which he had repaired at the reckless outlay of thirty shillings, flourished there in the person of one John Stevens until 1849.

Polperro, like other places, had to deal with jealous neighbours, who corrupted its euphonious other name Polstoggan, into the opprobrious Polstink, alleging that the town was well christened since the scourings of fish filled it with a reek that made those not born to love it go about holding their noses. This of course is the voice of jealousy, prompted by the exceeding prosperity of Polperro men in those days when there were better things than fish to be picked up on the seas. "Surely," cries old Fuller, "divine providence did not make the vast body of the sea for no other use than for fishes to disport themselves therein."   True, dear Fuller ; he did not. Polperro men found quite a number of other uses to which it could be put ; in fact had you asked them in the last century, they would have answered that fishes were "poor trade" and that their luggers had something better to do than attempt to catch them.

The staple industries of Polperro, in the good days when protecting the revenue was deemed too difficult to be worth the trouble, were smuggling and privateering ; and in both it excelled to a degree which makes it really classic ground. The deep seacleft, as Mr. Couch points out, was particularly adapted for smuggling ; and he adds with truly Cornish pride that " all joined in it ; the smith left his forge, and the husband-man his plough ; even women and children turned out to assist in the unlawful traffic and received their share of the proceeds." The ships employed were built at Polperro, " fine craft too they turned out, clippers, which when manned by skilful and intrepid sailors, would scud away from the fastest of the government cruisers, and offer them a tow rope in derision." Lusty seamen these, bearing no malice even when the revenue men scored a point, as we see from the kindly and pious epitaph on a smuggler shot in the discharge of his duty.

> In prime of life most suddenly,
> Sad tidings to relate,
> Here view my utter destiny
> And pity my sad fate.
> I, by a shot which rapid flew,
> Was instantly struck dead.
> Lord, pardon the offender who
> My precious blood did shed.
> Grant him to rest, and forgive me
> All I have done amiss ;
> And that I may rewarded be
> With everlasting bliss.

The smugglers could well afford this kindly attitude towards the coastguard men, for indeed the efforts of the latter to interfere with their lucrative pursuits resembled nothing so much as the antics of a podgy terrier whom you may see on a garden lawn capering about breathlessly after the swallows, which, with a keen zest in baffling him, skim by under his nose, and leave him staring up to the sky with a ludicrous air of breathless perplexity. It was a fine breezy, lawless, defiant life, the natural continuation, as I have said before, of one much wilder and

more lawless, of which the two, taken together, formed during
long centuries of daily peril and seawarfare that type of hardy

Polperro.

reckless sailor who won our battles in our time of need.   Let
it be recognised that it was not idling in a fishing boat that bred
the qualities of dash and resource which we expect in seamen.

The pressgangs which swept along the Cornish coast in days of
war knew that they were entering a huge storehouse of the finest
fighting material that could be wished, an inexhaustible reserve
of men whose daily trade was to encounter enemies either with
force or guile, and whose ancestors for untold generations had
been doing just the same, till there was not a lad born upon the
coast who did not inherit the tradition of deeds of daring which
would make a modern veteran illustrious.   For the point I insist
upon is that there has never throughout our history been peace
upon the western coasts until within the last three generations.
If the seamen were not fighting with the enemies of England
they were fighting with its law ; and the result in training them
was just the same.   I say nothing of the morality of the life.
I insist only that it was that which produced the thing we wanted
when we went to war.   Take the Polperro privateering.   Who
would have supposed in visiting Polperro to-day, a sleepy, idle
place where half the population are basking in the sun on shore,
and the other half basking in their boats—who would have
supposed, I say, that this little town was ever able to deal doughty
blows at the enemies of England ? Yet the Polperro privateers
were famous. And what were they ? They were smuggling vessels,
manned by smugglers, who sometimes built them larger ships
when they found a need for them.   And how did they conduct
themselves upon the sea ? We will answer that by taking from
Mr. Couch's book another story told him by a descendant of
the officer concerned.

" Mr. Nicholas Rowett of Polperro, during the French war,
commanded the *Unity*, a hired armed lugger ; and when
cruising in the Channel, off Ushant, he was very much surprised
to find himself one morning at dawn between two French frigates,
one on either side, who hoisted English colours, but from their
build and rig he had his suspicions as to their nationality.   All
doubts however were dispelled when a shot was fired across his
bows to bring him to ; and both immediately displayed the
French flag.   The nearest hailed him, and considering the

Unity to be their prize, ordered him to lie to while they
boarded her. This order Capt. Rowett feigned to obey, and for
the moment shortened sail ; but when under the lee of the enemy
who were both lying to, quite contentedly lowering their boat with
the sails aback, he suddenly spread all sail, passing ahead of
both frigates, took the helm himself, ordered the crew to lie
flat on the deck to escape the perfect shower of balls rained
from the bow chaser and muskets of the enemy, which in their
anger and disappointment at so unexpectedly losing their prey
were fired on them. The *Unity* soon escaped out of range
without any one being hurt, and with only very slight damage
being done to the sails and rigging, and had the satisfaction of
seeing the Frenchmen occupied for a considerable time in
trimming and spreading their sails for the pursuit, while they
were at a safe distance. Being close hauled by the wind they
were soon on the weather bow, and by breakfast time far on the
weather gauge of both the heavy, lumbering frigates."

I do not reproduce this gallant tale in order to argue that
the seamen of our own day would not do as much. I assert
nothing more than that whereas their daily life a century ago
was made up of such incidents, it never contains them now.
Very probably it was for the world's advantage when law grew
potent ; but it has destroyed the finest school for sailors that
ever existed, and it is idle to fancy that any course of gunnery
instruction, or any training, however careful, on a hulk in
Plymouth Sound, will do for the seamen of to-day what was
done by a dozen trips to Brest or Roscoff when liberty, life and
fortune, hung together upon perfect seamanship.

There is a whistling sound in the salt air which warns us of
breaking weather. The sky has turned dark grey, and the black
water is surging heavily around the jagged harbour cliff. Every
sign promises a dirty night, and we have far to go. For though
the distance to Fowey, where all the greatest sea traditions of
Cornwall lie clustering together, is but seven miles, yet the road
is so hilly and withal so ill provided with signposts, that it is

no more than common prudence to let it count as ten. The way lies back up the valley by quaintly named Crumplehorn again, and then up a steep hill on the left till the lofty summit of the ridge is reached, and we go winding in and out by farms and cottages each one of which could tell its own wild stories of lawless gains and perilous night adventures. Somewhere on these hillsides dwelt a worthy man who owned a movable duck pond. It was not merely a scientific curiosity, as might be hastily concluded. Quite the contrary. It was an invention of his own, and possessed the highest practical utility, for when this excellent man entertained the revenue officers, which he was fond of doing, his pond was like all other ponds, and the ducks floated peacefully about its surface, or tilted their tails up in the slime, after the manner of their kind. But when there was no prospect of government intrusion, the duck pond with its quacking burden swung aside upon a pivot, and disclosed a deep recess which could and did hold quantities of things about which inconvenient questions might have been asked, had the excisemen seen them. Ah, merry lawless days ! what Cornishman can in his heart condemn them ?

There is an old manor house among these lanes where centuries ago a raid was carried out which brings home vividly how dangerous life was in seaboard districts of Cornwall when the seas were open to sudden French descents and every war was signalised by a number of petty expeditions, piracy legalised for the nonce. The lord of this manor had a French servant in piping times of peace. The man left him. War broke out, and the nimble-witted servant conceived the bold idea of plundering his former master. He landed on the coast without having been observed, led a party up the cliff by secret paths which he knew well, entered the house, and seized the luckless owner while he sat at supper. There is a cunningly constructed hiding place within the house, which is said to have been built to guard against the risk of any such mishaps in future. There was very little to prevent them in ancient days, and though all,

or nearly all the details of life in those wild regions are now
lost, it may be fairly surmised that such raids had been
successful on other occasions also, and that they had their
counterparts in action taken by the Cornish seamen in
France.

The town and river of Fowey, on which we are moving as
we run across this ridge, lie so deeply in the valley that nothing
is seen of either till the road has emerged upon an open hillside almost overhanging the convolutions of the estuary; and
the suddenness with which this view discloses itself adds
immensely to its effect. One moment there is nothing to be
seen but the windings of an unlovely road. The next there
has opened far below a dark green highway, broad and spacious,
branching among hills. Deep down at the foot of the descent
lie the roofs and cottages of Bodinnick, with its heavy ferry
boat lumbering across to Fowey, of which quaint hillside town
more and more is seen at every winding of the road, till at
length one's sight is drawn off it by the disclosure of that noble
view which roused old Carew to eloquence nearly four centuries
ago, and which still remains an unforgettable memory with
those who have once seen it. "In passing along," says the
squire of Antony, "your eyes shall be called away from guarding
your feet to descry by their furthest kenning the vast ocean,
sparkled with ships, that continually this way trade forth and
back to most quarters of the world. Nearer home they take
view of all sized cocks, barges and fisher boats hovering
on the coast. Again, contracting your sight to a narrower
scope, it lighteth on the fair and commodious haven, where
the tide daily presenteth his double service of flowing and
ebbing, to carry and recarry whatsoever the inhabitants
shall be pleased to charge him withal, and his creeks, like a
young wanton lover, fold about the land with many embracing
arms."

The salt air mingles strangely with the scent of violets as we
descend the hill, and the sweet odour of the woodlands unites

with a decided savour of tarry rope.   One could drop a pebble
on the roofs of the four or five houses which stand about the
higher end of the sloping pier, pretty whitewashed cottages, of
that neat aspect which sometimes enables the Cornishman to
recognise the dwellings of his own people in other countries.
For the Cornish peasant's garden is full of stocks and roses.   I
know not what it is that is peculiarly Cornish in the growth of
these common flowers, or of the valerian that flames crimson
on the low walls, or the tamarisk that surmounts it, or it may be
something that I am not observant enough to detect and
isolate.   But whatever it may be, certain I am that a Cornish
garden may be known far away from Cornwall, and I myself
have recognised one at a glance in the wilds of Donegal, where
the stocks and roses bloomed as sweetly under the shadow of
Muckish and Horn Head as ever they did in Fowey or Bodmin,
and the true sense of Cornish kinship blossomed sweetly too
in the heart of an old Saltash woman who, for many a year had
not heard a Cornish tongue, and could not make enough of it
when found, but laughed and cried and chattered all at once
till she brought to mind in very soberness that great passion
which beset Sordello on the Mount of Purgatory, when
he heard Virgil speaking in the tongue of his own city,
Mantua.

I might pause here to say much of the intense feeling which
the Cornish cherish for their homes and for their own wild and
beautiful country, a feeling which neither years nor exile can
do aught but strengthen, and which, as far as I know, has been
little recognised in literature.   Perhaps the reason may be that
which makes me stay my pen, and refrain from writing down
for other men to wonder at what is too strongly felt to be easily
expressed.

The dusk has fallen while we are waiting for the ferry boat.
The few vessels lying in the harbour have lit their lanterns.
Across the water come the faint noise of a wheezy hurdy-gurdy,
and the cries of children ; and one sees on an open spot beside

the quay a tent in which some rustic tragedy is being acted. We are landed on a dark and slippery jetty, and go through the dim old town too weary to notice more than that its streets are steep and tortuous, and that through many openings and court-yards we see the dark water washing to and fro.

CHAPTER XIV

I said in my last chapter that all the greatest sea traditions of Cornwall are locked up in Fowey. I might have gone somewhat further; for indeed there was a time when this Cornish harbour led the kingdom in matters of seamanship, and not London, nor Plymouth, nor Dartmouth, nor even Yarmouth, nor any one among the privileged Cinque Ports could furnish such a gallant fleet or sailors so well used to speak with England's enemies in the gate. For the town sent to the fleet which Edward III. collected for the siege of Calais the majestic contribution of forty-seven ships and no less than 770 men. Yarmouth sent forty-three, Dartmouth thirty-two, London twenty-five. No other port than Yarmouth approached the Cornish contribution.

This is quite enough to show that in the past history of Fowey there lies some story well worth telling, some long maturing greatness, some steady growth fostered by wise counsels and guided by the hands of prudent governors. Consider what is involved in the capacity to furnish and equip so large a fleet. Grant that they were not all Fowey ships, which is likely enough, for Fowey may have been in some degree a rendezvous for the adjoining coast. Yet making all deductions, enough remains to show that Fowey was a great and mighty town, far different relatively to the rest of England from its present lowly condition. And what was it then that checked

the growth of a town so splendid, and thrust it back on insigni-
ficance?   Why, very largely the weak or timid counsels of an
English king, who broke the strongest weapon he possessed, and
tossed away the splinters chiefly to gratify a foreign sovereign.
But before entering on this story look round Fowey, and see
what manner of place it is.

Fowey.

The first thing which strikes a stranger coming to Fowey from
the east is its singular similarity to Dartmouth.   Here is the
same deep harbour, fenced round by lofty hills ; the same narrow
entrance guarded by twin towers, and once closed nightly by a
chain ; the same winding river, flowing down a channel no less
lovely than the Dart, from a town as beautiful and ancient as
Totnes ; the same little rival town on the hillside across the

harbour, Polruan facing Fowey, as Kingswear faces Dartmouth
But the town of Fowey, if less studded with relics of old magnificence, is to my thinking more picturesque than Dartmouth,
more hilly, its streets more tortuous, and its houses built with a
strange angularity and jutting quaintness which is little matched
in Devon, but is characteristic of the Cornish fishing towns.   I
think of Fowey, and straightway there pass before my memory
steep flights of steps ending in dusky archways through which the
blue water of the harbour is seen, rippled by a light landward
breeze ; ancient gabled houses which stand out squarely into the
street and force it suddenly aside ; ships lying so close beside the
houses, that it is easy to credit the story of a lady who was
disturbed at her toilet by the yard arm of a ship entering her
bedroom ; a fine church old enough to have seen many vicissi-
tudes of fortune ; and rising over all, giving a mediaeval character
to the whole town, the old fortress-mansion of that great family
of Treffry, whose history is the town's history, and out of
which rode forth that gallant John Treffry, who was made
knight banneret on the field of Crecy.   If the family tradition
may be trusted, it was he made prisoner the French King John
at Poictiers ; and certainly none but some very signal service of
this sort would have won him the permission he received to
quarter the arms of France with his own.

No one knows the origin of Fowey ; but looking out across
its deep set harbour, and recognising the ease with which its
narrow entrance could be held against all comers, the same
thought comes into mind as occurred not unjustly at Dartmouth
also—that the men who first chose this stronghold for a dwelling
place must have been singularly moral if they did not practise
piracy. And indeed it cannot be claimed for the men of Fowey in
any age to which history reaches back that they were so far set
above the common failings of mankind.   In fact it must be
admitted that they were somewhat notorious for piracy, which
would of course distress me very much, if I did not know how
difficult it is even in much more recent days to define a pirate.

Most naval warfare, I take it, in the days of the Plantagenets, was curiously like piracy, and bore that name whenever the monarch of this country was displeased with those who conducted it, while at other times a gentler term sufficed.   Upon this western coast at any rate, as I have already insisted, life was made up of expeditions of Bretons against Cornwall and of Cornishmen against Brittany, which were sanctioned by nobody at all except the ingenious persons who took part in them. " During the warlike reigns of our two valiant Edwards, the first and third," says Hals, " the Foyens addicted themselves to backe their Princes' quarrels by coping with the enemy at sea, and made return of many prizes, which purchases having advanced them to a good estate of wealth, the same was heedfully and diligently employed and bettered by the more civil trade of marchandise ; and in both these vocations they so fortunately prospered that it is reported 60 tall ships did at one time belong to the harbour . . . Hereon a full purse begetting a stout stomach, our Foyens took heart at grasse and chancing about that time—I speak upon the credit of tradition—to sail near Rye and Winchilsea, they stifly refused to vaile their bonnets at the summons of those towns ; which contempt, by the better enabled seafarers reckoned intolerable, caused the Ripiers to make out with might and maine against them ; howbeit with a more hardy onset than happy issue ; for the Foy men gave them so rough entertainment as their welcome, that they were glad to depart without bidding farewell—the merit of which exploit afterwards entitled them gallants of Fowey."

Dear gallant Cornishmen ! Did they not cast back the Kentish lubbers nobly, tossing back defiance on the points of their boarding pikes ! They were ill counselled that quarrelled with Fowey men in old days ! Let us take another instance, and this is a very curious one, since tradition has preserved for us in ballad form the story of a fight against a Genoese Corsair, hired by the King of France for service against England, and commanded by no less a person than " John Dory," otherwise

Giovanni Doria, of the great Italian family of that name. We
do not know who Nichol was with whom Doria fought, but
tradition tells us that he was a widow's son, and dwelt upon
Fowey Harbour.   Doubtless he was a churl—but let the ballad
tell its own tale.

> As it fell on a holy day,
>   And upon a holy tide a ;
> John Dory bought him an ambling nag,
>   To Paris for to ride a.
>
> And when John Dory to Paris was come,
>   A little before he gate a ;
> John Dory was fitted, the porter was witted,
>   To let him in thereat a.
>
> The first man that John Dory did meet,
>   Was good King John of France a :
> John Dory could well of his courtesie,
>   But fell down in a trance a ;
>
> A pardon, a pardon, my liege and my King
>   For my merry men and for me a ;
> And all the churls in merry England
>   I'll bring them bound to thee a.
>
> And Nichol was then a Cornish man
>   A little beside Bohyde a ;
> He manned him forth a goodly bark,
>   With fifty good oars of a side a.
>
> Run up, my boy, into the maintop,
>   And look what thou canst spy a ;
> Who, ho! who, ho! a good ship do I see,
>   I trow it be John Dory a.
>
> They hoist their sails both top and top,
>   The mizen and all was tried a,
> And every man stood to his lot,
>   Whatever should betide a.

The roaring cannons then were plied,
    And dub-a-dub went the drum a :
The braying trumpets loud they cried,
    To courage both all and some a.

The grappling hooks were brought at length,
    The brown bill and the sword a ;
John Dory at length, for all his strength,
    Was clapt fast under board a.

The good King John of this ballad was doubtless the
unfortunate monarch taken prisoner at Poictiers ; and these
rude verses seem to be almost, if not quite, the only record of
the great deeds of the Fowey men during those French wars
in which the county of Cornwall bore a very honourable
part. This was the great period of Fowey. Its galleys
sailed far and wide and won a reputation for heavy handed
dealing both with friends and foes. " The people of Fowey,"
Hals goes on to say, " grew unspeakably rich, proud and
mischievous." Hals, I am afraid, was a little too much of a
nursery moralist to be a fair judge of the practices of Channel
seamen. Certainly he writes with an animus against Fowey
which suggests that had he lived in those days he would rather
have had his throat cut and his house burned by Breton raiders
than that anything should have been done in his defence
which was not warranted by the principles of the Sermon on
the Mount. Thus he evidently thinks it an instance of the
wrath of heaven falling on a wicked city when " the Lord
Pomier and other Normans " obtained from the King of
France " a commission of mart and arms to be revenged on
the pirates of Fowey town, and carried the design so secret
that a small squadron of ships and many bands of marine
soldiers was prepared and shipped without the Fowey men's
knowledge. They put to sea out of the River Seine in July
1457, and with a fair wind sailed thence across the British
Channel and got sight of Fowey Harbour, where they lay off at

R

sea till night, when they drew towards the shore and dropt anchor, and landed their marine soldiers and seamen, who at midnight approached the south-west end of Fowey town, where they killed all persons they met with, set fire to the houses and burnt one-half thereof to the ground, to the consumption of a great part of the inhabitants' riches and treasures, a vast deal of which were gotten by their pyratical practices." Really Hals is intolerable ! In his eyes the Norman enemies of Fowey appear to rank as the just executors of a lawful doom. Does he suppose that the Lord of Pomier was a nursery moralist like himself, or that the men who followed him had never slain and plundered on the high seas without a warrant ? But let him go on with his unctuous account, since it is the best we have. " In which massacre the women, children and weakest sort of people forsook the place and fled for safety into the hill country. But the stoutest men, under conduct of John Treffry Esquire, fortified themselves as well as they could in his then new built house of Place, yet standing, where they stoutly opposed the assaults of the enemies, while the French soldiers plundered that part of the town which was unburnt without opposition in the dark. The news of the French invasion in the morning flew far into the country, and the people of the contiguous parts as quickly put themselves in arms, and in great multitudes gathered together in order to raise the siege of Fowey, which the Frenchmen observing and fearing the consequences of their longer stay, having gotten sufficient treasure to defray the charge of their expedition, as hastily ran to their ships as they had deliberately entered the town, with small honour and less profit."

Now here, written by a half unfriendly hand, is the story of one of those nights of terror to which the whole west coast of England was exposed during many centuries. What the watch in the castles on the headlands were about to allow the French to land their troops on a July night without being seen must remain an unsolved riddle. Doubtless the harbour mouth was closed as usual by its chain, and the French may have landed in a little stony creek half a mile west of the entrance, a place of debarkation only possible in calm weather. There is but one path by which the invaders could have come ; and it is not easy to traverse it in the summer dusk without thinking of the silent march of enemies across the headland, the sudden onslaught in the dark, the screams and battle cries breaking the stillness of the warm night, the swords flashing in the smoky torchlight, the race of frightened women with their babes up the hills and across the harbour, and then the day breaking slowly over the smoking town, and the first light of summer dawn glinting downwards on the mansion where a grim handful of fighting men stood side by side with cold hearts and murderous fury in their faces watching the Normans harrying their homes.

We need not doubt that the men of Fowey took a heavy toll of vengeance for this onslaught, and that many a Norman town and village smoked before the Cornishmen held the balance to be even. In fact Hals, always apt at setting the deeds of Fowey men in the worst light, says that not long after, "our Fowey gallants, unable to bear a low sail, in their fresh gale of fortune began to skum the seas with their often piracies. . . as also to violate their duty on land by insolent disobedience to the prince's officers, cutting off among other pranks, a pursuivant's ears." Now this was an action which we cannot judge until we know what the pursuivant had been doing. There are certainly circumstances which might render it a knightly and a pious deed to cut the ears of a pursuivant, or indeed of any other person, say an historian, who had been inclined to take part against his countrymen. But Hals does not think it necessary to give us the facts, preferring to hasten on to the great act of treachery which destroyed Fowey, that lusty town which should have been till now one of the chief bulwarks of England.

Now it seems that King Edward IV. was annoyed at the treatment of his pursuivant, and had received complaints from the King of France against Fowey men. At any rate he sent

commissioners to Lostwithiel, who seem to have conceived
some fear of sharing the fate of the pursuivant, for instead of

Fowey Ferry.

opening their complaints directly and plainly with the men
whom they concerned, they feigned to want help in a coming
expedition, and the Fowey men came up the river gladly to

put their ships and all their skill at the King's command for
service against his enemies. But they were no sooner all
arrived than they were seized, their goods confiscated, their
leader hung, and—worst blow of all—the men of Dartmouth
were brought round to take away their ships and even the
great chain that barred their harbour, leaving them helpless
and exposed to the onslaught of any fleet that might sail in and
slay them.

How the Fowey men bore this blow we cannot tell. It
ruined the mighty town which had played a chief part in
Channel warfare for more centuries than we can guess. Never
again was Fowey quoted among the chief ports of England.
The treacherous and ill guided policy of an English king had
shattered what neither he nor any other man could build up
in time of need. Now and then the old spirit flashed out and
the dry bones of dead traditions stirred and moved. It happened so in 1666 when the Dutch fleet was off the Cornish
coast, having chased thither our Virginia fleet of eighty sail,
"which escaping their cognisance," says Hals, complaisant for
once towards the ruined town, "safely got some hours before
them into this harbour, and on notice given of the war, sailed
up the branches thereof as far as they could and grounded
themselves on the mud lands thereof . . . . Notwithstanding
which a Dutch frigate of seventy guns doubly manned, sent
from their main fleet that cruised before the haven, resolved to
force the two forts and take or burn the Virginia fleet.
Accordingly it happened on that day, a pretty gale of wind
blowing, the ship entered the haven, and as soon as she came
within cannon shot of those forts fired her guns upon the two
blockhouses with great rage and violence, and these made a
quick return of the like compliment or salutation. In fine the
fight continued for about two hours time, in which were spent
some thousand of cannon shot on both sides, to the great hurt
of the Dutch ship in plank, rigging, sails, and men, chiefly
because the wind slacked or turned so adverse that she could

not pass quick enough between the two forts up the river so as
to escape their bullets, but lay a long time a mark for them to
shoot at, till she had opportunity of wind to tack round, turn
back, and bear off to sea, to the no small credit of Fowey's
little castles."

Such is the shadowy outline of a great and noble history,
which if some skilled writer would undertake to tell in full,
humanising dusty documents, making good with a restrained
imagination the missing pages of the tale, and building not
only on a knowledge of what Channel seamen wrought elsewhere, but even more upon a full acquaintance with the people
who dwell there to-day, a sympathy with their natures and a
familiarity with their lives, he would produce a book which
would astonish and fascinate the world. Is it not time that
some one should begin to write local history after this fashion?
If a man's life, truly told, is, as is said, invariably of poignant
and vital interest, how keen ought to be the delight of reading
the history of a community of men who have jointly played
a part far beyond the reach of any individual! Yet I take up
volume after volume filled with patient dusty gleaning of
names and dates and deeds and leases, and find nowhere
through all the labour of years any perception that the town
or district described was filled with men of like passions with
our own, men who in their blind human way did at all times
aim and struggle after something, and were no shadows or
abstractions, but flesh and blood even as we are. This feeling
of reality in past ages is the chief thing worth having in local
history, and if a man cannot produce it, he would do well to
leave the work alone.

It is time to pass onwards up the river. But before leaving
this ancient town it is worth while to walk out by the higher
road along the harbour, pausing to look back and see how
grandly the castellated tower of Place House rises out of a
little grove among the houses, which cluster round it like
small children about a big protector, while just below the

fine square tower of the church stands darkly in the shadow,
making with the castle and the seamen's houses a full epitome
of mediaeval life.   A little further walk brings us to Point
Neptune, a pretty creek of shingle, and on climbing through
the wood upon the further slope we emerge on the headland
high above the ancient crumbling tower which, if stones could
speak, would tell such wondrous stories of the galleys which
swept out of the lovely harbour in old days, of the prizes they
brought back, and of the fierce turbulent sailors who led so
wild a life, but are now so long forgotten.   Here is little
change.   The furzy headland, the church, the castle, the twin
towers, all are looking to-day much as they looked 500 years
ago.   The harbour is as deep and tranquil.   The same hills
shelter it.   Nothing is wanting but the desire of greatness and
the energy to achieve it.   Yet the harbour is so lovely that we
lay aside regrets for the days that have been, and bear away
an exquisite memory of green water lying calmly amid the
deep foldings of the hills and the old town sleeping by its
shore so peacefully that we turn away saying over to ourselves
the words, graven as an epitaph on the tomb of one who loved
this spot so well that he desired to lie here always, "And so
he bringeth us to the haven where we would be."

There may be several roads from Fowey towards Lostwithiel, but there is only one for the judicious, and that is the
water road which starts from the old quay.   Let the cyclist
therefore pack his wheels into the stern of a big tarry boat, and
talk to the redbearded giant who rows him like a friend, and
he will find him the best of good fellows, goodnatured, slow,
and tolerant of all things save disparaging remarks on Cornwall,
which is as much as to say that having himself the natural
good taste and feeling of a gentleman, he expects to find the
same in strangers and resents its absence.   This burly sailor,
if the tide be caught at its first flowing, will be in no hurry,
but will be content to let the oars lie on the water while the
boat drifts up slowly under the deep woods and the hillside

villages while he talks in his broad sleepy accent of what he
has seen and learnt while plying up and down the lovely
river.   No men are better worth talking to than such a Cornish
boatman ; but we cannot stay to listen to him now.   Already
the beautiful creek of Lerrin lies behind us ; the church of
St. Winnow, so finely placed on the very margin of the river
drifts slowly past and is hidden by its woods, and now the

Lostwithiel.

country opens into level water meadows, and a little way ahead
the spire of Lostwithiel church stands out among the lower
hills.

At this point we touch the loveliest inland scenery in
Cornwall.   Nowhere else does the surface of that rugged land
fall into valleys of such richness as that through which the
river Fowey flows downwards from the point at which we left
it on the downs above St. Clear, or those lesser clefts and

gorges which radiate away among the hills and pinewoods till
they are lost in the moorland which is never far distant from
any part of Cornwall.

In the richest pastures of this luxuriant valley stands the old
town of Lostwithiel, a cluster of some half dozen streets,
rather picturesque, an old stone bridge which is the joy of
artists, and a church whose spire the late Mr. Street went so
far as to call "the Glory of Cornwall." Indeed its octangular
lantern is singularly graceful, and has fortunately survived all
the perils it passed through in the civil wars, when it was not
only a mark for the cannon fired from the fort on the beacon
where the King's troops lay discharging these pretty compliments at the Earl of Essex in the town, but even by some
marvellous chance escaped the danger occurring when two
Cavalier prisoners, rich men of Cornwall, who had been put
into the church for greater safety, got up into the steeple and
pulled up the ladder after them, and sat there jeering at the
Provost Marshall who was waiting to march away, being indeed
in a great hurry to go. The Provost Marshall seems to have
been a dull fellow, devoid of humour ; for, instead of sitting
down and flinging back jest for jest like a courteous gentleman,
he brought "mulch and hay" and growling out, "Ill fetch you
down," set fire to it. The incivility of this proceeding made
the two rich men of Cornwall obstinate, and they sat tight upon
their perches, which so annoyed the Provost Marshall that he
bethought him of a barrel of gunpowder lying close at hand,
and sent that spluttering up the tower, yet only succeeded in
blowing off a few slates, while the prisoners jeered more than
ever.

Having adverted to the civil wars again, it will be well to
explain what the Earl of Essex was doing at Lostwithiel. He
had marched thither in pursuit of Sir Richard Grenville,
brother of Sir Beville, but widely different from him in character,
and husband of Lady Howard, of whom we heard so much at
Tavistock ; and Sir Richard, who had been besieging Plymouth,

but drew his men off as Essex approached, retreated so far into Cornwall that Essex hesitated to follow him, not being quite clear how he should get out again. He would have done better to think of this before ; for indeed if the mouse gets into the leg of the boot, while the cat is entering by the tops, there is almost sure to be a difficulty in getting by. However, Essex lay at beautiful old Lanhydrock, which we shall see presently, while Grenville kept him amused by occasional attacks, and all the time the King himself, with a strong army fresh from his victory at Cropredy Bridge, was closing all the outlets, and hemming him in beyond escape. At last the King reached Boconnoc, some four miles from Lostwithiel, and his artillery poured shot into the town from that battery we mentioned, while every day skirmishes occurred which read more like some tale of ancient chivalry than the fighting of what were almost modern times. For one hundred Roundheads, all mere striplings of from sixteen to twenty years of age, led by one Colonel Straughan, challenged a like number of the King's troops to combat on St. Winnow Downs, and the challenge was caught up by Lord Digby. On a set day the two troops met in sight of both armies, Straughan having "nothing on his head but a hat, and on the trunk of his body nought but a white linen shift." Digby and his followers advanced firing their pistols before they were in easy range ; whereupon Straughan and his boys charged furiously at them, and poured the contents of their pistols in so close, that half the Royalists were slain on the spot and there was scarce horse or man but received some hurt.

There were Cornishmen on both sides in this unnatural warfare, at which a tree in Boconnoc Park was so shocked that it put forth only variegated leaves from that time. But not to make the tale too long, the King completed his investments so thoroughly that Essex first retreated to Fowey, and then fled disgracefully by sea, leaving his army to surrender, which it promptly did, though by the incompetence of Goring, the

Roundhead cavalry slipped through his lines in the night before
the capitulation was brought to a close, and thus the triumph
was shorn of something of its splendour.

There are two places which every one ought to visit from
Lostwithiel, the one is Boconnoc, the other Lanhydrock.   Now
Boconnoc has not only the finest park in Cornwall, but is
doubly interesting as having been the birthplace of Pitt the
Commoner, whose Nabob father bought the estate with the
pagodas shaken off that tree which seems to have gone out of
cultivation in India to-day.   I always love visiting the deep

Restormel Castle.

glades and glorious woods of Boconnoc , and had promised
myself the pleasure of wandering round its forest paths at
leisure, chatting the while of Lord Mohun, who had the place
before the Pitts, and of Lord Camelford, that wild scamp and
desperate duellist of whom there are still plenty of stories to
be picked up.   But I have indulged myself too long at Fowey,
and must give up Boconnoc, like a child who has been idle and
is deprived of his treat.   Lanhydrock I cannot give up, since it
is on the way to Bodmin, where I ought to have arrived a full
chapter ago or more ; and so I will set forth from Lostwithiel

by the road towards Restormel, and running for a mile or so along the hillside under cool woods where the bluebells are already withering on the deep grass and the foxglove spires are growing lofty and bursting colour, I find myself at the foot of the castle mound.

This is a rarely lovely spot. The keep, which is the only part of the old building left erect, occupies the summit of a natural mound, whence one looks out over the river winding through its western hills much as we saw the Dart from the ramparts of Totnes. The keep is exactly circular; and so covered up with ivy that at a little distance it is not easily distinguished from the woods that creep so closely round its old enclosure. It is a solitary place. There is no semblance of a town or village ; but only woodland, rich and exquisite, and a ruin which as far as possible has shaken off the aspect borne by the work of human hands, has cast away magnificence, and let its strength slip from it, and dropped the coping of its battlements stone by stone, and gathered to itself every seed of tree and creeper which the wandering wind brought near it, and rooted them and cherished them till now they shade it everywhere, and the ruin has put on a forest dress. The old Dukes of Cornwall would not know it now ; and the Black Prince, who was the first duke, and stayed here twice, would ride past his old palace without dreaming that it was here his knights jousted and his gay train rode in and out.

A pretty path leads along the hillside in the direction by which we came. It is a shorter and pleasanter way than the highroad, and it leads quickly through wood and coppice to the gate of Lanhydrock, whence we pass up a long and noble avenue of sycamores to an ancient gatehouse of rich and beautiful workmanship, beyond which the old mansion lies around three sides of a quadrangle, a low granite two-storied building, somewhat wanting in dignity, but picturesque and ancient, and in truth, until an unhappy fire occurred there some years ago, but little changed since the Roundhead Lord Robartes built

it, and Essex planted his head-quarters at the foot of the
park.

It is a situation of perfect beauty in which the old house
stands, high hills sloping upwards from the gardens, a little
church nestling on their first slopes, a wide, open, undulating
park in front, studded with noble trees. The footway to Bodmin
passes by the house, and emerges on a road which is still
beautiful, and the three miles into the old capital of Cornwall
go by between deep lanes where the yellow ferns are fast
uncurling, and the primroses glisten wet and dewy, and tall
bluebells hang drooping with their own weight, while under all
there runs a tangle of ivy and wild strawberry blossom, and
briony and a hundred other things, among which the eye loses
itself in a maze of greenery and shadow.

And of Bodmin what shall I say ? Why, if this book was
intended to contain a sympathetic description of that straggling
hilly town, it should have been entrusted to a Bodmin man,
for I know no one else who would be likely to succeed. It
may not be known to all the world, whom indeed it does not
much concern, that Cornwall, and indeed Devonshire also, is
full of local jealousies, and that the dwellers in contiguous
towns and villages often hold each other in low esteem. There
is frequently some deadly taunt hurled from town to town, as
for instance, the Zennor people ask St. Ives men, "Who
whipped the hake ? " while the St. Ives man, if indeed he does
not answer with his fists, sums up an infinity of concentrated
scorn in the rejoinder, "Who built a wall round the cuckoo ? "
I cannot digress now to explain the origin of these injurious
taunts, which will be discussed with others in their proper
place. But I mention them as illustrations of the kind of
feeling thrown by other Cornishmen into the saying, " Into
Bodmin and out of the world." Indeed, Bodmin has a very
sleepy aspect. It is one of the few Cornish towns which are
wholly inland, and has not even a bridge to bless itself with.
But I ought to be superior to inherited prejudice. I really

will not depreciate Bodmin before the "foreigners" who may
read this work ; and as I do not seem to be able to describe
the town without belittling it, I will set down a curious piece of
local tradition picked up on the sea coast some sixteen miles
away.

Long ago, when news travelled very slowly, and many weeks
passed before the dwellers in Cornwall knew what was happening in London and the north, there came into Bodmin certain
carriers with a string of pack mules, laden with goods the like
of which had never been seen in Cornwall before.   There
were plumed hats and rich robes of every kind, silk and velvet
dresses and gloves and ribands for the women, such as were
worn by high ladies, but were retailed by the carriers at prices
within the reach of all.   Half Bodmin went mad about this
rare opportunity.   The carriers sold their stock out in a few
days, and left the town as suddenly as they had come.   They
had hardly gone before sickness broke out ; shiverings and
faintings seized the people, some had lumps upon their sides,
some bled from the nose, and all those so afflicted died.   The
word ran round the town that the gaudy clothes were infected
with the plague.   They were collected and burnt, but it was too
late.   The fearful pestilence marched through the town, slaying
all whom it encountered, and the dead were carried far away
from Bodmin and buried in a field at Crantock, on the north
coast, where the surface is still broken into little heaps and
mounds, and the peasants believe that if any one stir the
earth by setting in it so much as a spade the angel of death
will be at once released, and go flapping over their village
with his heavy wings.

CHAPTER XV

As a child whose father has done some great and famous action, led a cavalry charge or planted the first storming ladder against a well defended fortress, will never cease from talking of him till his hearers grow weary and smile at the lad's honest boastfulness, so a Cornishman is ever garrulous about his country; and I vow it rends my heart to go by so many lovely places as we must pass unnoticed in this chapter. For we have come to a sad pass ; and if we are ever to get round Cornwall at all, we must go faster. I feel like a German pastor with whom I once walked seven miles in four hours in the Black Forest ; and who looked back sadly when we had done, remembering all the wondrous things he had failed to shew me, and sighed "wir sind zu schnell gegangen." It is even so. We have gone too fast, and yet we must go faster ; and since that is our hard case, we may take pleasure in the fact that we are approaching ideal roads, firm and smooth and not too hilly. For if Devon is sometimes trying to the cyclist's temper, Cornwall repairs the mischief done. Up, therefore, good cyclists, and spin quickly through St. Austell and along the wide and breezy road through ancient Tregony—which since the sad day of disfranchisement following the great Reform bill, has never known enough excitement to wake up the ducks from their slumbers in the very middle of the main street—and so by pretty wooded valleys to the slow ascent of a ridge, whence there bursts suddenly upon the sight a wide green landlocked sea, running far up among the hills, with countless indentations

St. Austell.

and dark woods sloping to the water, and green fertile meadows on the heights. Far away, on the shore of the furthest creek, one sees a mass of houses straggling irregularly along the waterside and climbing up the hill behind. That is Falmouth ; and beyond it the tower of old Pendennis castle rises dark and gaunt over a fretwork of golden furze.

So much is seen in running onwards ; but the road has left itself so little lateral space in which to get down to the water, that it has to drop almost sheer ; and so there is no time for contemplating views until we have crawled down into the ancient seaport of St. Mawes, where haply we may find a steamer starting for Falmouth, or if not, we may be very well entertained by strolling up and down the quay, talking to the sailors, or wandering round the old castle which guards the eastern entrance of the harbour. Indeed, St. Mawes is quite old enough to have a curious history, and were it not that Falmouth kills all other interests upon this noble harbour, I should gladly stay and probe it. But the greater town calls all our thoughts away, and as the little steamer puffs and blows across the blue water they run before it to the streets and quays of a modern borough which caught up the crown of naval greatness when it had long since slipped away from Fowey, and wore it with all the majesty and splendour of the older times.

I do not know where any sight can be seen more fair and lovely than Falmouth harbour on a golden evening, when the water lies all smooth and oily, when the houses on the quays are mirrored in its tranquil surface, and the light evening clouds tinge it with rosy stains. Then as the blue shadows deepen into purple, each boat and yacht runs up a little glowing lamp, and one by one the stars shine out, faint golden points in the warm sky. It is thus that Falmouth returns upon my memory, a place which is exquisite at all times and seasons.

This, the most westerly of the great harbours which we pass upon our journey, is almost, if not quite, the most beautiful ; and the river which flows into it, though its course is short, can show in the limit of a few miles beauties which are surpassed by no other river than the Tamar. The Fal has no upper course worth visiting. Its grandeur lies wholly where the salt water struggles with the fresh ; and indeed this invasion of the river channels by the sea is one of the most marked features of the whole West country.   For here and there as you wander through the inland districts, perhaps many miles away from Falmouth, you will suddenly find the dusty road which you are following descend to a small stone bridge under which a sweet fresh air is blowing over banks of ooze, and while you wonder whence the freshness comes so far inland, and the salt fragrance over mud which should be stagnant, suddenly you see a tide is stealing fast across the banks, and behind it comes a mighty flood of joyous water rushing up amid the trees which flank the winding valley, drowning the marsh, and scattering the thick inland air with all the breath and bitter odours of the sea.   Such is any one of the numberless creeks which open right and left as you cut across the still waters of Falmouth Harbour, creeks of which each one is different from the last, some wooded, others banked with sloping fields and villages out of which some ancient church tower stands gaunt and square, while your boat is heading so directly for the shore that it seems impossible it should not run aground, and it is only when the land is so close that you could almost leap to it that you see a channel or opening among the hills, and a winding gorge piercing the thick woods.   On both sides the trees are dense and high, the river flows down through a series of land-locked lakes of a beauty quite surpassing description.   Four miles or more it keeps this character ; and then the banks grow lower, the trees fall away, and in the distance the city of Truro rears itself against the hills.

I have not much to say of Truro.   It is an old and quiet town, permeated by the sound of running water, which hurries down either side of the main street in a fresh pure channel. It contains no buildings of consequence save the new cathedral, and what may be the precise merits of that triumph of nineteenth century art is a question into which it is the less necessary for me to enter since Mr. Pennell has set them

Truro Cathedral from the River.

before the curious reader with a vividness which makes other
description superfluous.

I spoke of Falmouth as a modern town, and it is true that
it has by no means the antiquity of most Cornish seaports.

Three centuries ago only a few cottages stood there, clustering round the mansion of Arwenack, the home of the Killigrews,

Street in Truro.

one of those very ancient Cornish families from whose recorded practices we derive our few trustworthy ideas of the state of life in this wild corner of the country during bygone centuries.

Now the more we inquire into the history of the Killigrews, the more we find ourselves plunging into an atmosphere where right and wrong were shaded off till neither had clear outlines, and the sea was regarded as a kindly friend which used his storms to enrich the house of Killigrew. The State Papers contain many references to little incidents which, judged in combination with what we know to have occurred elsewhere in the neighbourhood, throw a world of light on the practices of this ancient family. In 1582 John de Chavis and Philip de Ovyo, both apparently of St. Sebastian, complain to the Council that their ship had been stolen out of Falmouth harbour by certain of Killigrew's servants "and others," as is cautiously added. Of course so grave a charge could not be left unheard by due authority : and happily the very highest possible was on the spot, Sir John Killigrew himself being Commissioner of Piracy, and the person duly authorised to protect the King's lieges in all such difficulties as this. So Sir John constituted his court ; and to ensure the greater impartiality, joined to himself his neighbour Godolphin, an excellent and worthy gentleman, whose father had been accused – doubtless very unjustly—of appropriating a large part of the treasure carried by a Portuguese ship wrecked at Gunwalloe— we shall tell this story presently—and who, having thus suffered in his own family from the tooth of slander, was the better fitted to deliver judgment on this occasion. These two wise judges set themselves solemnly to execute justice and maintain truth, from which fact alone we might surmise that the scandal had become public. The thieves, whoever they were, had taken the ship to Ireland ; and as twelve of Killigrew's servants, who would have been quite enough to navigate her, were missing also, it seemed not impossible that the charge against them might have some foundation. A pinnace which played a leading part in the affair belonged to Sir John himself, as was testified most inopportunely at the inquiry ; but nothing seems to have transpired reflecting in any way upon Sir John's honour, which is very satisfactory to know, for no man is to be otherwise than pitied if his servants do that which he condemns.   So the Commissioners of Piracy reported to the Privy Council that they were afraid there was not much doubt that Killigrew's servants were guilty, and suggested outlawing those bad men, which was done accordingly ; and as all this righteous indignation did not go far to recoup the poor merchants of San Sebastian for their losses, the Council allowed them to export, duty free, a hundred and fifty quarters of wheat, out of which no doubt they made a pretty penny.

A year before this happened it had occurred to some one of the Queen's councillors, perhaps it was the terrible Cecil, who for some reason or other disliked pirates, that it would be useful to have a little list made out of the names of certain Cornishmen who were charged with being aiders and abettors of pirates, with particulars of their incomes.   A copy of the list lies before me as I write.   Nothing would induce me to break the secrecy of three hundred years by revealing all the highly respected names which it contains ; but as the Killigrews are dead and gone, I may say that Peter of that family stands near its head.   The amount written opposite his name is fifty pounds, though whether this was his whole income, or the part of it which Cecil made him pay for the frolic life he led, is not clear.   In the margin of the list is this horridly suggestive note by Cecil himself, " Half of the value of the goods, three years rent of lands where no goods are, and of these the best."

Was there ever such a spoil-sport ?   Really I know no man in life or fiction who could characterise this note of Cecil's as it deserves except the immortal Major Monsoon.   " No more fun," the Major moaned, " No more jollification, no more plunder, and how I did do it !   Nothing like watching one's little chances.   The poor is hated even by his neighbour." Just so Peter Killigrew may have expressed himself as he sat by the lonely western sea, and bewailed himself over Cecil's inability to appreciate a joke.

A few months later Killigrew's servants were once more in evidence, having attempted to rescue forcibly Captain Hamond, a notorious pirate, from the custody of John Norris and Lawrence Simons, who had been lucky enough to catch him and were conveying him whither all the King's lieges ought to have been glad to see him go. But Killigrew's servants were of a different opinion, and would have liked to see the bold captain scouring the seas again. Doubtless Sir John was very shocked at their behaviour, and made it plain that he was displeased. One's sympathy goes out to a Commissioner of Piracy whose servants were so constantly giving him away.

I am not well informed about the Killigrew pedigree; but I think it could not have been long after the time of this Sir John that Lady Jane, who may have been his widow, was sitting at her window in Arwenack one wintry day when she saw two Dutch ships, half disabled by the storm, running into the harbour for shelter. The arrival of strangers was always interesting to the Killigrews; and so the Dutchmen had no sooner anchored than the boat from Arwenack went out to see what they had on board. They had a good deal, so much, in fact, that the boat went back to Lady Jane for further instructions before taking any action; and she, with a laudable desire to see everything done properly, declared she would go out to the ships herself. Dutch sailors are proverbially rough; and there were two Spanish factors, moreover, who might be hasty. So Lady Jane thought it prudent to have a larger boat and a stronger party, and dealt out arms so that they might not be defenceless if attacked; and, thus provided, she went on board the first Dutch ship and notified the amount of the contribution she would take, while the rest of her party boarding the second ship made her wishes known there also. The Dutch were very fairly reasonable about the matter, recognising with the coolness of their race that they were outnumbered and could do nothing; but the more excitable Spaniards were noisy and obstreperous, and got themselves killed, some say at a signal given by Lady Jane, and one of them was inconsiderate enough to curse her as he died. The curse did not afflict her ladyship much, though it is said to have worked itself out among her descendants ; and she rowed cheerfully home with "two hogsheads of Spanish pieces of eight which she converted to her own use," while all her crew had picked up some pretty trifle or other to reward them for the trouble taken in visiting strangers in distress.

There was a good deal of worry about this afternoon's amusement, and Lady Jane was brought to trial at Launceston Castle, and even condemned to death, though the sentence was not executed.   Here we will leave the Killigrews, and also the subject of piracy and wrecking, about which there will be more to say as we continue to follow the coast of these wild western regions.

The best part of a hundred years had passed from the days of Lady Jane before Falmouth began to grow to any size ; and when it did, the impulse was due to the General Post-Office, which chose the port in 1688 as a station for its newly established Spanish mail boats. Few people in these days remember that Falmouth was to our grandfathers all that Plymouth or Southampton is to us ; and that when they contemplated ocean passages to Lisbon, Brazil or the West Indies, it was on the Falmouth coach that they took their seats and made their long journeys to the west.   All through the last century Falmouth and the packet service grew together ; and in the long and almost constant wars, which made the ocean highways unsafe for any ship that was not fully armed, the post-office vessels fought as desperately as the navy, and with less reward.   There was no very wide gulf between the packets and the king's ships.   For while on the one hand naval officers were far in those days from being the exclusive caste which they have since become, the commanders of the packets held by virtue of their office the equivalent rank of commander in the Navy, and received commissions from the Admiralty as such, in addition to those which they held from the postmaster-general.

xv OLD FALMOUTH LIFE 265

There is in the autobiography of that singular character, James Silk Buckingham, who was born at Flushing, a village immediately opposite the town of Falmouth, a description of the place as he saw it in his childhood, which reproduces vividly the aspect of the port during the wars of the last century. "The port of Falmouth," he says, "being the nearest to the entrance of the British Channel, there were permanently stationed here two squadrons of frigates, one under the command of Sir Edward Pellew, afterwards Lord Exmouth, the other under the command of Sir John Borlase Warren. The former as commodore hoisted his broad pennant in the *Indefatigable*, the latter in the *Révolutionnaire*. Each squadron consisted of five frigates, of thirty-two and thirty-four guns each; and in addition to this there were continually arriving and departing from Carrick Roads, the outer anchorage of Falmouth, line-of-battle ships and smaller vessels of war; while prizes taken from the French were constantly brought into the port for adjudication and sale. There were two large prisons with open courts for the reception of the French prisoners thus taken, both near the borough of Penryn, at the head of Falmouth harbour, and every month added many to their inmates. Both the naval commanders as well as such captains of the frigates as were married had their families residing at Flushing; and the numerous officers of different grades, from the youngest midshipman to the first lieutenant, were continually coming and going to and fro, so that there would be sometimes a dozen men-of-war's boats at the quay at the same time, including the barges for the commanding officers, and the cutters, gigs, launches, and jolly boats on duty; the boats' crews mostly dressed in dashing marine trim, with blue jackets and trousers and bright scarlet waistcoats, overlaid with gilt buttons in winter, and striped guernsey frocks and white flowing trousers in summer; while the little village literally sparkled with gold epaulets, gold lace hats, and brilliant uniforms.

"In addition to these squadrons of the navy, Falmouth was

also then enriched and enlivened by the presence of a fleet of handsome mail packets, in the service of the post-office, including from thirty to forty full-rigged three-masted ships, small in size, but of the most elegant model, built indeed exclusively for speed and passage accommodation, carrying the royal pennant, as the ships of war ; the officers all wearing handsome uniforms, and the crews being picked men, well dressed and generally young and handsome, the service being so popular that it was a matter of great difficulty to get into it. Dinners, balls and evening parties were held at one or other of the captains' houses every evening ; and not a night passed in which there were not three or four dances at least at the more humble places of resort for the sailors and their favourite lasses. The ample supplies of wages and prize money furnished all the naval officers and men with abundant means to meet every demand, and the profits of the officers and crews of the Government packets were not at all less abundant."

Such was the brilliant aspect of Falmouth and Flushing in days of war ; and such it may be again when the long peace is broken, for Falmouth can never be other than an important position for watching the French coast. Sir Edward Pellew, who commanded here as commodore, is one of the peculiar glories of Cornwall, descended from a family of some antiquity in the district between Marazion and the Lizard, and a man of such great physique and such reckless bravery as must have made him a popular hero in any age. Steeped and soaked as this splendid fellow was in Cornish feeling, it was his pride to man and officer his ship with Cornishmen, so that his triumphs, and his life was one long triumph, might be those of his own people. And so the lists of officers on the *Nymphe* and on the famous *Arethusa* and the still more famous *Indefatigable* form a roll of the best known Cornish families, and what they did and how they did it has become a part of English history. But as there have been mentioned in this chapter certain matters on which the "foreigner" may not look with the same indulgent eye as the born Cornishman, I shall proceed to recreate a good impression by showing how these men of Falmouth kept the sea when England was in peril.

Now, it is matter of history that when the French war broke out in 1793, this country was less well prepared for it than her adversary was; and some anxiety was thus felt for the result of the first actions, which might be expected to have so great an effect on the morale of the sailors. Pellew, who had made his reputation in the American war, offered his services to the Admiralty as soon as hostilities were declared, and was appointed to the *Nymphe*, a handsome frigate, which, however, in the dearth of sailors then existing he had great difficulty in manning. Now, Pellew knew very well what excellent fighting material there was in Cornwall; and if he could not have Cornish sailors he resolved to have Cornish landsmen, and asked for volunteers among the miners. About eighty of these sturdy fellows leapt at his offer, and joined him in the shortest possible time at Spithead. With this nucleus of a crew, Pellew came round to the west and picked up as many stout sailors as he could, and so put to sea, the whole ship's company in such a state of eagerness to meet the enemy that two at least of them have left on record prophetic dreams corresponding closely with the actual facts. There was not long to wait for the verification of these dreams. At daybreak on the 19th of June, they met a fine French frigate, named the *Cleopatra*, off the Start, commanded by Captain Mullon, a distinguished officer, who had served with Suffren in the East. At six o'clock the two ships were so close together that Pellew was able to hail the French captain, hat in hand. The French officer waved a red cap of liberty; and almost at the same moment a sailor ran up aloft and nailed it to the mast head. For a few minutes more the ships lay in silence on the summer sea; but the *Nymphe* was forging up. As she reached the starboard quarter of the *Cleopatra* Pellew raised his hat to his head, and at that signal the frigate rocked and quivered as her broadside crashed at close range into her antagonist. For three quarters of an hour the day was doubtful, for Mullon handled his fine ship most nobly. But Israel Pellew, the captain's brother, who had dreamt of this frigate, and dreamt, too, that he shot away her wheel and took her, had taken charge of a gun, and had already slain more than one French steersman, and at length, a few minutes before seven, sent the wheel itself flying into splinters. The *Cleopatra*, thus bereft of guidance, came round with her bow to the Cornish broadside; and almost at the same moment her mizen mast fell over the side and her deck was swept into a wild chaos of confusion. Instantly the signal for boarders rang out shrill along the Cornish decks. Pellew himself leapt upon the bulwarks, and a crowd of gallant fellows followed him down into the body of the *Cleopatra*, where in a few minutes of hard fighting the day was won.

Now, all the rest of Pellew's achievements must be read elsewhere, though I would that I had space to speak of them. For when I think of how he danced into Brest harbour in the *Indefatigable*, when Hoche's fleet was coming out, and headed saucily the whole French armada, confusing their signals with blue lights and false fires, so that more than one of them mistook its course and blundered into the wrong channel and went aground, while Pellew stood on and off and mocked them as he pleased, a very Puck or Hobgoblin of the ocean,—when I think of this, and remember too, that it was he, cruising with one other English captain, who saw the only fighting that came of all that armament, picking up the *Droits de l'Homme* as she laboured slowly homewards through the winter dusk; and how the two English bulldogs fastened their teeth in the great 80-gun ship and held on all night till the three vessels ran together on the breakers, and only his noble seamanship saved Pellew while the other two were lost,—when I remember all this greatness I am inclined to estimate Pellew as well-nigh the finest of all single ship commanders, hardly second to Cochrane himself.

So much for the king's ships at Falmouth; and if it were not that in another place I have told all I know of the great and splendid sea fights of the packet service, I should detail many of them here. For the packet service is most undeservedly forgotten. England owes a debt of gratitude to the sailors who, tempted by no prize money, rewarded by very little public praise or honour, shed their blood so freely and fought with such noble courage and resource to defend the mails and keep open those communications on which the life of this great ocean empire hung. I make my compliments to these dead heroes. I hold them up as an example which our own generation may have need to imitate, and which it cannot afford to forget. Never since the years in which Napoleon threatened Europe, have dangers so great and numerous hung about this country as now. It will be well with all of us if when the storm bursts and the day of trial comes, those who are responsible for our ocean services do their duty as devotedly as officers and men alike performed it at Falmouth in old days.

I add the story of one of these great fights, chosen from among the rest not because it exceeded them in valour, for there were many in which the courage was as high, and the obstinacy of resistance no less great ; I select the action of the *Townshend* simply because it is even less remembered than the rest.[1]

On November 22nd, 1812, the *Townshend* packet, armed with eight 9-pounder carronades, a long gun of similar calibre for use as a chaser, and a crew of twenty-eight men and boys under the command of Captain James Cock, was within a few hours of dropping her anchor at Bridgetown, Barbadoes, when the first light of morning revealed two strange vessels cruising at no great distance.

These vessels proved to be American privateers, the *Tom*, Captain Thos. Wilson, and the *Bona*, Captain Damaron. The

---

[1] This story I have quoted, with slight abridgments, from my *History of the Post-Office Packet Service between* 1793 *and* 1815, published by Messrs. Macmillan and Co. in 1895.

former was armed with fourteen carronades, some 18- and some 12-pounders, as well as two long 9-pounders, and carried 130 men. The latter had six 18-pounders, with a long 24-pounder mounted on a traverse, and a crew of ninety men. The forces on each side were therefore as follows, assuming that the *Tom* carried as many 18- as 12-pounders :—

	Weight of metal in pounds.	Number of men.
Privateers	360	220
Packets	78	32 (besides four passengers who rendered some assistance).

This enormous preponderance of force was greatly increased in effective power by being divided between two opponents. A single enemy might be crippled by a lucky shot; but if good fortune rid the *Townshend* of one antagonist in this way, there still remained the other to be reckoned with, more powerful at every point than herself.

If ever circumstances justified surrender after a short resistance they were present in this case. It might even be thought that resistance was a useless sacrifice of life; but such was not Captain Cock's view. He held it to be his plain duty not only to keep the mails out of the hands of the enemy—which could be done effectually by sinking them at any moment—but to use every means in his power to preserve them for their proper owners, and not to abandon hope of delivering them at the office of the post-office agent at Bridgetown until every chance of doing so was gone. Now, there were still two chances in his favour: first, that he might hold out until the noise of firing attracted some of the British cruisers which were probably in the immediate neighbourhood; and secondly, if that chance failed, he might run the *Townshend* ashore on some shoal of the coast where the privateers could not follow him. Both these chances were desperate enough; but Captain Cock saw his duty clear before him, and cared nothing for the consequences. All his preparations were quickly made, and every man was at his post before the privateers came within range, which they did about 7 a.m.

At 7.30 a.m. the *Tom* had placed herself abeam of the packet to larboard, while the *Bona* lay on the starboard quarter, and both their broadsides were crashing into the *Townshend* at pistol shot distance, all three vessels running before the wind. This lasted till eight o'clock. The Americans, as was usual with them, made great use of "dismantling shot," *i.e.*, chain and bar shot; the effect of which upon the rigging of the *Townshend* was most disastrous. It was not long before her sails were hanging in ribbons, and her spars were greatly damaged, and in some momentary confusion from this cause the *Tom* seized an opportunity of pouring in her boarders, while the *Bona* redoubled her fire, both of great guns and musketry, to cover their attack. After a fierce tussle the Americans were driven back to their own ship; but this success was won by the loss of four of Captain Cock's best hands, who received disabling wounds in the fight.

Thereupon both privateers resumed the cannonade, maintaining the positions which they had taken up at the commencement of the action, and for another hour the *Townshend* endured the fire of her enemies' heavy guns, the courage of her commander and crew remaining as high and stubborn as ever. But the packet was by this time so much shattered that she could with difficulty be handled. Again and again the *Tom* bore down upon her and hurled fresh boarders up her sides. Time after time Captain Cock led his wearied men to meet them, and each time drove them back.

But the post-office men were now so reduced in numbers that it was with the greatest difficulty that Captain Cock could continue to serve the guns and at the same time collect sufficient men to meet the constantly recurring boarding attacks. It was plain that this situation of affairs could not last; there was no sign of succour on the sea, and when Captain Cock looked aloft he could not but admit that in the crippled condition of his ship all chance of running her ashore was gone. The *Townshend* was, in fact, a mere wreck. Her bowsprit was shot in pieces. Both jib-booms and head were carried away, as well as the wheel and ropes. Scarcely one shroud was left standing. The packet lay like a log on the water, while the privateers sailed round her, choosing their positions as they pleased, and raking her again and again. Still Captain Cock held out. It was not until ten o'clock, when he had endured the attack of his two powerful enemies for nearly three hours, that he looked about him and recognised that the end had come. There were four feet of water in the hold, and the carpenter reported that it was rising rapidly. The packet was, in fact, sinking. Nearly half the crew were in the hands of the surgeon. The rest, exhausted and hopeless of success, had already fought more nobly than even he could have foreseen, and were now being uselessly sacrificed. Still Captain Cock's pride rebelled against surrender ; and as he saw the colours he had defended so well drop down upon the deck, it is recorded that he burst into tears. He had no cause for shame. Such a defeat is as glorious as any victory, and is fully worthy of the great traditions of valour on the sea which all Englishmen inherit.

Shortly after 1820 the packet service passed away from the post-office, which had conducted it with very marked success, and was taken over by the Admiralty. The first proceeding of that distinguished board of naval experts was to alter the type of packet which long experience had shown to be the best, and to substitute 10-gun brigs of a model which all old seamen declared to be most unstable. Pellew was emphatic in condemning them ; but the Admiralty were obstinate, and the result was, that whereas under the post-office management wrecks and losses were of very rare occurrence, no less than six of the new Admiralty packets were lost with all hands, in six and a half years, and the 10-gun brigs quickly got the name of "coffin ships," by which they are remembered to this day.

A fine and level road leads out of Falmouth towards Penryn, skirting the deep inlet on which both towns stand, and having passed the latter ancient but uninteresting place, mounts fast upon the ridge of downs which form the spur of the Lizard Peninsula. An excellent surface and a breezy moorland make pleasant riding; and the road runs by quickly until Helston is reached, at which old town we will not pause now, for its great festival is approaching, and we shall see it to more advantage then. And so we pass onwards with the briefest pause, and take the road towards the Lizard, a fine and easy highway, of which nothing need be said until it runs out upon Goonhilly Downs, some four or five miles from its end.

Here we become conscious, suddenly, that the stones we are treading underfoot are like nothing we have seen before. They gleam with little points of ruddy fire, and now and then a glow of green or purple strikes upward from the roadway. The hedges, too, are built of blackish rock, which, where it is broken, shows the same brilliant colours. This is serpentine, a stone so common in the district that there is, in fact, none other for the roughest purposes. It is a strange experience to kick about the roads a material which elsewhere is so precious; and of this new sensation we may make the most, for it is the only pleasurable one on this dreary road. At length a few white cottages appear in the distance, and group themselves into a little town. That is the Lizard Town, and an uglier little spot it would be hard to find.

CHAPTER XVI

THE Lizard Peninsula is almost, if not quite, the wildest and most solitary district in Cornwall. The deep estuary of the Helford River on the one hand, and the Loe Pool on the other, give it in some degree the character of an island promontory. It is the most southerly land in England. It contains no town save Helston, which lies at its entrance ; and nearly all its centre is occupied by the great waste of Goonhilly Downs, a tract of country which, however interesting to the botanist, or to him who gloats on legends, is sufficiently savage to have been a terror to travellers of ages not very remote from our own, and is still a perplexity even to natives, when the sea mists envelope it with light wreaths of vapour, and the familiar landmarks seem to melt away, and drift by as impalpable as the fog. It has a coast line of great magnificence and beauty in the eyes of summer visitors, but pitifully dreaded by the mariner, and there is hardly one among its rocky coves or iron precipices to which some story does not cling of a night of death and terror ; so that when one walks around the cliffs they seem a trifle ghostly, as those regions must where, since the beginning of time, scarce ever a winter storm has blown itself out without sending some tall ship crashing to her doom. And it was not only the fury of the sea and wind that sailors driven on this coast had cause to dread, for the cruelty and greed of man wrought in the same direction ; and this is one of the districts in which the old tales of wrecking cling most persistently. In this isolated region a wild and lawless population was left to follow its own impulses, unrestrained by contact with men of other ideas ; and the result was a life vivid enough to set any man's imagination working, as he follows the cliff paths ; while if he be of a fanciful turn of mind, he cannot fail to notice how curiously the downs are covered with little jutting knobs of rock, so numerously scattered that, as one walks along, they seem to move and revolve behind each other, and from the corner of one's eye they appear suddenly above a hummock as if half-a-dozen little heads were thrust up suddenly to watch.

But let us go and see what the place is like before we speak of its associations. Following the bare road through the little township towards the coast, we become suddenly aware that birds are singing somewhere close at hand, though never a tree is to be seen ; and going on a little further, the old church of Landewednack reveals itself in a deep cleft of trees, somewhat stormbent, it is true, yet giving shelter to a host of blackbirds and thrushes, which sing there in the morning sun, knowing full well that for miles around there is no other harbourage. Below the church is a cluster of white cottages, which could tell strange stories if it would ; and a path springing from the houses leads up on the eastern cliffs, which, in this warm May weather, are stained with flowers like an Eastern carpet. A mile or so onwards is a little cove with pebbly beach. On either side the cliff drops with a fine, swift slope, lighted up here and there with patches of flowering whitethorn, while the grass is rendered infinitely lovely by multitudes of violets and primroses and tall bluebells, and countless little creeping flowers of pink and lavender, all glistening like gems in the fresh dewy air. Down below the tide is of many colours, steely in the sun, blue and green where the light falls less intense ; and a tall archway cleft by the storms breaks the darkness of the cliff with a gleam of warm blue waves. A deserted fish cellar with shattered roof adds a touch of melancholy to the scene, keeping be-

T 2

fore the memory the decay of one of Cornwall's two chief
industries.

Here, or somewhere in this immediate locality, one Lutey,
in days now long gone by, laid the foundation of the fortunes
of his family.   He was a fisherman by trade, and by inclination
doubtless a smuggler, if not worse ; and one idle afternoon he
was dozing in a cavern underneath the cliffs when he heard a
sound of sobbing not far off.   Now, people who get into
trouble at the foot of the Lizard Cliffs commonly find their
breath choked and their troubles over before they have time to
sob ; and so Lutey thought it worth while to go and see who
was making this unusual sound.   He picked up his heavy
carcase from the sand, and went rolling round the rocks just in
time to see a long-haired woman's figure slip down into a pool
from which the tide had receded.   He stooped down and
stirred the long fringe of seaweed, and with some difficulty
made out the figure he had seen nestling at the bottom of the
pool, casting now and then a frightened glance upwards through
the water.   Now, Lutey had seen mermaids before, though
never so close, and he was by no means alarmed, but resolved
to make the most of the good luck which had brought one
within his grasp.   So he put on his most wheedling voice, and
cooed and comforted her till she raised her timid head out of
the water, and told him she had gone into a cavern to comb
her hair, and the tide had ebbed without her noticing it, and
she would give him great gifts if he would carry her back to
the water.   With that she wept and sobbed and looked so
bewitching that Lutey took her on his back and carried her
down to the water, bargaining only that he should be made
wise, in the special sense applied to that word in the west.
The mermaid agreed very readily to these easy terms ; and
taking the comb out of her hair gave it to the lucky Lutey,
telling him she would come and teach him all he wanted to
know whenever he stroked the comb upon the surface of the
water.

So he put on his most wheedling voice.

[To face p. 276.

Now, Lutey's family is said to exist still, and it has always
been very famous for the possession of charms and other
valuable secrets which they say were learnt from the mermaid.
It may be that some readers will be interested to see a specimen
of the kind of lore which the mermaid probably taught Lutey.
It is taken from a manuscript book of charms which Mr.
Jonathan Couch found at Polperro, and which very possibly
had a mermaid origin also. It is as follows,—"'Bradgty,
Bradgty, Bradgty,' under the ashing leaf, to be repeated three
times, and strike your hand with the growing of the hare.
'Bradgty, Bradgty, Bradgty,' to be repeated three times before
eight, eight before seven, seven before six, six before five, five
before four, four before three, three before two, two before one,
and one before every one, three times for the bite of an adder."
This is not, as might be hastily concluded, to be repeated fast
in a single breath as a cure for the hiccups. Quite the
contrary. It is a grave and serious remedy for the bite of an
adder, rarely known to fail, and deserving every confidence.

There is little more to be seen on the eastern range of cliffs,
for the caverns which pierce them are accessible only by sea.
As for the cliffs in the contrary direction, the wise man will
walk along them all the way to Helston, in preference to
returning by the dull road which brought him hither. There
is scarce a yard of all the distance which is not fine and
striking; while almost at the beginning of the walk lies
Kynance Cove, which some assert to be the finest in all Cornwall. I do not quite endorse this judgment; but it is beyond
all doubt a place of singular beauty. It is approached through
a rocky gorge, whose deep sides are golden with sweet-scented
furze, and in whose bottom a rapid stream gushes over
boulders, foaming into little cascades and reedy pools, and so
courses onwards to a high rocky wall down which it leaps into
the sea. In the bed of this stream the stones of serpentine,
polished by the rushing water, gleam with points of fiery red;
and the steps cut in the rock beside it, by which one goes to

the beach, are like those of a king's palace, so green and ruddy
are their streaks and veins.

The rock forms on the beach are so well known to all who
have ever entered a picture gallery that I shall spend no time
in dwelling on them.

Nor may I pause to speak of the splendour of the black

Kynance Cove, The Lizard.

scarred cliffs which tower all along the coast from Kynance to
Looe Pool. Even Mullyon, with its striking island and its
formidable precipices, I shall pass by undescribed ; and I do so
with the less reluctance since an admirable local history of the
parish has been written by a former vicar. It is the eve of
Helston Flora day, and unless I reach the " Angel " ere nightfall, I may well find myself crowded out from that old hostelry.

But as I go up and down the sheep paths which thread the alternate heights and hollows of the uneven coast, while the insects hum heavily among the warm flowers under foot, and the sea breaks lazily below, all manner of wild tales of the life which has passed away come whispering in my ear. And among them is one which I promised in the last chapter that I would tell, about the wreck of a treasure ship at Gunwalloe. We are within sight of Gunwalloe now, a little cove with a church and village set in a dip among lofty cliffs, a terrible place to look on from the deck of any ship if the wind drives in from south-west, as it did one day in January, 1526, when the *St. Andrew*, a treasure ship belonging to the King of Portugal, was driven hither out of her course from Flanders to Portugal " by outrageous tempest of the sea."

Now, I presume Gunwalloe in those days may have looked precisely as it does to-day, for nothing changes less than the aspect of a solitary fishing village ; and the dark olive-complexioned sailors whom one sees there now are the very counterparts of those who watched the heavy galley driving on the rocks three hundred and fifty years ago. It is often charged against the Cornish that they not only plundered shipwrecked mariners, but slew them also ; and thus we may note that one Francis Porson, apparently an Englishman, who was on board the doomed ship acting as the factor of the King of Portugal, testifies in a document still extant that " by the grace and mercy of Almighty God, the greater part of the crew got safely to land," and that, assisted by some of the inhabitants, they saved a large portion of the cargo also.

The list of what they saved is enough to make one's fingers itch and tingle even now. On those lonely cliffs, guarded only by a score or so of half-drowned sailors, lay eight thousand cakes of copper, eighteen blocks of solid silver bullion, with silver vessels, plate, pearls, precious stones, chains, brooches and jewels of gold, cloth of arras, tapestry, rich hangings, satins, velvets, chamlets, sayes, four sets of armour for the King of

Portugal, a chest containing over six thousand pounds in ready money, and heaven knows what besides. I put it to those persons who are most apt at condemning what they call the barbarous practices of the Cornish,—what would they themselves have done had they been needy landlords in a lonely country, whither the long arm of law intruded only once in a way, and found so huge a treasure lying on the grass? Is there more than one human nature? Are we not all cut out of the same piece? Or if we ourselves should have come through the trial, what about our wives? Would they have welcomed us had we come back empty handed? Would poor frail mother Eve have been content to leave all the jewels and chains and brooches lying on the cliff till some one could take them back to the King of Portugal? Let us have done with cant on this subject. What the Cornish did, the men of any other county would have done, and thought themselves lucky to have the opportunity. "Do you think we tell the captain," said a Kentish boatman the other day, with a sly leer, "do you think we tell the captain when he shaves too close upon the Goodwins? Not we! Else what'd us get for 'elping 'im off?" Will any one deny that that speech was animated by the very spirit of the wreckers?

Well, the men of Gunwalloe prudently got the chief part of this great treasure ashore, and stacked it up on the cliffs,—so at least Francis Porson declared, for the facts are otherwise related. And to follow Porson's story for the moment, there appeared upon the scene when the landing was complete, or almost so, Thomas Seynt Aubyn of Clowance, William Godolphin of Godolphin, and John Milliton of Pengerswick, with about sixty armed retainers, who assaulted the shipwrecked men and took all the treasure from them

According to Mr. Seynt Aubyn's version of the matter it all happened very simply. He chanced to be in the neighbourhood of Gunwalloe, heard of the wreck, and rode thither with the truly charitable purpose of helping to save the crew. Godolphin and Milliton joined him on this pious errand, and are entitled to even more credit than he, for their houses are a good many miles away from Gunwalloe, and we can hardly suppose that chance brought them too with their retainers out on the cliffs so far from home on that wild January day. It must have been a very eager Christianity which animated these gentlemen ; and those who accept the story in this form will see from it how much the Cornish character has been maligned. Well, they saved the chief part of the crew ; but the cargo they could not save, except the merest trifle, worth some twenty pounds, which, seeing that the poor fellows were utterly destitute, they bought from the captain as an act of charity, paying him good honest money in exchange.

We may take our choice between these stories. Mr. Michell Whitley, who found this tale in the Record Office, inclined towards the latter. For my part I ask myself how Francis Porson could have dared to trump up a lie upon a subject of which the true facts were known by many people, and, himself a stranger, to charge men of high birth and influence with a robbery which a slight examination would show they did not commit. What object could he have had ? What possible gain could have resulted from it ? If the goods lay still in the ship, any tide might have washed them ashore and given him the lie. The risks of a false accusation were immense. The profit could be nothing.

There was a darker side than this to the tales of wreckers on the western coasts of Cornwall. "When the Tyners observe a ship on the coast," wrote George Borlase in 1753, "they arm themselves with sharp axes and follow those ships. They'll cut a large trading vessel to pieces in one tide, and cut down everybody that offers to oppose them. . I apprehend no person should be allowed to attend a wreck armed with axes or the like unless lawfully required. . . . I have seen many a poor man half dead cast ashore and crawling out of the reach of the waves, fallen upon and in a manner stript naked by these villains." I have no observations to make on this evidence,

except to hope that it is not true, and to admit that I am afraid
it is.   And indeed, to come down to quite modern days, is it
not recorded that when the first steamer went round the Lizard,
she was followed close by quite a fleet of boats, all the people
who saw her being firmly persuaded that the smoke from her
funnel meant that she was on fire, and would go ashore soon,
when they would have the plundering of her?   And as we may
as well trot out all the old chestnuts while we are about it, let
us call to memory also that good vicar of Breage or of Germoe,
he is differently described according as it is a Germoe or a
Breage man who speaks of him, who, when his sermon was
interrupted by the sudden announcement of a wreck, bellowed
out to the old clerk, " Anthony, shut that door."   Then as
the clerk, who knew better than to disobey, swung to the great
oak door with a clang, while the congregation stopped in their
tracks, dismayed at this unlooked for impediment, the vicar
slipped out of his pulpit, cast away his gown, elbowed his way
to the very front of the crowd, and then looking about him
with a genial smile, "now," he said, "now, my Christian
brethren, we'll all start fair."

There was a pretty verse said to have been current in old
days about the two seaboard parishes just mentioned.   It ran
thus :—

> God keep us from rocks and shelving sands,
> And save us from Breage and Germoe men's hands.

And with this I drop the subject of wrecking, which pastime I
beg my readers to believe was by no means peculiar to Cornwall.   If any one says it was, a few hours spent on the
Calendars of State Papers will quickly convince him of his error.

Two hundred and fifty years ago all this coast suffered to a
degree which seems to us incredible from the ravages of what
were then called Turkish pirates, but which were in reality
Algiers and Sallee rovers.   We saw some way back how a
Plymouth ship fought with one such rover in this very neigh-

bourhood; but it seems strange to read that in such comparatively recent times the fishermen were afraid to put to sea, while
the dwellers in the cliff towns feared with reason that they
might be kidnapped in the night. The justices of Cornwall
complained to the Lord-Lieutenant that in one year the Turks
had taken no less than a thousand Cornish mariners; while
Looe alone, in the ten days before the letter was written, had
lost eighty men. A letter dated July 10th, 1636, and quoted
in the State Papers, says that seven boats and two and forty
fishermen were taken by the Turks off the Manacles between
Falmouth and the Lizard, "last Wednesday was three weeks."
These numbers prove the existence of widespread misery, for
each man so captured was a bread winner, and few of them saw
home again. Two or three years later Sir John Pennington
was cruising between Mount's Bay and the Lizard when he saw
"five sail of Turks men of war standing in for the Channel."
They turned and fled when they saw Pennington's fleet; and as
unfortunately the wind was very light, Pennington did not
succeed in taking any of them. "Clean, light, nimble vessels,"
he said they were, "and would have done a great deal of spoil,
and made many a poor soul captive."

At low tide one may walk from Gunwalloe Cove to the
sandy spit which divides Looe Pool from the sea; and this is by
far the pleasantest way of reaching Helston, for the Looe Pool
is a beautiful stretch of fresh water, winding like a river through a
forked valley, richly wooded. Oak coppice falls sweetly to the
water's edge; and the sloping banks, through which a
winding path runs near the water, are covered densely with a
tangle of ivy, bluebells, and the white stars of mountain strawberries in bloom. Here and there is a clump of arbutus dying
in its lower limbs, or a chestnut tree shedding white and rosy
petals on the water, while a deep glade cuts far back into the
hill, and up its banks the azure bluebells run riot, and pink
sprays of campion wave over them, with a few late primroses
growing humbly at their feet. At the head of the lake the
water yields to shelving meadows, where red and tawny cattle

graze under a group of noble trees, beeches, sycamores, and
darker elms, on whose branches no more than a faint green
flush has yet been cast by the budding spring. This is the
park of ancient Penrose. The old house stands on a rising
ground looking down the lovely winding water, which the reflection of the sunset clouds are staining rose and purple. But
the short spring dusk is nearly past. The warm gold light
fades out of the valley, the trees grow shadowy, and when I
reach the wide hilly street of Helston the lamps are lighted in
the porches of the hotels.

All night I am lulled by the song of running water, for the
one beauty of Helston is a double stream which gushes fresh
and copious down either side of its precipitous main street ;
and early in the morning the sound of a band awakes me to
the consciousness that the festivities of Flora Day have begun.
I dress hastily, and go out to find the volunteer band peram-
bulating the town, playing in slow time, and with a strongly-
marked accent, that quaint old hornpipe tune which will be
familiar enough before the day is over. A crowd of men and
boys marches with the band ; but Helston has not got its blood
up yet, and they step out gravely, keeping time as if it were a
solemn duty, while none but a few impulsive youngsters seize
each other by the waist and twirl round to a clumsy dancing
step. The general opinion is that the time for these levities
has not come yet ; and thus the band goes quietly about, and
the women stand in their doors tapping out the time with
restless feet, and laughing merrily as the crowd goes by.

A little later in the morning brakes and carriages begin to
arrive in crowds. Enormous numbers of people throng the
streets, booths are erected by the footways, and such mountains
of sticky things are being piled on them as may serve to give happy
moments to all the boys and girls of western Cornwall. Down
in the meadows by the river at the foot of the town a circus
tent is being put up as fast as the crowd of children will permit ;
and by and bye the procession goes through the streets. It is
historical and educative. First comes William the Conqueror,

all clad in silver armour a little battered, as the corselet of such
a mighty warrior would naturally be, his half-fed destrier neatly
ticketed on the flank with the designation and date of his
illustrious rider.   William the Second follows him, wearing a
splendid ermine cloak, beneath which a pair of very ordinary
blue serge trousers peep forth rather quaintly ; and after him
come riding solemnly a long row of English monarchs as far as
Richard the Second, where a hiatus occurs, and we skip
suddenly to Queen Mary, her of Scots, and after her there are
no more than her rival of England, with Queen Anne in
company, and lastly her reigning Majesty and Empress throned
high on a triumphal car, which has been rigged up with un-
sparing grandeur.   Truly a very moving pageant, though a
little incomplete !

But how this sight has drawn the people out !   Burly farmers
in corduroys and gaiters, smart servant girls and farm wenches
in new straw hats and bright print bodices, labourers in their
ill-fitting Sunday clothes, a sprinkling of ladies in gay summer
dresses, a countless multitude of boys, a party of sailors from
the *Ganges*—all these seething to and fro, pushing, struggling,
shouting, laughing, swearing, cracking jokes upon each other,
swaying every way at once and trampling each other down the
centre of the street.   Outside the corn market the throng is at
its densest, for from that point the first party is to start at one
o'clock on its time-honoured errand of dancing round the town,
thus celebrating the old spring festival which has been kept
in Helston with hardly a break since the days, so very long
ago, when the faith and reverence which it excited were real
and living.

This is why the streets are dressed up with green boughs
and garlands and strings of flags ; and this it is which has
drawn all this mad weltering impatient crowd out of the
scattered hamlets and lonely farms of a thinly populated
country side.   There is a long delay ; but at last the police-
men rush out of the corn market and charge everybody in
violent excitement.   The booming of a drum is heard.   The

volunteers in uniform emerge and form up as well as the
crowd alllows them, followed by a procession of ladies and
gentlemen gaily arrayed, in number no more than . . . No, I
will not reveal how little Helston cares for keeping up her
ancient ceremonies.   Now the band has begun solemnly, yet
gaily, to play the ancient well-marked melody.   The crowd
surge back, and the party come tripping down the steps,
looking by no means joyous, but oppressed with the consciousness that the most venerable institution of their mother town
is in their hands to maintain or to disgrace.   And now they
dutifully twirl each other round, and smile and try to look as if
they were at ease ; and so the whole procession sweeps round
into a street where they disappear bodily into the back door of
a shop, while a few minutes later those who are able to see
anything at all in the press behold them issuing triumphantly
from the shop door, ducking their heads to avoid the swinging
hams and sausages, headed by their music trumpeting loudly
for very joy at having got over their first fence and left none of
their number in the ditch.   High spirited and joyful they all
are as they emerge, and they twirl each other round and
change partners outside the shop door on the pavement, and go
on again, disappearing and emerging, among the shouts and
laughter of the crowd.   And indeed there is something highly
quaint in the sight of those uniformed musicians with their
train of top-hatted men and bright-dressed ladies marching
solemnly into the kitchen entrance of some quiet house, while
the crowd fights and quarrels as to where they will come out,
and the servants rush to the upper windows and look down on
them from above.   And so they go in, and take their jollity
among the pots and pans, and come out again and take it on the
pavement, still dancing and twirling, while the sailors from the
Ganges follow on behind dancing together, two and two,
wholly in their element.   But the crowd cannot forget itself as
they do.   No one copies them.   It is a good-tempered throng
enough, but it has no joyousness, no verve, it is afraid of
looking foolish, and, indeed is more than half convinced that

the dancers are a pack of fools, and they themselves who
stand squeezing each other in the street the only wise ones.

How different this might be were the spirit of the ancient
ceremony not yet dead! Can no one even now revive it?
Then this solemn capering, all weighted and burdened by the
fear of ridicule, might become what it was once an act of joyousness and true rejoicing with one's neighbours over the glory
and the beauty of the spring. There is room enough in
modern life for such a festival : for a day set apart on which for
once the heavy weight of labour and responsibility might be
shaken off their shoulders by all ranks and classes, making
open profession together of a joyousness which clears the heart
and sweeps away the mists of winter and ushers in the season of
warmth and sunshine in which all things equally begin to bud
and blossom.

Helston, like most other parts of Western Cornwall, has
been hard hit by the closing of the mines. The great
discoveries of tin in the Straits Settlements, followed by the
equally great ones in Bolivia, have scattered desolation through
many a thriving district of the Duchy, and sent the bread
winners to toil in foreign lands. It is a distressing subject, and
I take no pleasure in writing of it. We shall pass one mining
town which is now almost a city of the dead ; and it will be
enough to speak of what we see there. Besides, here at
Helston the state of things is not so bad as elsewhere ; for the
town stands in the centre of a rich farming district, and dairy
work is carried on with success.

In speaking of the wreck at Gunwalloe, I named Milliton of
Pengerswick ; and as not much is to be said of the pleasant
road to Marazion but that it is high and breezy, and commands
occasional snatches of fine coast, it may be as well to beguile
the way by telling some of the wild tales which are still remembered of him. For Milliton of Pengerswick was an
enchanter. There are strange stories of his youth, and of evil
practices which forced him to flee no one knows where. He
was absent many years, and came back without warning one

day when he was already half forgotten, riding up with a strangely lovely lady and no more than two attendants, who spoke none but some Eastern language. The castle was almost ruined, but Milliton summoned spirits to aid him, and in three days the walls and towers rose more splendid than before : and in this wondrous dwelling, Milliton and his wife shut themselves up, mixing hardly at all with the other gentry of the neighbourhood. Often in the night there were strange sounds and fearful cries from the tower, where Milliton sat wrestling with the spirits called up by his enchantments. The air would throb and the sea rise black and awful, and all the aspects of heaven and earth appear to threaten some great outburst of primæval forces, till the soft music of the lady's harp came stealing through the burdened air, soothing all things like a note of heavenly peace ; and as the twangling strains spread out upon the night, the sky cleared and the moon shone out, while in her beams countless spirits floated to and fro above the rippling waves, guarding the castle from the onset of all ill things.

After many years a stranger came one day to Marazion ; he had an outlandish look, like one who has travelled far and dwelt among strange peoples, yet no one could induce him to say whence he came, or what his errand was in this far part of England. He lived alone, and spoke willingly to none, but went out at nightfall, and sat till dawn on the sea shore, doing no one knew what. There were those who said that since he came neither the lord's enchantments nor the lady's music had been heard ; but, whether that were so or not, certain it is that one night there came a mighty tempest, and that in the midst of the darkness and the storm a sudden awful glare broke out, a pillar of flame shot up the sky above Pengerswick, roaring and scintillating with myriads of sparks and volumes of black smoke, till at last the flames sank as suddenly as they had risen, and the black night swept back across the sky. In the morning the wondrous castle was a pile of ashes, and neither Milliton nor his lady nor the bronzed stranger was ever seen again.

This is but one of many tales about the castle ; another,

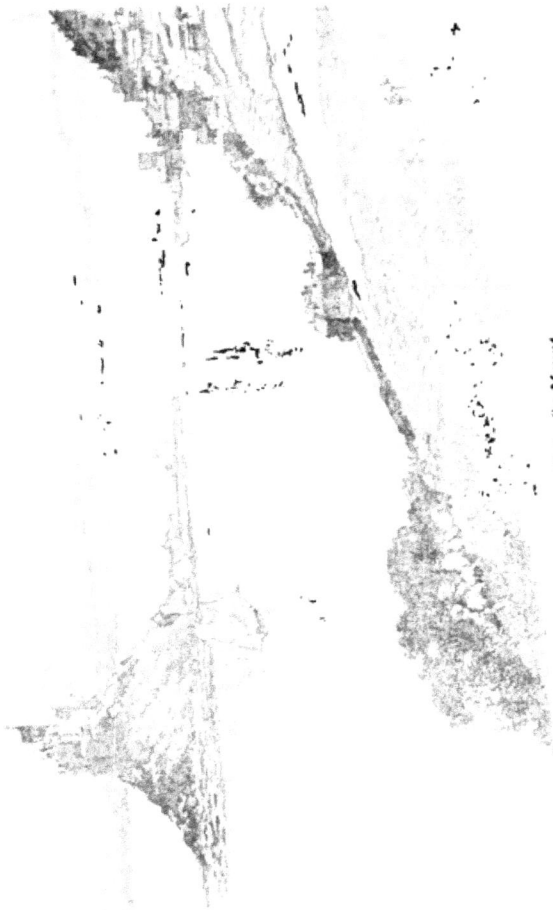

St. Michael's Mount.

U

hardly less striking, tells how Pengerswick and a company of guests were banqueting in a stately barge upon the blue waters of Mount's Bay. The barge was splendidly equipped, the table was of solid silver, and was spread with plates and vessels of pure gold. There was music too, and laughter rippling across the summer sea, when suddenly without warning the whole company sank and disappeared. All along the coast the children are still searching for the silver table. If you see a bare-legged urchin digging in the sand, he will tell you he is after bait, but he has the silver table in his heart; and his father, if you win his slowly given confidence, will tell you that often when his boat has been drifting slowly over the deep transparent water, he has seen the whole company seated far below him, and watched them drinking to each other from their cups of gleaming gold.

St. Michael's Mount.

St. Michael's Mount. The Causeway.

CHAPTER XVII

I HAD walked out to Newlyn in the early morning hoping to
see a fish auction, and found nothing save a countless host of
gulls screaming and fighting up and down the mud of the large
empty harbour.   All Mount's Bay lay in haze.   Westwards
half a score of fishing boats were standing out to sea.   On the
east the fine cone of St. Michael's Mount lay dark and solemn,
looking infinitely distant in the soft mist ; while behind it,
hardly seen, ran a low shadow which might have been cloud if
one had not known it to be land.   Suddenly the light began to
fall and spread around the Mount. A long gleaming line flashed
out across the sea.   The jagged promontory of Cudden began
to show his scars and clefts, and a widening patch of silvery
light dropped down in front, changing and growing brighter
every moment, till at last the haze had risen altogether from the

sea, and clung only about the pinnacles of the Mount, where it
hung remote and solemn, while the sea gleamed and glittered
round the rocks below.   An hour later blue sky was chasing
cloud all down the heavens.   The bay was full of blue laughing
water, dashing joyfully on the beach as the tide flowed in.   The
Mount was green and grassy and the hills behind it clear.   The
sight was unforgettable ; for while the curving shores of Mount's
Bay have nothing either so grand or so beautiful to show that it
cannot be matched and surpassed elsewhere in Cornwall, the
Mount itself lifts the whole prospect to a higher level, and gives
it rank as one of the three most interesting views in Cornwall.
The other two are those which include Pendennis and Tintagel.

Just so the whole bay must have looked on that July
morning in 1595 when, as Carew tells us, "soone after the
sunne was risen and had chased away a fog which before kept
the sea out of sight, four gallies of the enemy presented
themselves upon the coast over against Mousehole, and there
in a fair bay landed about two hundred men, pike and shot,
who forthwith sent their forlorn hope, consisting of their basest
people, unto the straggled houses of the country, about half a
mile compass or more, by whom were burned not only the
houses they went by, but also the parish church of Paul, the
force of the fire being such as it utterly ruined the great stone
pillars thereof.   Others of them in that time burned that fisher
town Mousehole ; the rest marched as a guard for the defence
of these firers."

This was a sad sight to see at breakfast time when least
expected ; and it may serve to bring home to our minds the
various excitements of life in a Cornish coast town in old days.
We have already seen how lively the Sallee Rovers kept the
coast ; and now we find the Spaniards dissipating dulness.
Of course neither one nor the other was always on the spot.
But when life threatened to be tedious through the lack of
foreign enemies, the fishermen might generally be trusted to
find some bright and merry way of enlivening it.   Let us take

St. Michael's Mount and Bay

an instance.   Early in February 1634-5 there was brought into
Gwavas Lake, as the anchorage off Newlyn is called, a Spanish
galleon taken from the Dutch.   She was a good deal battered
when brought in, and riding there in the rough wintry weather
was cast away.   The Dutch "endeavoured by contract with
certain gentlemen of those parts, aided by Mr. Bassett and
others, to save the goods,"—one would like to know the
details of this contract—while the Spanish resident by warrant
from the Admiralty arrested the ship, and what came out of her.
Here was a pretty rivalry of conflicting claims, but there was
one more to be preferred with which neither the Dutch nor
the Spaniards, nor apparently the gentlemen of the county, had
reckoned, though they at all events might have anticipated it.
For all the endeavours of these various interested parties to
save the cargo were opposed "by a riotous mob of the inhabitants of Mousehole and Markajew, who maintain their riot
with the word 'one and all,' which is usual among sea
mutineers."   This is rather cutting.   Like most other Cornishmen I have always been proud of my county motto.   I did
not know it was usual among sea mutineers; but I profess I do
not like it the less on that account.   For the conduct of these
"sea mutineers" of Markajew and Mousehole was so very
human.   They wanted the goods.   Had I been there I
should have wanted them too.   It is for its humanity that I
love my duchy, and fresh proofs that it was compact of flesh
and blood rather than of some high spiritual essence will not
make me love it less.   But to return to the story.   There were
some Admiralty officials sent to look after the interests of the
Spanish resident.   They got out to the wreck but were surrounded
by "at least a hundred men and women and children,"—observe
the pluck and courage of the little prattlers who went out to beard
Admiralty officials—"hunted them ashore with weapons, and
not only threatened to kill them, but would have done so if to
save their lives they had not all three leapt down a steep cliff."
Really, I was quite glad when I read in the State Papers that

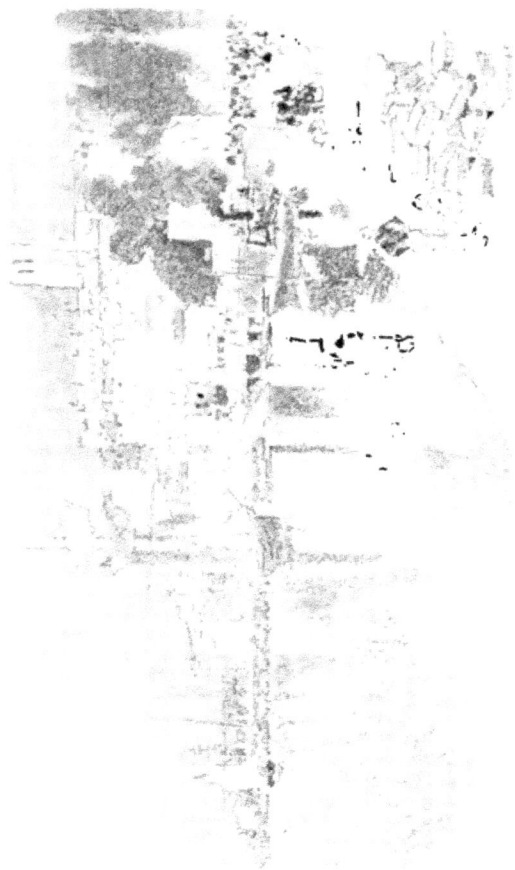

the Admiralty officials leapt down this cliff, for I am half afraid the sea mutineers meant what they said about killing them. These mutineers were the best of good fellows, kindly and staunch to a degree ; but they believed that wrecks were their

Market Pen Street, Penzance.

title-deeds, and they were a trifle peremptory about insisting on their rights. This story had a sequel of prosecutions ; but that is a vulgar trivial affair of law courts, and we need not dwell on it.

There is not much to say about Penzance ; while the settlement of certain distinguished artists at Newlyn has made that
little fishy town as familiar as Kensington.   The prettiest view
of it, at least in spring time, is from a spot half-way up the hill
beyond, where there is a low wall topped with apple trees, and
through their pink and rosy blossom one looks down upon the

Newlyn.

harbour, blue and radiant in the sun.   A single fishing boat is
hoisting her brown sail and forging slowly past the pier head,
and on the wide bay a hundred more are sailing to and fro.
The bulk of the boats are away at Scilly now, for the mackerel
season has not long begun, and there are lively times at St.
Mary's, where boats from Mount's Bay, Lowestoft and even

Scotland put in to hold their auctions in the early morning. Old Fuller was of opinion that fishermen could not be kept up "unless the publick eating of fish at set times be countenanced, yea, enjoyned by the state," and fearing evidently lest the great heart of the people might revolt against the compulsion of such public banquets, he goes on to point out that it is quite a mistake to suppose there is any sin in eating fish. "Some suspect," he cries scornfully, "as if there were a Pope in the belly of every fish, and some bones of superstition in them which would choke a conscientious person, especially if fasting be observed. But be it known that such customs grew from a treble root of popery, piety and policy; and though the first of these be plucked up, the others must be watered and maintained, otherwise the not keeping of feasting days will make us keep fasting days." Alas, fasting days are growing common in the duchy which was once a land of plenty; and still no minister arises with courage enough to try old Fuller's remedy.

It is a long road from Newlyn to the Logan Rock, but by no means a dull one, to those at least who care to turn aside to see stone circles or monoliths. The road goes in full sight of the "Merry Maidens," a fine cromlech of nineteen upright stones, while over the way, at a convenient distance are the huge monoliths which represent the pipers, they who made sweet music on a Sunday, and led the poor Maidens into so sad a plight. It is a weary trudge from the Maidens to what the cottagers speak of briefly as "fishing cove" but at last a side road turns towards the coast, and a few windings among the furze bring us to the brow of a hill, whence we look down suddenly on a deep, ragged cleft, set between high slopes of grass and broken jags of granite. A sea mist is creeping inwards. About the summit of the cliffs it hangs dense and voluminous; but the sun catches the breaking water round their base and sparkles brightly on the white crests of the little surges. Three or four boats are tossing in the cove. The sailors are hauling up another with a windlass; the sound of its keel

scraping the pebbles mingles with the creaking of the winch
and the low song of the men straining at their task.

Newlyn.

What was it that planted the first cottages in such a spot as
this, so wild and lonely and difficult of access?   It was neither

in this generation nor the last nor in many previous to it, that
the first smoke rose along these grassy slopes. But what
kindled the fires on those hearths? Was it fish that brought
men to a place where there was none to buy it? But what
then, if not that? for even in these days there is little tillage on
either hills or valleys of that storm-swept region. There was
surely suitability for something in this cove, which made it seem
a desirable abode. I conclude it was its very loneliness that
fitted it for occupations which thrive best when seen by fewest
eyes.

But whilst I am still pondering on this, I have reached
Treryn Dinas, that great splintered headland on which the
Logan rock stands. But the Logan is a trifle, a toy, beside the
strange and wonderful beauty of the headland. For nowhere
on this coast is the granite so rent and shattered, so split into
spires and pinnacles and minarets and towering gigantic blocks of
masonry, all of which touched by the light wreaths of the sea mist
which somewhere behind it has a hot bright sun, appear as
unsubstantial as a fairy palace. Around the base of this superb
medley of rock forms, the clear blue water laps and sparkles
brightly. There is no living thing in sight save a single gull
whose snowy plumage gleams as he skims the surface of the
water, and again fades and disappears as he rises into the region
of the mist.

It is a singular good fortune which has brought this weather;
for in the struggling of the sun and fog we can realise both
aspects of this coast, so wildly beautiful and so steeped in
fanciful romance, the tangled wreckage of a fierce and lusty
life which was lived upon these shores more centuries ago than
one can count. As the mist flows around the headlands, little
palpitating flashes are cast upon it by the hidden sun, so that
the solid blocks and columns of the granite appear to quiver,
while out at sea, beyond the blue bay where the sun falls, coming we see not whence, the sight loses itself at but a little distance in a gray soft cloud which sets one's fancy working as the

senses fail to pierce it or discover what it hides. Out of such
a cloud might have sailed that spectre ship which haunts
Porthcurno, the fine bay with a beach of lovely driven sand
which lies a few minutes' walk away across the cliff. Out of
the mist she always came, a black square-rigged vessel, sailing
right up upon the beach, taking the sand without a shock or
quiver, and pursuing her course as steadily over dry land as on
the sea, till she vanished in a smoke wreath higher up the
valley. There are several forms of the legend which accounts
for the first coming of this ship; all centre on a stranger who
came to dwell at Chygwiden, up the valley, with a single
servant, and who kept a boat at Porthcurno in which he and his
man put out to sea in the worst of storms. There was clearly
something about this pair of strangers which awed the fishermen ; but even tradition has forgotten what it was, and the tale
remains a vague trace of former days almost as impalpable as
the mist.

A little way beyond Porthcurno lies another fishing hamlet,
named Porthgwarra, which one may well suspect of owning a
history of more incident than arises naturally out of nets and
trawls ; and a short climb above this cluster of white huts brings
us out on the summit of Tol-pedn-penwith, the holed headland
which takes its name from a deep circular chasm, formed
doubtless by the falling of the roof of a sea-cave hollowed far
underneath the grassy slopes by the ceaseless beating of the
waves. There is no grander sight in Western Cornwall than the
sheer dropping of this mighty headland to the sea. Its dark
jutting shoulders and huge buttresses impress the mind to-day
as they did of old when every peak along these coasts had its
tale of witches gathering to watch and help the growing storms,
or sailing through the air on stalks of ragwort towards Wales,
whither they migrated at certain seasons. On the top of Tol-
pedn is a rude recess among the cubes of granite which keeps
the name of Madgy Figgy's chair. Madgy was one of the
blackest of all the Penwith witches ; and often when the winter

storms were rising, and in the great stream of commerce entering the Channel all the skill of seamanship was being used to keep the great ships off the rocks, Madgy Figgy was seen swinging to and fro with exultation in her chair screaming out her incantations till the storm rose into ungovernable fury, and the ships drew near and nearer to the reef. Then when the crash was imminent, Madgy Figgy would sail off from her chair on a stalk of ragwort, and float shrieking up and down the air, while far below her the wreckers stripped the bodies cast ashore and gathered up the spoil.

There was once a richly laden Indiaman cast away by Madgy's spells, and among the bodies found was one of a lady richly dressed, with chains of gold and many valuables about her. This body Madgy declared bore a mark which boded evil to those who robbed it, and she would allow no one to touch the spoils which were upon it. All the gold and jewels she collected, and stored them in a chest in her hut, while the body was buried at a little distance. That night when darkness had settled down upon the cove, a bright light appeared on the grave, passed along the cliffs and rose up to Madgy's chair, where it remained burning brightly; and night after night the signal fire wandered from the grave to the chair, until at last a stranger, who could speak no English, came, and made known by signs that he wished to see the graves of the drowned. All day he sat there by himself; but when night came, the light rose up more brilliant than ever before, and went before him to Madgy's hut, where it rested on the chest which contained the treasure, and without a protest Madgy opened the chest and gave the stranger all the gold and jewels. "Ah, one witch always knows another, dead or living," she remarked when he had gone.

There is a certain sameness about the grand range of headlands which lie between the Logan and the Land's End. Wherever one's eye falls the sight is of granite, split and weathered at the joints, so that it looks as if piled by human

hands, while here and there the angles are so worn away by the
ceaseless beating of the storms that one sees a rocking stone,
or Logan, in the making.   An exquisitely springy turf runs to
the very margin of the cliff ; and one walks along crushing
wild thyme and little vetches and numberless sweet-smelling
things at every step, while tufts of sea-pink blossom beside the
scattered boulders, and here and there lady's fingers, crimson and
yellow, are opening their first buds.   This cliff, if there be any truth
in tradition, did not always border the seashore.   That wide
space of ocean was once solid land, a rich and fertile country,
dotted with no less than one hundred and forty parish churches,
the Lost Land of Lionesse ; and those countless isles of Scilly,
which we should see now were the fog to clear away, are the
peaks and high grounds of that vanished country, which stood
up above the inrush of sea waves that drowned the lower lands
fathoms deep beneath the ocean.

Is there any truth in this old story ? Was there ever such a
land stretching westwards from these cliffs ? The story runs that
when the flood rushed in one of the Trevilian family was riding
a fleet white horse, which sped so fast before the following
waters that it brought him safe to Perranuthnoe, where a cave
is pointed out as that whence he looked back in safety on the
drowning of the fields and cities which no man has ever seen
again.   Is it true ? or is the story only another version of the
Keltic superstition which clings so closely to white horses, the
same tale substantially as that of the O'Donoghue rising from
Lough Neagh ?

There are certainly submerged forests all around the coast of
Cornwall ; and in some parts of Mount's Bay beech trees have
been found with the nuts still hanging on the branches, which
seems to show that the destruction was sudden and that it
happened in the autumn.   If so large a tract of country was
really swept away in historic times, it is strange that legend, which
remembers so many things in the West, has not much to tell us
of the day of so great a doom.   There are in the Saxon Chronicle

notes of two great inundations of the sea which happened in the eleventh century. Under date 1014 is written : "This year, on St. Michael's Mass Eve, came that mickle sea flood widely through this land ; and it run up so far as never at no time before ; and it drowned many towns, and mankind too innumerable to be computed." And again in 1099 the chronicler writes : "This year eke sprang up so much the seaflood and so mickle harm did as no man minded that it ever before did."

There is no reason that I know of to distrust these notes. Doubtless two mighty storms and sea floods did occur at the time the Chronicle records them, the first drowned many towns and the second was more awful. Now there is one other slight indication which may be pierced together with these. A certain charter of Henry 1st gives to the monks of Tavistock "all the churches of Sullye with their appurtenances and the land as ever the monks or the hermits in a better state held it during the time of Edward the King." One is struck by the words "in a better state." What was it then that had happened since Edward the Confessor died in the year before Senlac to throw the Scillies into a state so markedly worse as to be worth naming in a charter ? The second and the worst of these storms was but fifteen years old when the charter was delivered.

A good deal of heavy raillery has been cast on the legend of Trevilian, and it has been criticised as stupid people criticise all fragments of tradition, condemning it because his horse could not have swum through a sea which must have driven over the doomed land mountains high, and raging furiously. But not all forms of the story claim that his horse did swim ; and even if all did, the rejection of one circumstance does not prove the whole story false. It would be strange indeed if a tale could roll on through eight centuries without some accretion of falsehood. For my part I claim that tradition is rarely altogether in the wrong. What she tells us contains a kernel of truth, however twisted or concealed by careless repetition ; and it would in my judgment be far stranger if this definite and

precise story had grown up with no other foundation than if it
were in truth an actual recollection of that great tragedy which
can have had no parallel in the history of this country and but
few in that of any other.

Whatever the truth may be a certain fascination, such as the
wisest of us feel when we hear a tale of lost cities, or of buried
treasure, will always cling around the wide sea view which lies
below the most westerly cliffs in England ; and indeed the
stories current three hundred years ago, when Carew rode round
these coasts, of doors and windows brought up in fisher nets,
are still heard by those who haunt the cliffside cottages, and
many a burly giant will drop his voice to an awed whisper as
he tells you how he has seen towers and houses far down in
the depths of the transparent water, and long oarweed waving
round the steeples which once summoned the folk of some
wide parish to prayer.   He does not know himself how much
of what he tells is the creation of his rich Keltic fancy, stimu-
lated by the constant plying over lonely waters which do but
change from one to another form of exquisite beauty.   The
man has never seen what is common or ugly, and thus his
thoughts run quickly into the land of pure imagination.

The charm of the Land's End itself is one of mere idea.
The cliffs are neither so lofty nor so beautiful as at many other
points of the seven miles which lie between Old Bellerium and
the Logan ; nor, if the truth must be told is this, however fine,
the grandest portion of the Cornish coast.   I do not see how it
can be questioned that the range of cliffs lying between Padstow
and Tintagel far exceeds the better known west both in height
and beauty.   But it is needless to anticipate.   The western
range leaves unforgettable memories ; and we turn away through
Sennen with the regretful consciousness that one of the chief
interests of this journey round Devonshire and Cornwall has
been tasted and enjoyed.

The wise cyclist has sent his wheels on to Sennen and
done this journey on his legs ; but the moment has now

come when he may very well take to his wheels again, for as
much is to be seen from the road as it is at all necessary to see.
But before leaving Sennen, it is well to walk down through

Land's End.

two fields to Sennen Cove, for though the whole of
Whitesand Bay, in the deepest part of which the little hamlet
stands, lies spread out in full view from the road, yet the place
had so ill a fame in past ages that one is curious to have a

closer view. The wide curving strand lies very lonely now,
and it is many a day since any shipping has been seen there
save the fisher boats, which are of the smallest kind, or an
occasional telegraph ship bent on repairing cables. But in old
days it was a frequent haunt of pirates. In fact, there was no
bay along the western coast where these desperate characters

Land's End.

congregated in such numbers, unless indeed it were at Padstow,
or at Lundy, and though the chief part of the wild deeds
wrought on these lonely shores are long since forgotten,
with the very names of the men who did them, yet a few still
linger to confirm the more sober entries in the State Papers,
which invariably give this bay the worst of characters.

Once long ago—so Mr. Hunt tells us, and there is no better

guide to the legendary wealth of Western Cornwall—once long
ago the fishermen of Sennen Cove watched a pirate sail into
the bay and land a man who was laden with heavy irons.
His comrades removed his manacles upon the beach, and in spite
of his fierce struggles to regain the boat, rowed away and left him
there. Now this unwelcome stranger settled down where he
had been thus marooned, and proved to be a most desperate
and murderous wrecker, one who not only plundered drowning
sailors, but hacked their hands off with a hatchet as they strove
to climb out of the surf. The easy consciences of the natives
were troubled by the deeds of the man, and they watched age
creeping on him with a certain longing for the time when he
would be no more among them. It came at last in the days
of barley harvest. "Two men," says Mr. Hunt, "were in a
field on the cliff a little below the pirate's house, and there was
not a breath of wind to stir the corn. Suddenly a breeze passed
by them, and they heard the words, 'The time is come, but the
man isn't come.' Looking out to sea they saw a black, heavy,
square-rigged ship, with all her sails set, coming in against wind
and tide, and not a hand to be seen on board. The sky became
black as night around the ship, and as she came under the cliff,
the darkness resolved itself into a lurid storm cloud, which extended high into the air. The sun shone brilliantly over the
country, except on the house of the pirate at Tregaseal,—that
was wrapt in the shadow of the cloud. . . . The dying wrecker
was in a state of agony crying out in tones of the utmost terror,
' Put out the sailors with their bloody hands.' . . . The parson,
the doctor, and two of the bravest of the fishermen were the
only persons in the room. They related that at one moment
the room was as dark as the grave, and at the next it was so
light that every hair on the old man's head could be seen standing on end. . . . All this time the room appeared as if filled
with the sea, with the waves surging violently to and fro, and
one could hear the breakers roaring as if standing on the edge
of the cliff in a storm. At last there was a fearful crash of

thunder, and a blaze of the intensest lightning. The house
appeared on fire, and the ground shook as if with an earthquake.
All rushed in terror from the house, leaving the dying man to
his fate. . . . The black cloud which was first seen to come in
with the ship, was moving with a violent internal motion over
the wrecker's house. The cloud rolled together, smaller and
smaller, and suddenly with the blast of a whirlwind it passed
from Tregaseal to the ship, and she was impelled amidst the
flashes of lightning and roarings of thunder away over the sea.
. . . They tell me the coffin was carried to the churchyard, but
that it was too light to have contained the body, and that it
was followed by a black pig, which joined the company no one
knew where, and disappeared nobody knew when. The bearers
of the coffin were obliged to leave it by the stile, and rush into
the church for safety from another storm which raged with
violence, and all was as dark as night. A sudden blaze of
light was seen, and those who had the hardihood to look out
saw that the lightning had set fire to the coffin, and it was being
borne away through the air blazing and whirling wildly in the
grasp of such a whirlwind as no man ever witnessed before or
since."

Now if any man claims that this terrific story grew and
spread from no root at all, I venture respectfully to differ from
him. If the sober records of history had depicted those who
dwelt on Whitesand Bay in past days as a race of sweet and
godly men whose community constituted, so to speak, one vast
Sunday school, such tales as this might have been set down as
the imaginative exercises of the good, who love to depict
villains in their leisure, just as bad and reckless people rejoice
in the accurate description of old maiden ladies and young
curates. But history does not sketch this gentle picture. It
tells us bluntly that Whitesand Bay swarmed with pirates; and
knowing this we need make no scruple in believing that such a
wrecker did die at Tregaseal; and though we may deduct something from the tale of appalling natural phenomena which ac-

companied his death, we must add just so much in wickedness, or we shall not be able to account for the terror which set men's minds devising or fancying these terrible scenes.

From Sennen Cove to St. Just is but five miles, and five very ugly miles, while St. Just itself is not a thing of beauty. It is a mining town, deserted by its miners; for of all the great and famous mines which sustained a crowded population in this district, one only is open, namely Levant. Yet it is odd that one mine in a whole district can be worked profitably, while all the rest have failed. Is it conceivable that the ore in none other was so rich? Or does not the fact point to some default of management? It is a question which perplexes men wiser far than I, and it is not my business to decide it. I pass on through Morvah, famous for its mermaids, following the Zennor road, through country which is neither beautiful nor grand but only wild and waste. The road skirts the coast; but the views are never more than ordinarily fine, except at Gurnard's Head, which is well worth diverging to visit, though in my judgment it has been over-praised, and can in no way be compared with the grander headlands of the north. A little further on lies Zennor, commonly known as the place where the cow ate the bell-rope; and indeed when one glances round at the scarcity of provender one is not surprised. The village lies in a little hollow. The church is on its furthest slope, a worn gray building which harmonises well with the welter of granite blocks that strew the hillsides. They breed a superior kind of man at Zennor, as may be seen from an epitaph within the church, which claims for one worthy who died in the last century that he was "hospitable, sociable, peaceable, humble, honest, and devout. In manners he excelled his equals, in piety he was their example. He met death with composure, and is here interred with his wife of spotless fame and virtuous character." This is excellent testimony, and I think it only fair to mention it in advance since the men of St. Ives, giving rein to that discord between adjoining parishes which is not the

least charming of Cornish qualities, entertain a low opinion of
men of Zennor, and are in the habit of asking superciliously
when they meet one, "Who built a wall round the cuckoo?"
This taunt, which is sometimes levelled also at the men of
Towednack, the next parish, is founded on a striking incident
in the past history of Zennor. Some natives of that bleak
village, noticing how closely the pleasant spring was connected
with the coming of the cuckoo, resolved to keep the warm
weather always with them by detaining him. So they caught
him, and began to build a wall round him, but had only
completed two or three courses when the bird flew out. "Ef
us 'd got another coorse an, us 'd a kep'n in," they said regret-
fully as they watched their treasure fly away.

But the St. Ives men, when they bring up this ancient gibe,
expose themselves to a terrible rejoinder; and indeed it needs
no more than the smallest reference to the word "hake" to
reduce them to tears of rage. And what is it in the name of
this succulent fish that can prick these worthy men so deep?
Why, the story is that long ago, probably about the time when
the Zennor men caught their cuckoo, the fishers of St. Ives
were much distressed by the ravages made by the hake, then
very numerous along this coast, among the mackerel, which
were an important part of their subsistence. It was quite
necessary to stop the misdeeds of the greedy hake, so the
fishers took the natural and simple course of catching the
largest they could find, a sort of king among the hake, whipped
him soundly with little rods to teach him better manners, and
then put him back to tell his brothers what he had under-
gone.

Just such are the relations between Camborne and Redruth.
Camborne men inquire scornfully, "Who crowned the donkey?"
and Redruth men remember with contrition an act of jeering
disloyalty committed on the accession of George the Fourth.
Another taunt flung at them is that they have all three chocks
in their heels. Chocks are slits: and though I do not re-

member that I ever saw the heels of a native of Redruth, yet I
incline on general grounds to disbelieve this slander. Yet it
breeds bad blood, so there may be something in it.

But this dissertation has brought us near St. Ives; and when
we climb the hill above the station the whole of the noble bay
lies spread out at our feet. There is such infinite variety in
these Cornish fishing towns. Here is no huddled hump of
houses tumbling one over another in a cleft of precipices, but

St. Ives.

a wide bay forming an almost perfect arc, and having on its
left a sheltered tongue of land, rising to a height at its extremity, thus forming a natural breakwater against west and
south-west winds, a bay within a bay, a safe anchorage in
heavy weather. Round the shelving strand the old town
clusters. The ancient church stands there, close to the water's
edge, right in the centre of her work, surrounded by a labyrinth
of fisher houses, which break away at last into a beach, where

the fishing boats are hauled up in safety. It is a sweet and
sunny place, a harbour full of clear green water, the sandy
shores of the wide bay curving round past Phillack and
Gwithian, past Godrevy Island, where the lighthouse gleams
tall and white against a background of blue sea, and so on
past Portreath and Perranporth to the dim line of that grand
northern coast which holds the finest scenery in Cornwall.
Here nothing is grand, but soft and sunny and exquisite ; and
always some little fishing boats are slipping in and out of the
harbour or scudding to and fro on the blue bay.

CHAPTER XVIII

THERE are wondrous fables of fairies and of giants along the shores of St. Ives Bay ; and as I am so unfortunately constituted as to care more for idle tales than for some matters of practical utility, I should willingly sit me down upon the towans and decline to stir until I had discharged my childish recollections of these follies. But that may not be. We have an immense distance to go, and must ride fast to accomplish it. There will be little time for examining the mining country, which is not an unmitigated misfortune, since in the eyes of all but mining experts it is ugly to the last degree, while the most patriotic of Cornishmen can now take little pride in an industry which has few associations left but those of poverty and exile.

It will hardly do however to leave the country of the giants without any reference to them, and therefore while we run on through Hayle and Gwinear we will pass the time by telling the story of Jecholiah, of which there are several inaccurate and imperfect versions. This however, which was taken down from the lips of a peasant on the north coast, may be accepted as the true story ; and its scene is St. Agnes Beacon, a lofty hill which we shall see presently standing out most conspicuously on the left.

Jecholiah, the first of that name who made any figure in profane history, was the last, or thousandth, wife of the Giant Bolster, a hero of ancient times when giants were common in the world, or at least in that important portion of it which is now called Cornwall. The deeds of Bolster would fill a volume; but it is only with his views on matrimony that the story of Jecholiah is concerned. In Bolster's opinion the proper and natural duration of that state was one calendar year. There appears to be in some quarters in the present day a dis-

St. Agnes.

position to approve of varied matrimonial relationships; and in such quarters interest will be felt in Bolster's simple and direct method of securing the desired sequence of wives.

An ideal which had worn out was to him a thing of jest; and so every year, on the anniversary of his wedding, his practice was to set his wife on the top of Saint Agnes' Beacon and throw rocks at her until he killed her. The blocks of granite still lie all over the hillside, proving the truth of the story; and so the system went on bringing annual relief and satisfaction to its author until he married Jecholiah.

Now Jecholiah seems to have been a good wife in everything but her reluctance to go away when she was no longer wanted. She could not rise to the height of self-denial which her husband expected of her; and when her year of office had nearly expired, she appealed to Saint Agnes for help. Saint Agnes came to the rescue willingly, not having been entirely pleased this long while with the use to which her beacon was put; and she made a treacherous suggestion to Jecholiah, who demeaned herself sufficiently to entertain it, thus showing how quickly even the best of wives fall to pieces morally when they begin to conspire against their husbands. Saint Agnes gave Jecholiah full instructions, and despatched that deceitful woman home again to meet her husband with a smiling face.

The next morning Jecholiah, still wreathed in smiles, led her husband up to the shaft of a mine which opened on a pleasant hillside overlooking the sea; and there Bolster, throwing himself at length on the turf, opened a vein in his arm. This was his invariable custom as the time for putting his wife away came near; for the exercise was severe and he found it well to carry off any little surfeit in advance. He always bled himself a mine-shaft full, no more and no less; and though he had not used this shaft before, he thought it would do as well as any other, while Jecholiah seemed to wish to go that way. So she sat by his side singing softly some sleepy song, and from time to time looking behind his head at the sea which was now beginning to be covered with a dark red flush. Bolster grew drowsy; he looked again and again to see if the shaft were not full, but there was still no sign of blood near the top. At last, full of strange suspicions, he rose tottering to his feet and looked around him. The sea as far as the horizon was red with his blood, flowing like a river, leagues on leagues from land. The very sky had caught the reflection, and flamed like a brilliant sunset. The mine had an exit to the sea, and the life-blood of the trustful giant had flowed out before he saw the trick.

The mining country is upon us now, and all the land as far as one can see on both sides the road has grown waste and sterile, covered with huge heaps of slag, and dotted with tall chimneys, of which I would with all my heart that I could see the whole number belch forth smoke again as they did not many years ago, when the miners were prosperous at home, and the population had not been drained off from Camborne or Redruth to toil for foreign taskmasters at Johannesburg or Kimberley, while their wives, left behind to keep up the cottage whither the breadwinners hope always to return, look weekly for the remittance which never fails to come over the sea. For the men's hearts are in the valley underneath Carn Brea, though their bodies are sweating in the heat of an African mine. Cornishmen do not accept exile for ever, but there are weary days in the mining valleys now, and it gives me a pang to see on the gable of every barn the coloured placards of the "Castle" line of steamers to the Cape and to Natal. The manhood of the duchy is being drained out of it, and the air between it and South Africa is crossed and recrossed with flying thoughts and hopes and memories and visions of some clean white cottage where the hearth is kept clear swept and the lamp bright burning for the day when at last the man may come home once more. There was once a simple poet, very little read now, who understood with what feeling the men of Keltic race regard their homes, and cast it into eight lines so exquisite that I shall quote them in preference to dwelling further on this subject.

> In all my wanderings round this world of care,
> In all my griefs, and heaven has sent my share,
> I still had hopes, my latest hours to crown,
> Amidst these humble bowers to lay me down.

And as a hare whom hounds and horns pursue
Pants to the place from which at first she flew,
I still had hopes, my long vexations past,
There to return, and die at home at last.

It is unfortunate that I have no science ; otherwise I might
have made a striking description of some one among the fairly
numerous mines which are still working prosperously.   Unhappily, when I strive to recall what I saw when I visited a
mine, I can discover no clear impressions save a deafening
noise of stamps, a bewildering chaos of beams and engine rooms
and washing-pans, and copper-coloured men and boys emerging,
half naked, from the bowels of the earth, and streaming their
bodies in deep basins of hot water in the vain endeavour to
wash the blackamoor white.   It was all very picturesque and
interesting, but it seems to need an expert to describe it clearly,
and I am not an expert, therefore let us go on our way, and not
try to talk of what we do not understand.

Far and wide as we journey through the mining country,
desolate and grimy in its aspect, we catch sight of the noble
outline of Carn Brea, towering against the skyline with a
grandeur which absolutely compels attention.   Such a potency
of influence it exercises still, this lofty, rugged crag, so strangely
different from the rounded hills which stand about it on every
side, that it proclaims itself at first sight to be one of those
places where the reverence and superstition of ancient races
must have centred, and where their traces may be sought as
confidently as on Roughtor.   The sides and summit of the hill
are covered with immense blocks of granite, piled in utter
confusion, now propped vertically side by side, now ranged so
symmetrically in a cairn that it is difficult to credit the absence
of human agency, so strangely has the random operation of
natural forces simulated what man might do.   On one of the
tallest of these cairns, in far distant mediæval times, a castle
placed itself—surely the strangest foundation ever used by man,
for the cairn to which the ancient building clings is so far from

solid that the sky shows through the interstices of the boulders, and the whole erection, walls and pediment alike, looks as if a gentle summer breeze might puff it over, and send it rolling shattered down the slope. Yet the fiercest storms of heaven knows how many centuries have not been able to stir the castle, which digs its talons into the granite boulders and holds on, defying tempest, and looks forth still over the wide valley full of mines, beyond which, in both directions, one can see the Channel.

On this hill the relics of old settlers in the age of stone are very plentiful, and they have recently been dug out by Mr. Thurstan Peter of Redruth, whose investigations and discoveries are of the most striking interest, and mark clearly the momentous change which, as I have already said, has come over archæology during the last generation, removing that pursuit from the domain of speculation to that of experiment, and so giving it, for the first time, a claim to the title of a science. Imagination has been superseded by the spade, and the result, in the hands of investigators so shrewd and capable as Mr. Peter, is already great enough to justify the hope that many a secret may be revealed which has been hidden no less by the hasty guesses of previous inquirers than by the long grass and piled up stones and earth.

The road to Newquay goes through Truro as far as Mitchell, and then strikes off northwards. It is long and dull, and as there is nothing else to do, we may as well turn our minds to the question of witches, who abound in all this region. The following authentic tale will serve to start the subject.

There once dwelt in this region a small farmer named John Hocken, who seems to have been a worthy person with a rasping manner. At any rate, he was by no means so popular among his neighbours as his solid virtues might have led one to expect — in fact, Hocken had enemies, as he was soon to discover. One morning he was on his way to market with three fine calves, for which he hoped to obtain a good price. On the way he met a neighbour, who stopped to pass the time of day. "Wheer be gooin', Jan?" Jan explained, and the other turned to look at the cattle. "Vine beasts," he admitted, after a critical examination, "What do 'ee want for them?" "What I can get," replied John, cautiously; whereupon the other bid ten shillings a head, an offer which John put aside as too foolish to need an answer, and went on his way, leaving the keen bargainer casting sour looks after him. When John reached the fair he saw no calves so good. Everybody admired, but no one bought; and when night came he had no choice but to drive them home again, which he did in a very bad temper. But a worse misfortune was in store for him, since next morning he found all his fine young calves dead in the cowhouse. This was a heavy blow ; but John had still three pigs fit for sale, and he set out at once for St. —— where it happened to be market day, driving the pigs before him. The road was not the same by which he had driven the calves, so it was the more curious that when he had got about halfway, he again met the man whom he had encountered on the previous day. There was something about the man's look, too, which John did not like, so he kept a rigid silence when accosted, and deigned no answer to the question where he was going. The man walked on beside him for a little way, plying him with questions and at last turned down a byeway, observing with a sour look, "You might as well have dealt with me, John." John was glad to see him go ; but something seemed to be the matter with the pigs. They grunted, staggered about, and finally lying down in the dust, were, in a few minutes, as dead as the calves. John began to see that something more than common was the matter with his affairs ; but upset as he was by the serious loss he had sustained, his chief trouble was a conviction that the powers of darkness were employed against him. He drew the carcases under the shadow of the hedge, and set off home as fast as he could go. He was nearly there when someone looked over a stile and asked in a sour voice, "How's your

wife, John?" John needed not to look to see who it was.
Terror seized him, and he fairly took to his heels. When he
reached home he had at once to run for the doctor, since his
wife was in a fit and lay dangerously ill for many days.

There is no mystery at all about these events in the judgment of the Cornish. The would-be purchaser of the calves
had clearly " laid a load " on poor John Hocken. It is by no
means an uncommon occurrence, and there are a considerable
number of people who derive a handsome income from the
useful occupation of taking off such loads. There was one
who did it by rubbing his patients all over with "something
that smoked," but he shared the fate of many other friends of
humanity and became obnoxious to the police. I add another
tale of witchcraft, which came within my own experience, and
which is a fair sample of the transactions now taking place
from day to day between the peasants and those white witches
in whom, for the most part, they have a confidence far
exceeding that which they bestow on any doctor.

The circumstances were these. A girl, the daughter of poor
parents, was seized with fits—epileptic, I should imagine—but
no one can speak with any certainty about this because no
doctor was called in. The witch, however, was consulted.
She shook her head, said the case was serious, and in all
probability the girl had been bewitched by somebody. They
had better take her away, try to discover who it was, and
bring her back in a week. Before the week was up the witch's
intelligent suggestion had produced its effect. The girl began
to dream every night of a stout elderly woman with a very red
face, who approached her in a very threatening manner, and
the parents hurried off to report this new and alarming symptom
to the witch. Of course the witch was triumphant. There
could not be a doubt that the red-faced elderly lady of the
girl's dream had wrought the mischief. It only remained to
identify her. Did the parents know anybody who answered to
the girl's description ?

Now there lived at no great distance from the girl's cottage an old widow lady, charitable, popular, and highly respected, but stout, and having an unfortunately red face. No one had ever suspected her of any but kind and benevolent actions; but this fact, the witch argued, really made the case against her stronger, since it was well known that all persons who practised magic were extremely apt at diverting suspicion from themselves. It is human to err occasionally; so that when you find any one who appears not to err at all, you will do well to suspect some agency which is not human. Besides, if the old lady had not bewitched the girl, what was she doing in her dream?

There was no resisting these arguments. They would have been ample 150 years ago to set the poor old lady swimming in the river, which, of course, would have been much the best way of breaking the spell. As that, unhappily, was impossible, the next best way was to go by night to the old lady's house, take a stone from her garden wall, and put it into the kitchen fire at the girl's house. When it was charred away the fits would cease; and, indeed, they would cease earlier still if the cure could be helped by hanging round the girl's neck the finger of a man who had hanged himself; but such things were hard to come by.

Fortune favoured the girl. A man hanged himself that very week in a hamlet near at hand. The suicide's finger was secured, used as the witch had directed, and the fits ceased almost immediately. This case occurred in the year 1887.

Far and wide as we ride through the undulating country between Mitchell and Newquay we see the spire of Cubert Church outlined against the skyline, surmounting one of the highest ridges near the sea. It is a handsome spire, and there are features of interest about the church; but that which leads me to follow a cross road heading in that direction is the attraction of its singularly lovely well, which is like no other in Cornwall, and was sanctified so long ago as to give to the

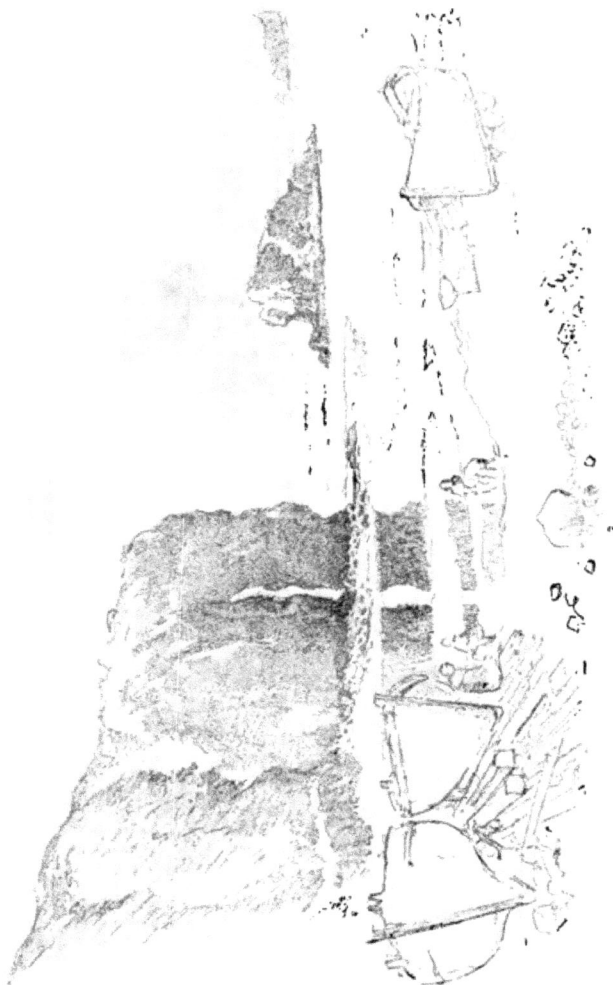

Perran Porth.

beach by which it stands the name of Holywell. When we stand beside the church at Cubert we look out westwards over an immense waste of blown sand which is said to cover the site of a great and ancient city, overwhelmed in a single night by this doom. It is easy to credit some part of this tradition ; for it is only in the last few generations that any effort has been made to restrain the movements of the sand ; and the swaying to and fro of the vast restless mass has in present memory destroyed both farms and fields. Legend, which is so positive about the lost city of Langarrow, declared with equal certainty that the ancient church of St. Piran, the first founded by the Irish bishop when St. Patrick despatched him into Cornwall, lay buried here underneath the sand, and in 1835 it was discovered. In this case, therefore, legend did not lie. It rarely does ; but it is little likely that the towers and streets of lost Langarrow will ever be laid bare, for the growth of reeds and couch grass has checked the motion of the hills, and fixed their outlines, and strewn a thin turf over them which will grow yearly thicker till some day the dunes will be fertile ploughing land, and the lost city will not come to light till in some future age occasion arises for digging there.

But let us go onwards to the shore. A road leads down from the church to a fine bay, shut in between two lofty headlands, off which a couple of large rocky islets on the western side stand mysterious and dark, the haunt of innumerable breeding sea-birds. In the eastern cliff, at the head of a deep gully into which the tide runs swiftly near high water, a spur of rock is cut into deep steps, worn out no less by the feet of pious pilgrims in past ages than by the fretting of the waves. At the head of these steps, in a grotto in the cliff, a spring of the purest water issues from some crevice in the rock and drips from basin to basin of a beauty which exceeds description. For the whole grotto has suffered a sea-change ; and its roof and walls are tinted with colours richer than were ever shown by seaweed washing in a still pool, or by anemones which

display their gems of emerald and carmine when the sea has
run out of some lonely crevice of the wet rock. All shades of
green and pink and purple stain the roof and walls of this
lovely cavern. Stalactites hang from the roof, and the water
overflows from one pink basin to another till it drips away
noiselessly among the boulders and gravel which form the
pavement of the grotto.

It is little wonder that a place so exquisite should have been
counted holy in past days ; and we read that in old times, when
faith was stronger on the earth, mothers came hither in incredible numbers, and from distant regions, bringing deformed or
sickly children to be dipped for the cure of their infirmities.
The waters were very potent then ; and many a cripple left his
crutches in a crevice near the well and went bounding home
across the sands without them. Even yet there are those who
trust in the virtue of the well ; but they are few, and for the
most part one sees little on the lonely beach but the coming
and the going of the tide.

The shortest way to Newquay from Cubert is across the river
Gannel, but as there is only a narrow plank-bridge, the way is
troublesome for cyclists. Yet we will take it ; for the river is
not only picturesque but is the scene of superstitions which are
worth mentioning.

The Gannel is a tidal river which flows down to the sea
through a deep and wide valley, or rather a gorge in the hills.
The fresh-water stream winds like a narrow riband over the
wide expanse of sand which fills the bottom of the valley ; and
at low tide foot-passengers cross the water on a bridge consisting of a single plank, while vehicles of all kinds drive through
a ford close by. At the proper time this is safe enough ; but
when the tide begins to flow, the salt water races through the
gorge with astonishing speed ; the little foot-bridge is submerged, and the ford, even at the first coming of the tide, is
easily missed.

The river has an evil reputation. Countless disasters have

occurred there ; and the souls of drowned men and women are perpetually flitting to and fro across the waste of sand, in the guise of little birds, pointing out to the traveller where the footing is secure. So runs one of the traditions ; and indeed the valley is infested by flocks of birds. But there is another sign of warning in this river bed, especially by night and when the salt water is streaming fast over the sandy flats. Then as the wayfarer pauses in doubt whether he can reach the foot-bridge, or the farmer in his gig hesitates before dashing into that wide stream which is fast drowning the ford, while his mare snorts and plunges as the water ripples round her feet in the darkness, suddenly a hoarse shriek resounds close beside him, a wild inarticulate cry, which the least superstitious man might interpret as a note of warning. It is the crake, and for many miles there is no man, woman, or child who, having once heard that scream, will not turn and go five miles round rather than cross the river-bed that day. Whence the warning comes, if indeed it be one, I know not. Some say the shriek is from a bird ; others again philosophise about noises in the wet sand ; while most of the peasants can tell a wild story about a wicked man who perished at the crossing in the endeavour to bring a priest to the bedside of a dying woman. His one good deed rescued his soul from utter damnation, and won for him the privilege of flying for ever about the scene of his act of self-sacrifice, gifted with the power of warning others in this wild way against the danger which proved fatal to himself.

There is an easy wisdom in smiling at such stories when one reads them in a warm well-lighted room ; but I have not always felt them ludicrous while driving down into the river valley on a winter evening. On such a night, when the hills are shrouded with vapour, the very sound of the surf beating on the rocks is enough to fill a man's fancy with strange thoughts : and I take no shame in admitting that it is sometimes an effort to drive the traditions from my mind.

There is another superstition on this coast, for an account of which I shall revert once more to the recollections of my friend the doctor, who gave me an interesting story quoted some way back about a fairy's grand-daughter, and whose popularity among the peasants has enabled him to collect great numbers of curious and striking scraps of traditional and superstitious learning.

" I was driving home in the dark one wintry evening," said the doctor, "when I saw a little group of people entering a solitary cottage by the roadside. The woman who passed in first was in tears, she was the tenant of the cottage and wife of a sailor whose ship was long overdue. Another woman, who seemed to be trying to console her, passed in with her, while the third member of the party, an old fisherman with whom I have held many curious conversations both before and since that evening, remained standing by the roadside. He greeted me and I dismounted. 'Any fresh trouble there, Peter?' I asked. 'Ez, zur,' he replied; 'poor Jan's drooned.' 'Then you have heard that the ship is really lost?' 'Naw, zur,' was the reply; 'oonly poor Jan.' 'Is the ship safe then?' 'Uz doan't knaw about the ship, zur. Betty, she said hur couldn't goo on like this waitin' and waitin' and not knawin' whether her man was dead or alive. So she went and called 'n on the shore,— down by the watter,' he added, seeing that I did not understand him. 'Well and what happened? Did you go with her?' 'Ez, zur,' he answered in his slow way; 'and Tamson Rickard over to Polmorth and Betty, her stood at the edge of the watter, crying out, "Oh, Jan, my man, my good man;" till Tamson catches her by the arm and tells her to hush: an' then, just very low, we heard 'n answer.' The old man shook his head and stepped back to allow me to proceed. There was something in his manner so solemn and dignified as effectually to check any disposition to pry further. He had the aspect of one who had indeed been present at an actual communing with the dead. The widow called her husband. They all heard the spirit answer; so much might be told, but what remained was sacred

to the bereaved woman's grief. I rode on after a few words of
sympathy ; and as I followed the coast road beneath which the

The Port, Newquay.

winter surges were beating heavily in the darkness, and glanced
out at the line of foam across which the drowned sailor had

answered the cry of his desolate wife, I began to wonder whether there might not be truth in some things, at least, across which we have long since drawn the bar of incredulity."

On Newquay Head a strong breeze is blowing off the land; and all the sea in that wide bay which lies between the great headland of Trevose far away to eastward, and Pentire, on the west, is ruffled over with white splashes, which come and go and change perpetually upon a bed of that glorious dark colour which is neither green nor blue. The coast-line is half veiled by a little haze, shadowy, faint, and opalescent, so that one can hardly say where the cliff meets sea till some sudden flash of white surges up from a breaking wave and goes again in haze as the swells come back and the broken water passes. Far away the dim line stretches, past Porth Island, with its blowhole spouting high as each wave rushes up the gulley, past Watergate, where huge dark caverns open upon golden sands, past Mawgan Porth, that loveliest of coves, where towering headlands enclose a beach as firm and even as a ball-room floor, past Bedruthan Steps, its strange rock forms all mingled and lost in the fine dim shadow, till, at Trevose, the land ends suddenly and nothing further east is visible. In the opposite direction great rollers are curling in across the mile-wide Bay of Fistral, torn into clouds of flying spray as they curve and break and scatter into whirlpools of lashing foam. Often when the afternoon sets towards evening, there are seals diving and plunging in quiet spots around this headland: and I recollect climbing down to the caverns which, from old tales of smuggling, derive the name of the "Tea-Caverns," and hearing in the dark recesses a long-drawn bellowing, which rose and fell and sometimes was like the sobbing of a child frightened by the darkness, and the slimy rock and the rattling of the pebbles dragged down by the waves on the little beach outside. A scanty light fell on a patch of sand, and on it lay a baby seal, left quite alone, and crying as if he feared he knew not what.

The most marked objects on the fine cliffs in sight from
Newquay are two barrows, which stand side by side on the
summit of the lofty headland of Trevelgue. From far and
near these twin mounds catch the eye ; and there is a tale told
among the peasants of two kings who fought all day long upon
that height until at last each killed the other, and they were
buried where they fell. In 1872 these graves were opened and
examined. Mr. Borlase inclined to think they were the
tombs of strangers in the west. If not, they were older than
most other interments in Cornwall ; but, whether native or
stranger, they were men of such consequence who lay here, that
fires were heaped up on the capstones covering the hollows
where the bodies lay, and kept burning for weeks, if not for
months, while all the time the funeral feasts were doubtless in
full progress on the cliff, and the longships lay beached in the
little cove below, where often, in these days, we may see a tiny
schooner canting over on the dry sand, while the country carts
come down for her cargo of heavy slates.

There is no choice of ways from Newquay. Mawgan is the
point for which all travellers make, a lovely village set among
tall elm trees which give a shade the more refreshing since the
surrounding country is so little wooded. Mawgan is at the
seaward extremity of the Vale of Lanherne, which runs from
St. Columb to the coast, and is all lovely. Every one will
stay there, to admire the fine old church and the beautiful
manor house of Lanherne, formerly the seat of one branch of
the great family of Arundel, of which another branch was
planted at Trerice ; a far more splendid house, three miles from
Newquay in the contrary direction, a place which should be
seen by all who visit this neighbourhood, not only on account
of its intrinsic beauty, but for the memories of old Sir John
Arundel, who defended Pendennis so nobly for the king.

Now the finest piece of coast about these parts is at
Bedruthan Steps, at no great distance from Mawgan, and it is a
place not to be missed, for the towering precipices are superb,

and the shore at low water is strewn with detached rocks and islands, which make up a scene unmatched in Cornwall, far surpassing the more famous beaches of the West. I could dwell at great length on its beauties and its grandeur ; but I am weary of descriptions which, after all, persuade few save those who are convinced already, and I shall therefore say no more about the coast until I am well into my next chapter.

I greatly doubt whether it can be understood by any save those who have lived among these people, how strangely their thoughts and actions are mingled with the traditions and superstitions of the past. Dead faiths and dead beliefs lie about this countryside like withered leaves in autumn. My feet rustle in them wherever I go ; and from day to day I encounter some hoary fragment of antiquity brought forth from a memory where the tradition of centuries has planted it, and displayed not as a curiosity, but as the ground of some important action.

A singular instance was presented to me not long ago. I had been visiting an old servant at a farm high on the border of the moor ; an aged woman, the widow of a freeholder, whose family record in the parish could be traced back almost to the first pages of the church registers. The old woman leads a lonely life in her distant farm, and is generally eager for such news as her visitors can give her. My chief piece of intelligence on the day in question was that a relation of my own, whom she had once seen, was about to be married. The woman was greatly interested, and asked the name of the bride. On hearing that it was Margaretta, she at once assured me that was a lucky name, and begged me most earnestly to let the bridegroom know how to reap the full advantage of the luck ; he must, it seemed, pluck a daisy on the eve of the marriage, draw it three times through the wedding ring, and repeat each time, very slowly, the words, "Saint Margaretta or her nobs."

But what, I asked, did this mystic formula mean ? To my

ears it sounded like pure gibberish, and I hinted as much.
But the old woman, though quite unable to assign any definite
meaning to the words, harped always back to the conviction
that they were lucky, and pleaded this so earnestly that I
should have given her real offence if I had seemed to doubt it.
Promising, therefore, that my relation should be duly warned
how to secure his luck, I took my leave, wondering rather idly
whether the nonsensical words had originally any meaning at
all. It was not until far on my homeward journey that it
flashed suddenly into my mind that the words were a prayer,
"Sancta Margaretta, ora pro nobis," a genuine Latin inter-
cession, handed down from Roman Catholic times. Who
knows with what rapture of devotion in days long past Saint
Margaret's prayer had been repeated in that very farmstead by
the lips of men and women taught to feel a personal attachment
to the saint. And though now even the holy character of the
words is forgotten, yet the fact that they have been kept in
memory through so many generations, in never so corrupt a
form, proves the strength of the feeling which once sanctified
them, showing that in some one's mind the prayer was stored
up not to be forgotten, with a lingering trust that it would
bring a blessing yet.

A somewhat similar fragment of antiquity lingers in the
neighbourhood of Redruth, where the country people when
they see a ghost say "Numny dumny," and it goes away. It is
not at all necessary to know what is meant by those words of
dread. The ghost knows, which is quite enough, and I leave
the riddle to be solved by any one who is curious enough to
undertake a useful piece of practice in unravelling the
corruption of language.

I cannot help it if my mind is stored with idle trifles. They
will out. There is a strange superstition in some parts of
Cornwall about the colour yellow. A man once called to see
my friend the doctor in great pain, which turned out to be due
to lumbago. But what he suffered from the ailment was as

nought to the astonishment which tormented him when he
found out its cause. He could not guess where on earth
lumbago could have come from, seeing that, since his last
attack, he had always worn a waistcoat made of the skin of a
cat killed on the 12th May—he did not know why that date
was especially effective, but it was no good to kill a cat on any
other. Was it possible that the remedy might have failed
owing to the presence of a few yellow hairs in the skin?
Everybody knew how bad yellow was for rheumatic people,
and indeed he had been acquainted with a man who walked
from Newquay to Bodmin in a yellow necktie and died of
rheumatic fever.

Alas! I must rein up my garrulity. There are such pretty
charms and fancies which I wanted to set down; but I should
have been long since on the high road to Wadebridge. Let
us climb up the hill out of Mawgan, and speed as quickly
as we may across the downs, past another group of merry
maidens with another piper playing on the hilltop, over a fine
furzy open road with a glorious view of dropping ground upon
the left, and far away a rugged coastline broken by the fine
inlet of Padstow Harbour, all shining in the evening sun.

It is a good and pleasant way to travel in bright spring
weather; but when the winter storms scud across the moors,
bringing up sleet and fog from the sea, it may go hard with that
traveller who is surprised upon this lofty road. Once, long ago,
a poor old woman went from St. Issey, which lies a little way
down the hillside towards the sea, to St. Columb on a market
day, and set out homewards when the dusk was falling. It
was winter time, and she would have done well to start earlier
on her long walk, but she had sold little and waited in the
hope of customers. As she trudged along with her heavy
basket the wind rose and the snow began to fall. Thick and
fast it whirled about her, falling heavier and heavier, and soon
it was quite dark, and the familiar landmarks were hidden by
the snow which drifted against every hedgerow and perplexed

her more and more till at last the poor old body stumbled off the road altogether, and the snow closed over her. There, buried in a deep drift she lay so long that she heard the bells of St. Issey Church ringing on two Sundays; and if she had sold out her basket she must have perished of hunger. As it was, her fingers and toes were lost by frostbite, but otherwise she was not much the worse when found.

CHAPTER XIX

I KNOW it is my duty in this work to refrain from obtruding my personal preferences on the reader; but this makes it very difficult for me to say anything about Wadebridge, which quiet little place I look upon with eyes reserved by every Cornishman for one place only in his native duchy. Mr. Pennell tells me it did not impress him; but he got there at low tide. It is as the tide is flowing that I like to think of the old town with its granite bridge of many arches. For, when the first signs of the coming flood sweep round the sandy bed from out the foldings of the hills, a cool salt wind runs up in advance, and almost before one has felt its freshness or tasted the briny odour on one's lips, the first wavelets are lipping already round the ancient buttresses, and great flocks of ducks and geese sail by with a portentous quacking, all noisily rejoicing in the flow of dark foamy water which rushes up more impetuously every moment, cutting off the corners of the large waste banks, and drowning them deeper and deeper under the rippling waves. When the tide is out, it is as if the town had lost its soul; but life and energy come back with the flowing water. A string of barges rounds the point on its way up from Padstow, and a couple of small schooners forge slowly onward underneath those hills which the sunset is dyeing rose and purple.

This valley of the river Camel is full of haunted lanes and houses. A mile or so up the river stands the ancient church of

Egloshayle. Under a night-sky the church is scarcely visible. But if the clouds roll back from the moon, and let a sudden blaze of light fall over the river bed, you will see the old gray tower clearly, standing out from a group of chestnut trees, and may even discern an open space beside the churchyard wall where the high-road meets the lane leading to the village. The road gleams beneath the moonlight; but you are too far distant to see any object moving on it.

A Cornish Mill near Wadebridge.

If it were otherwise, you might now see—but never save when the moon is bright—a white rabbit gambolling about this open space beside the churchyard wall; a pretty, long-eared rabbit with pink eyes, like any child's pet escaped from its hutch. It goes loppeting about among the grasses by the corner of the marsh; and if any one should pass, will sit and look at him with fearless eyes. And well it may. It has nothing to dread from any one dwelling in those parts. No villager would attempt to catch it. No boy would aim a blow

at it. If any one walking late sees the white rabbit lopping at
his heels, he makes no effort to drive it away, but quickens his
pace, and hopes some good angel may stand between him and
harm. A belated postman, terrified to find he could not shake
off the pretty white creature at his heels, lost his head and
turned and struck fiercely at it with his oaken cudgel. He felt
the stick fall on the soft back of the rabbit, such a blow as
might have killed a much larger animal. But the rabbit lopped
on as if nothing had happened. The cudgel it was which was
broken—shivered into splinters, as if it had struck upon a rock.

No one can tell the history of the rabbit; but our grandfathers knew and feared it as we do ourselves; and it was in
their time that the last deliberate effort to meddle with the
creature took place. The attempt was made by a stranger, and
it happened in this wise. A number of young men were drinking together in the bar-room of the chief inn of the town. As
the evening wore away, the talk grew high; and, at last, when all
the party were heated, somebody spoke of the white rabbit.
Instantly the stranger began to jeer—a silly story such as that
would never be believed outside a poky country town where
nobody had anything better to do than to listen to the first idle
tale told him. What harm could a rabbit do anybody? He
would like nothing better than to shoot it.

One of the others drew aside the shutter and looked out.
The street was as bright as day, and overhead they could see
the full moon sailing, free of clouds. "Tha'd best go now," he
said. "When the moon shines like this, tha'll find the rabbit
by the church."

A gun was hanging on the wall. It was taken down and
loaded amid a babble of jeers and angry retorts: and then the
party crowded to the door to watch the stranger stride down
the moonlit street, whistling merrily as he went. They saw
him pass upon the bridge, and then went back to their
bottles.

But some strange feeling of uneasiness had settled over them.

Not one seemed inclined to sit down again. They moved
restlessly about the room, and presently one of them went to
the door and looked out. The others asked eagerly if he heard
anything, though they knew the stranger could not have reached
the church ; and then one suggested that it was a shame to
allow a man who had no knowledge of his danger to encounter
it alone. The others agreed as readily as men will when they
have done what does not please them, and without more delay
they set off in a body. They trudged along saying nothing ;
but when they came near the church, they heard a report and
a loud cry ; and, with one accord, they ran to the open space
with beating hearts. Neither man nor rabbit was to be seen.
They ran up and down calling his name ; there was no reply.
He was not in the lane, nor on the high road, nor on the marsh,
where, under the bright moonlight, the motion of a water hen
could have been seen with ease. At last one of the searchers
leapt up on the churchyard wall, and sprang down on the inner
side, calling on his friends to follow him. There they found
him lying dead, with one barrel of his gun discharged, and the
contents buried in his body. That happened many years ago ;
but still the stranger may be seen leaning over the low wall,
pointing an ancient flint-lock gun at some object which moves
quickly in the long grass.

Does any one realise, I wonder, how large a part superstition
plays in the lives of persons dwelling in the West? This is not
the place in which to dwell at length on such a subject ; but as
it is one of those which come most prominently before all who
obtain more than a superficial acquaintance with Devonshire
and Cornwall, I think it worth while to enumerate very briefly
the stories which are told, whether on good authority or bad
makes little matter, of this one small country town and its
immediate neighbourhood.

On one side of the river is Tregeagle's parish. The manor
house in which that wild and wicked spirit dwelt in life is now
a farm. One autumn afternoon the farmer had occasion to go

down to the town just as dusk was falling. His wife accompanied him, and they left no one in the house. It was dark when they returned ; and they had no sooner set foot in the farm-yard than they saw the house was lighted up in all its windows. The shutters were unclosed. Strange forms in antique dresses were passing to and fro. A long table was set with bottles and decanters such as the farmer never saw ; and the most unholy noise was issuing from the room. Shouts, oaths, scraps of obscene song, bursts of wild laughter, appalled the two simple people who stood barred out from their home. At last the farmer plucked up **courage**, and marched up to the door. **He** had no sooner put the key in the lock than every light went out. The howls and cries dropped instantly **into** silence. The **sudden** absolute stillness was **as** awful **as** the noise. The farmer and his wife went from room **to** room, but all were empty, and of the riotous carousal there was not one trace.

Not far from the farm where this occurred stands another containing a **room** of which this uncanny thing is said—that if you are left alone in it by night, a small, cold hand **is** gently laid in yours. Nothing **is** seen, nothing is heard, but, softly, confidingly, as **if** human warmth were what it **sought,** this little icy palm **steals into** yours, and nestles there.

Again, in that same neighbourhood, there were found beneath the flooring of an upper room the bones of a full **grown man** with the remnants of a slashed doublet and other antique clothing of the Stuart time, relics of a **foul** murder done two-hundred years ago. The cavalier still revisits the scene. His lovelocks drop over his shoulder as **if he** were alive, and in the grey light of early morning his spurs ring sharply on the old oak floor.

I could extend this list **to** three times its present length, did I not fear that, to all but a chosen few, the recital of tales which are half forgotten and by many people wholly disbelieved must prove quickly wearisome. Yet it is **a** fact surely not destitute of value, or at least of curious interest, that beliefs of this kind are still so thickly strewn, like the dead leaves of former centuries, all over modern England.

There are several places which are visited more easily from Wadebridge than from any other town ; and among them is that range of coast which, however little known, I maintain to be beyond comparison the finest in all Cornwall. The distance from Wadebridge to Pentire Point is about seven miles ; and wise men will go right out upon the headland to its furthest point, where they will see a sight such as is not to be seen elsewhere.

For Pentire, which must not be confounded with the smaller headland of the same name near Newquay, has two points. The one first reached is the Western Horn, a buttress of amazing strength and massiveness thrust out far into the ocean. On the left hand lies Trevose, clearly marked by the light-house half way down its abrupt declivity as well as by a cruel reef of rocks which on the stillest days the blue sea marks with a patch of white. Nearer still the high grassy slopes of Padstow Point stand out grandly, topped by an ancient land-mark, and passing round it one looks up the whole depth of Padstow Harbour, so famous and so lusty in its enterprises until the vengeance of a mermaid choked up the port with sand. A brown discolouration stretches across the wide entrance nearly from side to side. That is the Doom Bar, and the woful name is truly earned ; for that ship which misses the narrow channel on the west, so narrow that her yard arms almost scrape the rocks, is doomed beyond all hope of safety. On this side of the harbour lies a sandy spit with low slate cliffs of a deep purple colour, parting it from a lovely bay whose wide firm sands and deep rock pools are the most beautiful upon the coast.

That is the western view. On the east the prospect seems almost boundless. Port Isaac Bay lies just below, sweeping far back into the land, half hidden by the Eastern Horn of Pentire which we have yet to visit. Across the bay, Tintagel lies

directly opposite, eight miles away over the sea, every crevice and
gulley of its riven island clearly marked in the translucent air ;
and beyond it the eye follows leagues and leagues of iron cliffs
towering far higher than any others in the west, and point after
point of noble jagged promontories, past Boscastle, set back a
little out of sight, past Bude and Cambeak, and rugged Moor-
winstow, till it rests at last on the dim line of Hartland Point,
full forty miles away as a bird would fly.

It is idle to compare any other view in the west country with
this either in extent or grandeur, or in the immediate beauty of
its surroundings.   It is little known, and rarely visited by any
but by shepherds.   Yet it is more easy of access from Wadebridge than the Land's End or the Logan from Penzance ; and
there will be some to whom its very loneliness is an additional
attraction.   However this may be, those who leave Cornwall
without visiting Pentire have missed its noblest scenery.

A sheep-path along the seaward brow of the great headland
leads us past deep jagged ravines which gash the scarred
face of the cliff full three hundred feet down to the blue sea
below.   Their slopes are covered with short sweet grass, and
wherever the peaks and spires of granite jut upwards through
the herbage, there ivy has rooted itself on the sheltered side
of the rock, and crept thickly over the stained surface.   The
sheep-path leads across a rising ground, and brings us suddenly
in sight of a bay of the most surprising beauty, a deep rect-
angular inlet on whose landward face a precipice of amazing
height drops down, sheer and straight, into water deep enough
to float an ironclad.   On the nearer side there is a steep and
dizzy slope of grass out of which project pillars and arches of
granite which are piled with quite unequalled beauty ; and on
the east the bay is closed by a high narrow promontory ending
in a lofty peak.   This neck of rocky land is one of the most
perfect of those strange cliff castles which to this day perplex
the antiquary.   There are triple mounds and ditches cut across
it, intended plainly for defence ; but who the people were that

took refuge in this lonely fastness, or from what enemies they were fleeing, are among the secrets which this wild western country has not yet disclosed. Landward foes, one may guess, they must have been ; for even on this perilous coast sober men do not take refuge from foreign pirates within arm's length of the sea. There are few headlands in Cornwall where such defences cannot be traced ; and the warfare must have been fierce and long continued which caused them to be dug and built.

Those quarrels of old times seem very distant as one paces by the grassy mounds, which are abandoned to the rabbits and the seabirds. Where is now the dense population which made these refuges? For miles around there are only scattered farms and hamlets ; and you may walk all day upon these glorious cliffs without meeting any creature more human than a seal. The rock forms are superb. There are deep caves and lofty islands, and changing colours, and beauty in such wild profusion that the day will surely come, when this range of coast will be the most famous in all Cornwall.

The cliffs from Padstow to Hartland may properly be treated all together, for indeed there is a certain unity among them, just as there is about the two districts of the Lizard and the Land's End, a unity of tradition, of history and of peril to the mariner. And to take the last subject first, since we shall not again stand in a position so apt for estimating the dangers of the sea upon this coast, we may set down here a rhyme which is current all around the district.

> From Padstow Point to Hartland Light
> Is a watery grave by day or night.

It needs but an unskilled glance over the cliffs within a line drawn from one to the other of those points to comprehend the force of this grim saying ; and never a winter passes by without drawing some ship across this fatal boundary, and sending her crashing on the rocks where there is neither beach nor landing, but deep water up to the very bases of the cliffs. Not many years ago, as I have heard from those who saw it, a tall three-masted ship was driven by October storms within the line, and lay slowly foundering off the island of Trebar-with, a little on this side of Tintagel. The sea ran mountains high, and the Port Isaac lifeboat could not get out, though she made more than one attempt. And so the people stood gathered on the cliff in the winter dusk, and watched in silence till at last there came a great spout of water towering high into the air from the deck of the ship, and in another moment she had disappeared. Now as the people turned away, one of them saw something white lying on the grass. It was the photograph of a girl, and the wind had blown it out of the drowning hands of one, afterwards identified, who did not let it go until both it and all other earthly things had passed beyond his knowledge. Nothing else than this scrap of pasteboard came ashore for many days.

All along this coast the stories one hears most frequently from the peasants are those which relate to a vessel called the *Black Prince*. Now this was a smuggling lugger owned by one whose name is infamous from Lundy to Padstow by the name of "Cruel Coppinger." I am not clear how far this worthy is historical. It may be that some half-formed myth has caught up his name and sported with it. There are features in his story which recall that of the pirate wrecker at Tregaseal. Like him Coppinger made his appearance from a foreign ship which was driven inside the fatal line already spoken of. By some marvel of strength or luck Coppinger reaches the shore, and has hardly done so when he springs on the crupper of a mule on which a timid maiden from some adjoining farm had ridden down to see the wreck, and urges the mule with its frightened burden back to the stable whence it came. What happened to the ship does not appear to be told in the fable; but Coppinger married the girl, using her with a cruelty which he displayed in all his dealings, and which was sufficient to establish in a brief time something like an absolute empire of terror over the wild seamen of the lonely creeks on the north coast, as well as over their more law-abiding neighbours. There were certain roads and paths which by Coppinger's orders were absolutely closed at night except to his own followers ; and strange as it may seem, his orders to avoid them were obeyed, and even enforced with shocking brutality on those few who dared to disregard them.

There is hardly any creek from Hartland to Pentire where the *Black Prince* and Coppinger are not well known even now. I have heard of them as far west as Newquay ; but that was beyond their usual beat, and the bulk of their deeds were wrought north of Pentire. There is however a cave in the latter headland which is supposed to have been in some way connected with Coppinger ; and Mr. Baring Gould selects it for the scene of his novel " In the Roar of the Sea," in which Coppinger is a central figure. Indeed it is not easy to say which part of the coast was most associated with this man who terrorised it all ; and when at last the country became too hot to hold him, and in answer to some signal a strange ship appeared off the coast to which Coppinger put out in a raging storm and was never seen more, one long gasp of relief ran along the villages, and in every cottage and hillside farm the people breathed more freely.

There will be more to say of Coppinger and of the Gauger who was as brave and fierce as he, when we get into the neighbourhood of Morwinstow ; but we have first to reach Tintagel ; and it will be right to look in at Port Isaac on the way ; for that little fishing town, which has been hard hit by the decayed condition of its only industry, is placed in a striking cleft of rock, and in some ways recalls Polperro. It lies at the foot of a hill which is famous all round the country side for steepness and for length ; and when one has climbed down the precipice, one plunges into a winding street of quaint white houses which are as much for the harbourage of fish as for that of human beings.

The streets are old and narrow. The harbour is deep and walled between high black cliffs. The tide comes lapping up a little shingly beach pleasantly enough in this spring weather; though none who have once seen it dragged back so far during the October storms that one might think it was about to leave the harbour empty, and then hurled forward mountains high

Port Isaac.

with the force and power of a battering ram, can ever look at it without dread again. There are pitiful sights to be seen in Port Isaac at such times ; and I have heard the women tell how they have watched the fishing fleet lie all day outside the harbour fighting with the tempest, but unable to get in, while they who stood trembling on the cliffs often lost sight of it in the trough of the sea for as much as a quarter of an hour at a

time, and held their breath lest they should never see any of
the boats again.

There are pretty lanes between Port Isaac and Tintagel, but
there is nothing of sufficient interest to detain those whose
minds are full of Uther Pendragon and the dwelling place of
King Arthur and his Knights. The approach is through a long

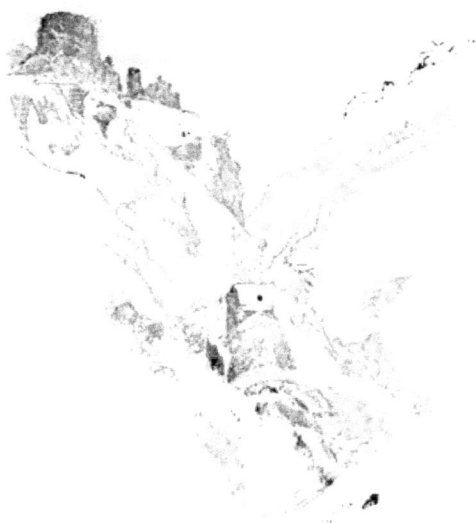

Tintagel, Arthur's Castle.

and winding village into a ravine which falls steep and narrow
towards the sea. Looking upwards when the shore is close at
hand, one sees that the spur of high ground on the left has
been cleft by a vast wedge-shaped chasm, leaving its extremity
connected by a tongue of rocks so narrow that it will some day
surely be an island. On both sides of this ravine are the
remains of old grey walls and towers, approaching the edge of

The Rocky Valley near Tintagel.

the cliff so closely that one can hardly doubt both to have been
integral parts of the defences. But what then has become of
the intervening space? Did ·solid rock once stretch between
the mainland and the island, and was the fortress continuous
between the two? Tradition tells us of a drawbridge which
spanned the gorge; but the width and depth are far too sheer
and awful in these days for any such expedient. Probably many
yards of the rock have slipped and slid away in modern times,
making the chasm much wider than it was of old; for there is
now no access to the island save by a climb so steep and
difficult as forbids the supposition that there was no other road
by which supplies could be brought in. It is a strange eyrie
which one finds at the top, a rough waste of grass slopes and
low walls, amid which one may yet make out the enclosure of
a chapel, a strange wild place in which to plant a human
dwelling, at the mercy of every storm that blows.

It is not easy to keep one's fancy in the present as one sits
or lies among the ruins of this famous Castle, watching the sea
pour over the black rock ledges far below, or gazing past the
old church on the headland, whose bells tolled without mortal
ringers on the day when the body of the blameless king was
borne away to its tomb at Glastonbury. But how these stories
vary! Here is not a word of Dozmaré, or of the valley of
Avilion! Who knows what the truth may be? All that great
age of chivalry lies happily outside the period of records, in the
far lovelier land of fancy and imagination, where those who
visit it may follow what paths they will, bringing their own
light with them, and dissipating the shadows as they please.
Even in this place where Bors and Lancelot might have still
been household heroes, their memories are absolutely lost; and
the peasants have retained nothing out of all the glance and
glitter of those days save the one fancy that the king did not
really die, but was changed by enchantment into the body of a
chough, and still flies mornfully about these cliffs, or perches
on the broken walls of his noble Castle, a lonely, pathetic soul,

still waiting till the spell shall be broken, and he himself ascend the throne again.

The whole neighbourhood of Tintagel is wildly and superbly beautiful. There is not from Newquay up to Hartland one single mile of cliff which does not repay a visit, yet of it all the finest lies between Tintagel and Pentire. On that stern coast the sea is rarely calm ; and for one day on which it ripples in upon

The Rocky Valley, Tintagel.

the beaches there are three on which a stiff breeze sends it flying white around the headlands, or a heavy ground swell brings long rollers thundering all across the bay. There are nooks of coast where even in fine summer weather a heavy sea is far more common than a smooth one. Trebarwith Strand is one of them, and on that lovely beach under a warm July sun I have seen a sea breaking in which neither boat nor man could live.

I might add many pages of description, but to what purpose? I have said enough. Boscastle, St. Nightan's Kieve, Bossiney, the Rocky Valley, I can use no words which will convey their beauty. I will go onwards, leaving it to the exquisite pencil of him who is associated with me in this work to hit that mark at which I discharge arrow after arrow all in vain.

That traveller who is wise will give a wide berth to Bude, with its strand, its unsafe harbour, and its new hotels, and seek out Stratton, that ancient town which lies fast decaying in a hollow of the hills, no more than a mile and a half away. For Stratton, deserted by the world, robbed by the tricks of time of all its old prosperity, still owns what no turn of fortune can deprive it of—charm of antiquity and of association. Nowhere in Cornwall are the cottages more picturesque, the streets more narrow or more obviously ancient. Into Stratton, that blighting aspect of prosperity which substitutes plate glass for antique lattices, and bull's eye panes, has never entered; and the consequence is that we see the place to-day, dominated by its ancient church, washed by its sparkling rivulet, gleaming among its apple orchards, the same angular pretty town as when Sir Bevil Grenville rode over from Stowe to do business at the Manor House where his giant servant Anthony Payne was born, or when the soldiery flocked down from Stamford Hill, after the great battle to seek food and rest in the little inns. To this day the townsmen can talk of little but Sir Bevil. You stay at the "Tree Inn," most comfortable of unpretending hostelries, a house of billowy corridors which rise and fall beneath your feet with the alternations of old age. It was the Manor House, and you are shown the room in which Sir Bevil did his business, the chamber in which his true-hearted servant died, and out of which his coffin could not be brought, so vast was the bulk which it contained, otherwise than through a hole cut out of the floor. You stroll over to the church and find the giant's grave; and the very children will tell stories of his strength and comeliness.

One Christmas Eve at Stowe the great fire in the hall had burnt low, and the servant sent into the woods with a donkey to gather fuel was long in bringing it, so that Lady Grace grew angry, and sent off Anthony to hasten him. The giant had not been long gone when he stalked back into the hall carrying both ass and logs together on his back, and under the great burden he strode out lustily, chanting, "Ass and fardel! ass and fardel, for my lady's yule." I have already told of the great and knightly act which he committed at Lansdown fight, when having seen the master whom he loved with every fibre of his great heart struck down and slain, he took the lad, little John Grenville, and set him on his father's horse, and bade him lead the Cornish troops to victory as his father would have led them had he lived. I think there is no finer story to be told than this; nor can there have been, since first men began to slay each other, many sights more noble than that of the child, tearful, excited, triumphant, set upon the great charger a world too high for him. and led up the hill at the head of his dead father's troops. When Sir Bevil fell. Lansdown fight was lost for the king, and in another moment the Cornish would have crowded down the hill. It was the quick nobility of Anthony Payne which won the battle; and the deed should give him an enduring place in history.

"Honoured Madam," wrote the brave retainer when the fight was done, "ill news flieth apace: the heavy tidings no doubt hath already travelled to Stowe that we have lost our blessed master by the enemies' advantage. You must not, dear lady. grieve too much for your noble spouse. You know, as we all believe, that his soul was in heaven before his bones were cold. He fell, as he did often tell us he wished to die, for the good Stewart cause, for his country, and his king. He delivered to me his last commands and with such tender words for you and for his children as are not to be set down with my poor pen, but must come to your ears upon my best heart's breath. Master John, when I mounted him on his father's horse, rode him into the war like a young prince, as he is, and our men followed him with their swords drawn and with tears in their eyes. They did say they would kill a rebel for ever hair of Sir Beville's beard. But I bade them remember their good master's word when he wiped his sword after Stamford fight; how he said, when their cry was 'stab and slay,' 'halt, men; God will avenge.' I am coming down with the mournfullest burden that ever a poor servant did bear, to bring the great heart that is cold to Kilkhampton vault. Oh, my lady, how shall I ever brook your weeping face? But I will be trothful to the living and to the dead. These, honoured madam, from thy saddest, truest servant, Anthony Payne."

There is a rare nobility in this letter, and it is a happy fate which has preserved it to our day. Trothful he was, a loyal, true-hearted servant all his days. And of him we may surely use those wistful words which we applied to his dear master: " If there be a dwelling for the spirits of good men; if as wise men think, great hearts do not perish with their bodies, rest thou there in peace." Ah, good Tacitus; how his heart yearned even while his lips rebuked its weakness! " If indeed there be a dwelling . . . . if . . . . if . . . ."

Ah well, the tears shed at Stowe are long since dried, and the trothful servant has slept in Stratton Churchyard, these two centuries and more, as soundly as his master at Kilkhampton. One goes on from Stratton through a pretty wooded valley. A noise of rushing water catches the attention, and one sees deep in the valley a thatched and whitewashed mill of many gables, half hidden by blossoming apple trees and the red bronze of newly opened sycamores. A shoot of water gleams and flashes in the sun, which lights up the dewy meadows on the hill and touches the yellow foliage of the trees with a golden sparkling. A little further on, from the rising of a hill, there is a fine backward view over all the lovely country to the sea coast lying dark in shadow as far as Tintagel; and after that a short run brings us to Kilkhampton, where we stay but a little while to

see the church with its fine pew ends and its poor monument
to Sir Bevil, and so push onwards to Morwinstow.

"Many a man still living will relate with glee," said Mr.
Hawker the famous vicar of Morwinstow, and I must observe
that he seems to tell these stories with less horror than is quite
becoming, "how they," that is to say the men of his piratical
and lawless parish, "used to rush at some well-known signal to

Morwinstow Church.

the strand, the small active horses, shaved from forelock to
tail, well soaped or greased from head to foot so as to slip
easily out of any hostile grasp: and then with a double keg or
pack slung on to every nag by a single girth, away went the
whole herd, led by some swift, well-trained mare, to the inland
cave or rocky hole which formed the rendezvous." Really all
this is very dreadful! Mr. Hawker even had a smuggler

gardener, one who had been kidnapped in his youth by cruel Coppinger, and from this aged reprobate he got many a tale of crime. Tristram Pentire was the bad man's name; and as I slander no one without giving the grounds of my ill word, I shall set down some of the conversations which Pentire had with Mr. Hawker, as they are reported for the eternal shame of Tristram in *Footprints of Former Men in Cornwall*.

"Sir," said old Tristram once, with a burst of indignant wrath, "that villain Parminter, the gauger, and his dog murdered with his shetting irons no less than seven of our people at divers times, and they peacefully at work at their calling all the while!" And with that Tristram plunged into an exciting story of how his friends were in the middle of landing a cargo on some beach not far away when, "just as the keel took the ground, down stormed Parminter shouting for Satan, his dog, to follow him. But the dog knew better and hung back, they said for the first time in his life; so in leaps Parminter smack into the boat alone, with his cutlass drawn; but"—with a kind of inward ecstasy—"he didn't do much harm to the boat's crew!"

"Because," I interposed, "they took him off to the ship?"

"No, not they; not a bit of it. Their blood was up, poor fellows, so they just pulled Parminter down in the boat and chopped his head off on the gunwale." The exclamation of horror with which I received this result elicited no kind of sympathy from Tristram. He went on quietly with his work, merely moralising thus, "Ay, better far that Parminter and his dog had gone now and then to the Gauger's Pocket at Tidnacombe Cross, better far."

It will probably be necessary to explain what the "Gauger's Pocket" was to which this wicked old man referred. It was a deep crevice in the ground behind the cross just named, into which the smugglers now and then, before any particularly desperate undertaking, used to slip a little bag of gold. Having done this, one of them would go to meet the gauger, and say to him when no one else was by, "Sir, your pocket is unbuttoned." Then the gauger, if he were a merry fellow, would reply with a twinkle in his eye, "Ay, ay, my man, but my money's safe enough." And then nothing remained but for him to walk out to the cross and make it safe, while the honest smuggler followed his calling in peace and friendliness.

Now if any one should feel impelled to remark that I have not always in this work professed such horror of malpractices upon the sea as I am evincing here, I do not know that I should be greatly troubled, for consistency has always seemed to me a thing scarce worth aiming at ; but I may point out that I am a great deal nearer to civilisation now, so that another attitude towards disorderly persons is natural and proper. Besides, did not the Latin philosopher remark sagely when puzzling himself as to why so few people confess their sins, "because they are in them still. *Somnium narrare vigilantis est*—it is only a waking man who can tell his dream." Well I have dreamt out my dream, and I beg that my morality may be judged by what I say when I am awake.

The most striking thing about the Churchtown of Morwinstow is that you do not know when you are there. In most places of the kind there are indications that you have arrived at the centre of the township ; but when you reach the heart of Morwinstow, you stand upon a scrap of barren common land, surrounded by three cottages, of which one calls itself an inn, and offers entertainment of the humblest kind. Of church or other houses there is not a sign ; nor does there appear to be room for them, since the edge of the cliffs is obviously close at hand ; and it is only on passing through a gate which seems to lead nowhere that you come at length in sight of the church, and of the vicarage built beside it in a spot where Mr. Hawker had seen the lambs resort for shelter from the storms.

Many strange things happened in this church during the

reign of the bad men I have been speaking of; and even
smuggled cargoes on occasion found a safe hiding place in the
ancient building. "We bribed Tom Hokaday, the sexton,"
said that unrepentant knave Pentire, "and we had the goods
safe in the seats by Saturday night. The parson did wonder
at the large congregation; for numbers of them were not
regular church goers at other times, and if he had known what
was going on he could not have preached a more suitable
sermon, for it was, "Be not drunk with wine, wherein is excess,"
one of his best sermons, but there, it did not touch us, you see,
for we never tasted anything but brandy or gin. Ah, he was a
dear old man, our parson, mild as milk, nothing could ever
put him out. Once I mind in the middle of morning prayer,
there was a buzz down by the porch, and the folks began to get
up and go out of church one by one. At last there was hardly
one left. So the parson shut his book and took off his surplice,
and he said to the clerk, "There is surely something amiss."
And so there certainly was, for when we came out on the cliff,
there was a king's cutter in chase of our vessel, the *Black Prince*,
close under the land, and there was our departed congregation
looking on. Well, at last Whorwell, who commanded our
trader, ran for the Gull Rock, where it was certain death for
anything to follow him, and the revenue commander sheered
away to save his ship. Then off went our hats and we gave
Whorwell three cheers. So when there was a little peace,
the parson said to us all, "And now, my friends, let us return
and proceed with divine service." We did return, and it was
surprising after all that bustle and uproar to hear how parson
Trenoweth went on just as if nothing had come to pass,
"Here beginneth the second lesson."

I have heard another story of an encounter between the
Black Prince and a revenue cutter which ended more murder-
ously than this Sunday morn's amusement off the Morwinstow
cliffs. I shall suppress some of the names of still existing
families which were mentioned by my informant; but as the

whole story is now a century old or more, there can be little
indiscretion in saying that the commander of the schooner on
this occasion was called John Moffat, and that he dwelt at
Lower St. Columb. Somewhere in the neighbourhood of Porth,
of which secluded little creek the smugglers made great use,
Moffat while following his calling met a revenue cutter who
disputed passage with him. The *Black Prince* had the heels of
most vessels on the coast ; but either Moffat did not choose to
run, or he had not time, for he fired into the cutter, boarded
her, took and scuttled her, and slew or drowned every soul
among her crew, save one small midshipman who swam ashore,
and was rescued for the time by a woman named Jessy Varcoe,
who hid him in a cave. But the smugglers rarely did their
work negligently. They discovered the cave, found the lad,
and slew him in the presence of his protectress who, having
pleaded vainly for his life, turned and cursed them and their
ship with a savage fury that appalled them.

Now Jessy's curse did not fall idly, for the *Black Prince*
which sailed shortly afterwards was never heard of any more.
But those were not days in which it was quite safe to curse at
smugglers, however much provoked ; and not long afterwards a
certain lofty peak upon Trevelgue cliffs gained the name of
" Jessy's Jump," and for many years the children used to peer
over affrightedly down the dizzy height which poor old Jessy
leapt to expiate her curse.

Who knows which is the fact out of all these stories that is
safe to lean on? I sometimes wonder whether in all the tales
of sea life round the coasts of western England, some brave,
some terrible, some supernatural, and all daring and adventur-
ous, there may not be the scattered pages of a great sea epic.
Perhaps some day a writer will arise who can gather up these
fragments, and purge away their grosser parts, and bring out
their grandeur, and set it down in words so that all men may
hear the music of the storm wind, and the crash of the great
waves pouring over the black rock ledges, and the cannon

thunder and the merry flapping of the canvas as the ships went into action, and thus at length may know and understand what that great drama was that has been played along these coasts. The stage is strangely silent now. Is the last act over? When England is in peril again, will not the first cannon shot rouse those dormant forces into action, and make the West once more the school of England's greatness?

A deep and narrow valley runs down from the church to the sea at Morwinstow, and the winding path which threads it has seen many a sad procession headed by the vicar in his robes repeating the services of the church over the bodies of drowned sailors; for there is no parish on the Cornish coast where wrecks are more frequent or more fatal, and Hawker's record both of help rendered to the living and reverent attention to the dead has won him a name which will be famous on the coast for many a generation yet to come. At length the path emerges on a low cliff between two precipitous grassy slopes. On the east towers Hennacliff, on the west another hill of almost equal height, while the tide ebbing not far below reveals a cruel reef of rocks, jagged and sharp, which have torn the life out of many a tall ship, and will so tear many another yet.

One needs good legs and wind to scale Hennacliff; but the view repays the effort. For there stretching westwards in the fresh clear air lie all the noble promontories we are leaving, the Dazard, Cambeak, Tintagel, and Pentire, rising one behind another, while a gusty wind scatters the flying water round their bases, and as far as one can see the dark blue ocean is roughened with white moving splashes. This glorious view is present with us all the afternoon as we walk eastwards to see the combes between Morwinstow and Hartland. It is heavy walking, for the combes follow quickly one upon another, and the hills above them sweep down sudden and abrupt from an altitude of 300 feet to the very level of the sea. The first is shallow, and its stream runs insignificantly through low scrub. But the next makes amends; for as you climb

cautiously down its break-neck slope, you become aware that
the glen is opening at every step, disclosing deeper and deeper
views of sloping woodland whose fresh verdure is a miracle of
loveliness. There, sheltered from the storms that beat so
close, the trees grow tall and straight, and ferns and trailing
ivy overhang the trout stream that brawls away beneath them
to the sea. Another hill surmounted, and one looks down on
a wide, open, grassy valley, filled with invigorating breezes, and
the loud sound of rushing water. For the brown stream which
sings out of golden woods higher up the valley, turns a mill on
the open ground near the sea ; and here also is a sawpit in
which two men are working busily. The sharp scent of the
sawdust is blown up to where I stand among the furze. A
little terrier discerns me on the height and resents the rare
intrusion. The men stop working ; the children run out of
the mill to see the stranger. It is their one excitement. In
this season it may be three weeks ere another comes. And so
I cross the stream in the bottom of the open valley, and climb
up the hill beyond, and regain the road which runs inland
from Morwinstow to Hartland.

CHAPTER XX

THE aspect of the corner of the world which we have attained is one of strange and beautiful surprises. For the roads, with few exceptions, run along the ridges of a bare and unlovely country, while the valleys into which they sometimes drop are as rich as the warm west wind can make them, bringing soft moisture and stimulating rain into the bosom of the woods and orchards. Never was a country so gashed with deep recesses ; and you wander all day through one more lovely than another, emerging again in sight of the rough coast with the rocks of Lundy in the distance, now faint and blue in the noonday heat, and now sharp cut in the clearer evening air, till at last you come down upon the ancient church of Stoke, standing grandly in full sight of the sea, a beacon and a watchtower for troubled mariners since its first stones were laid by the Saxon Githa, mother of King Harold.

There is a smithy outside the churchyard stile, and a wide-spreading tree makes a gloom through which the furnace fire flashes red and dark, while the merry tinkling of the anvil makes me linger on the stile to listen. I hear it clanking gaily as I wander up and down the cool aisles of the beautiful church, and as I roam onwards to the cliff the sound is with me still, mingling with the hum of insects among the countless flowers that blossom in the short turf. And so I look for the last time on the range of Cornish cliffs, and turning eastwards

see the wide opening of Bideford Bay, and the country which
none of us can ever think of without remembering Charles
Kingsley and *Westward Ho!* But in the wide sea view from
this point of cliff Lundy is the most noticeable object ; and it
is one on which we look in these peaceful days with small
comprehension of the feelings it excited in those who dwelt
along these coasts two centuries ago. For the little crag set so
menacingly in the track of ships coming up and down the
Bristol Channel, and even more in the stream of ocean traffic
to Barnstaple and Bideford, has not only a dismal record of
shipwrecks, but was a heaven-sent point of vantage for pirates
and for privateers. Indeed, if all the records of English
history were lost, one might safely assert that pirates must have
clustered on an island where the fattest prizes were constantly
passing within arm's length, and out of which nothing but a
strong fleet could drive them, and that only in favourable
weather. The uses of the island were so obvious that they
could scarce escape the dullest understanding ; and in matters
of acquisitive self interest the understandings of our ancestors
were by no means dull. And so a very superficial delving
among old records shows that the capabilities of this convenient
station were never wasted from at any rate the twelfth century,
when the piratical family of Marisco swept the Channel of
anything it might happen to want, until the commencement of
the present century, when, as I have often said during the
progress of this work, an era set in so strangely different from
any other in our history that it is not quite easy to prophesy
what may come of it.

But prophecy is not required of us ; nor is this the place to
enter into the merry story of the Mariscos, who married into
the Plantagenets and forfeited the island through their turbu-
lence, but defied everybody notwithstanding the decree of
forfeiture, and sought alliances with France, and were forgiven
again, and were sometimes hung and drawn and quartered, but
for the most part did just what they pleased and snapped their

fingers at authority, filling their castles with "devils and evil men." Life on Lundy is said to be very dull now; but this is the fault of our over-sensitive modern morality. Nothing like dullness was ever heard of at Lundy in old days; for when the Mariscos were at last dispossessed, other persons took up the game that they had dropped and played it with just the same gaiety. Captain Salkeld ruled it in the interest of a gang of buccaneers of which he was the chief. It does not seem to be known with precision what became of the gallant captain. Pirates even in later days than his were apt to drop out suddenly, and it was usually wasted breath to inquire where they were. A squadron of Sallee Rovers fixed their head-quarters at Lundy in 1625, and I should imagine they did very well among the Bristol shipping; in fact as nobody seems to have been at pains to drive them out, I conclude they made their fortunes and retired to spend them in the glowing east. Admiral Nutt was the next officer in command at Lundy; I do not conceive that his naval title rested on any higher authority than that of the pirates he had gathered round him. It took a fleet of a dozen vessels to repress the Admiral; and the fact that such an armament was got together for the purpose shows an excitement of public feeling from which we may infer that the Admiral's attention to business had been close and constant. Then came a Spanish Privateer, and after the Restoration French pirates possessed the rock, all gathering in large tolls, so that Lundy was in a sense the turnpike gate at the junction of the roads to Bristol and Bideford. There was always somebody to take money at the pike; and in the end I suppose the merchants taught themselves to look upon these forced contributions with philosophy, and allowed for them in their charter parties just as they did for "outrageous tempest of the sea."

Much worse than the pirates was the last famous occupant of Lundy, one Benson, who having obtained a contract from the Government for exporting convicts to Maryland, shipped

them off to Lundy instead, and employed them there as his
personal slaves. The idea was bold and original: but I take
no pleasure in writing about villains, and those curious about the
particulars of Benson's history must kindly seek for them elsewhere. I have said enough to show that the cruel reefs round
the southern end of Lundy were not the only nor the greatest
danger feared by those who saw its craggy outline rising out of
the sea on returning from some distant voyage. The island
was a lair of wolves. Its memories are all tragic, and a dark
Chapter of Channel history was closed when law gained power
over Lundy. The piracies of Fowey or Dartmouth were but
the rougher aspects of a life which had its noble side. But the
piracies of Lundy were not compensated by any services to
England. They were mere rapine; and the world was the
richer when they ceased.

It is very usual to speak of the country between Hartland
and Clovelly as bare and ugly. But surely there is something
effeminate in the taste which can see nothing beautiful in these
long ranges of rounded hilltop, so green, so thickly studded
with golden furze, hills on which the clouds stand piled in
fleecy ranks and over which the air blows with a freshness unknown in a tree-clad country. But if trees one must have, they
are not so far to seek, for every mile brings up a richer landscape,
till at last, when the road begins to drop towards the sea, the
outlook is across a prospect which in varied beauty has surely
few equals in this country. The ground dips rapidly, and
beyond the valley rise the park enclosures of Clovelly Court,
dotted over with red cattle grazing peacefully in the sun.
Further back a dark hill rises, lying sombre under a cloud
shadow, while the green and red fields higher on the slope
catch the sun, and just beyond them the sea stretches far and
wide, all tinted with the palest turquoise, with here and there a
darker patch upon it. Lundy lies like a flat table in the distance. Suddenly the sun shines out and the bay turns a deeper
blue. The path plunges downwards, tall trees rise around it

through which one catches glimpses of sea and cliff and a deep valley below, set in a frame of tender green and yellow foliage.

The Gateway, Clovelly.

A rich scent of flowers is in the air, and as yet there is no taste of the sea, but all around is green shade, and an azure mist of bluebells. Then suddenly the trees break away a little, and one sees far below a reach of brown water breaking on a shingly shore, and the roofs and chimneys of a little town. But the trees march with one up to the first houses of the town, and the blackbirds and thrushes whistle in the silent wood just above the street.

What is like Clovelly, and with what similitude shall I make clear the aspect of the most exquisite town in England? There is none. One is the richer in experience for having seen Clovelly; elsewhere there is nothing like it. I sit on the balcony of the New Inn, a pleasant hostelry with old bow windows. I have but this moment left the woods, and their green shade is close to my right hand. Below me lies a scene more exquisite than could have been devised by the wit of man deliberately set to produce what is picturesque. For it is surely very strange that this village, during all the centuries of its existence, has grown, if grown it really has, along lines of perfect beauty. How many villages one has seen defaced and ruined by the destruction of an old house front, or the building of new shops? But here is nothing, absolutely nothing, commonplace or ugly; not a modern house-front, not a shop, save here and there a cottage window filled with photographs or gaudy Barum ware. Not even a dissenting chapel breaks the perfect curve with which the narrow street drops down the hillside between high peaked and gabled houses and humbler slated cottages with deep bow windows and diamond panes, and the fresh red-brown Virginia creeper trailing over them. The street is cut in steps and paved with cobbles, and up it comes a string of donkeys limping from the quay, straying into the cool shade of every open doorway which they pass, while the women come out and hang over the green balconies above and scold and chatter at the luckless driver, who defends himself in his slow western speech, and at last with many thwackings sets the head of the poor patient donkey straight again, and goes up three steps more when the same process is repeated. It is warm and sunny. The white

clouds drift slowly over the tree tops. A little way below me
the street makes a bend, and over the houses I see the bay,
blue and brown and dotted with fishing boats ; and across it
lie the golden sands of Braunton and the dim high ground
which stands round Ilfracombe.

There is only one way by which any sober person dreams of
leaving Clovelly, and that is by the Hobby. A little way from
the entrance of this noble woodland drive just where the road,
after plunging inland, sweeps round suddenly towards the sea
again and a rustic bridge spans the valley, one looks down
again upon the town and sees how precipitously deep the
combe is to the sides of which it clings. The stream runs
down between high banks of overhanging fern, all blue and
white with wild flowers ; but further on the low oaks give way
to noble avenues of sycamore and beech, the bluebells vanish
and the slopes are covered with deep moss and strewn with
brown leaves of last year's fall. Soon the road passes over
another streamlet, hurrying down its winding channel to the
shore ; and then it rises, and from the opposite hill you look
back on the sea, framed by the noble sloping sides of the
combe all blazing with yellow foliage. Overhead a single bird
gives out a twittering note, but otherwise the silence is unbroken.

Then suddenly the road sweeps out on an open breezy
hillside amid fragrant furze and hawthorn bushes bursting bud ;
and you look down for the last time on the old world harbour
with its ancient pier slumbering at the foot of the steep white
houses ; and so the drive winds away out of sight of Clovelly
and our faces are set towards the eight miles of uninteresting
road between that little paradise and Bideford.

I did not mean to quarrel any more with Devon, but Prince,
who came sidling up again when I had half forgotten his
existence, really forces a dispute on me about the Grenviles.
Were they a Cornish or a Devon family? Can they be
classed as Bideford people with a country house at Stowe in

Bideford.

Cornwall, or are they more properly described as a Cornish family who kept a town house at Bideford, where they owned the manor? Who shall decide this problem, rendered doubly difficult by the fact that both at Bideford and at Stowe the settlement of the Grenviles dates back to a Norman of the name who conquered Glamorgan in the reign of William Rufus. Prince, who often hid a grasping disposition beneath a semblance of moderation, protests ingenuously that Cornwall cannot be allowed to have all the Grenviles, and then calmly appropriates them all for Devon. I, more honourably, have followed Fuller's principle. For he laid down that the Grenviles were enough to make one county proud, or two happy; and so in Cornwall I dealt with Sir Bevil only, conceiving that to the glory of his deeds, at any rate, Bideford can lay but little claim. For Sir Bevil's politics were little valued on the banks of the Torridge. Bideford, like Barnstaple, and indeed, most other towns in Devon, was heart and soul with the Parliament, and during the years preceding the outbreak, Sir Bevil's influence in Bideford must have declined as rapidly as it increased in Cornwall, where loyalty was a passion with all ranks and classes. There can be no doubt at all that the force Sir Bevil had the honour to command was rightly called "The Cornish Army." Devon men in some small numbers may have served in it. Some probably followed the gallant Slanning, but it was from Cornwall that the army gained its force and fire, and when it entered Devon it was in a hostile country.

This noble cavalier cannot, therefore, be claimed with justice as one of the long line of Devon heroes; but it is otherwise, I think, with his equally heroic grandfather, the great Sir Richard, who waged that immortal sea-fight in the *Revenge*, which will remain among the very greatest traditions of this country till all care for history has died away. I readily believe that Sir Richard, who valued sea-power as highly as all other statesmen of his age, was at Bideford for business, and at Stowe chiefly for recreation. There is no port along the northern coast of Corn-

Looking towards Westward Ho.

wall whence he could have launched the schemes which seethed
in his brain no less than in the heads of Raleigh or of Gilbert;
while Bideford, though by no means as great or powerful a
town in those days as Kingsley has described it, was as apt a
base as any sea-warrior or colonist could wish. Along the
shores of the Torridge and the Taw, there could have been no
lack of sturdy mariners, ready to follow Sir Richard wheresoever
he might lead them. I think, therefore, that his glory properly
belongs to Bideford; and, indeed, it would be useless to dispute
it, seeing that Kingsley has so twined his memory and that
of Bideford together in the hearts of all men, that were the
association as false as it is true, it would be impossible to break
it, and henceforth for ever, when men look on that wide water
flowing up over the spreading flats, past the Pebble Ridge, past
Braunton with its sandy burrows, past Appledore, that quaint
and dirty fishing village, past Instow, and a score of villages
and townlets, till it ripples round the buttresses of the old and
famous bridge, the first and last thoughts in their minds will be
of him who fought the deadliest and most hopeless sea-fight in
our history, giving his life freely to show that they who seek
prestige must not shrink from fighting when success is hopeless.
For by lost fights a nation gains as much as by its victories, if
they be but well lost; and those Spaniards who lay in their
great galleons round the little *Revenge*, fearing at last to attack
her any more, must have felt and known that in any equality of
number, the countrymen of Grenville would sweep them from
the sea.

It is tolerably well-known, nowadays, that Kingsley set the
naval greatness of the town he loved too high. Bideford, in
the days of the Armada, was not the busy and important place
which he describes. Barnstaple far outstripped its rival on the
Torridge; and there is reason to think that all the ships which
sailed out of the Golden Bay to join Drake's fleet at Plymouth
when England was watching for the Armada were really built and

Appledore.

manned upon the Taw, though doubtless there were Bideford men
on board them.   It was not until the following century was well
in, that Bideford became of much consequence.   But all this is of
little importance to the world.   The spirit of *Westward Ho!*
makes the book immortal, not its facts ; and it is a peddling occupation to dwell on the errors of a writer whose proved love for
England can be matched by only one other, who has also
left us.

I suppose it will not do to go away from Bideford without
mentioning the witches, Temperance Floyd, " Intemperate
Temperance " as the old pamphlet calls her, and her almost
equally wicked companions, all of whom were very justly
hanged at Exeter, in the year 1682.   " For my part," said Sir
Thomas Browne, " I have ever believed, and do now know,
that there are witches."   That settles the matter.   I am both
too humble and too deeply imbued with West Country
prejudices to feel any disposition to differ with the silver
tongued physician of Norwich.   Mary Floyd and Susannah
Edwards were the companions in guilt of Intemperate Temperance, " all three being stricken in years, which might have
taught them more grace."   Grace appears to have been the last
thing thought of by any of the three.   Temperance acknowledged
that she had been in league with the devil for more than twenty
years, and had commited many cruelties at his instigation.
Apparently this league was to be dissolved by any sort of legal
proceedings ; for though the devil obligingly saw Temperance to
the door of the prison, he did not go in with her, nor did he
render any further assistance either to her or her companions,
though they too " had not been idle in their hellish practices
but had served him faithfully."   These bad old women, it
appears, had conceived a grudge against one Mr. Hann, a
matter of mere spite, since he was of good repute and honest
conversation ; and " being all of one mind, began to exercise
their devilish arts upon him."   The first way of annoying him

that they thought of was to make his cows give blood instead
of milk ; which the poor beasts accordingly did, " to the great
astonishment of the milkers." A great many more pranks of
this description are recorded which it might be useful for any
one afflicted with doubts as to the existence of witches to study

Wear Giffard.

carefully. But as Sir Thomas has convinced us, we may pass
them by, and go on to cheerfuller things.

There is much lovely country round Bideford, of which I
should speak more fully were not my space so small, but I cannot
refrain from mentioning Wear Giffard which lies a little way off
the road to Torrington, and possesses an old manor house with a
banqueting hall of exceeding beauty, as well as a church which

stands so charmingly upon a slope above the Torridge that it is in itself an ample recompense for the small fatigue of going there.

Now those who are bound from Bideford to Ilfracombe may cross the bridge, if they will, and ride along a good road on the further bank till they round the parting of the Tamar and the Torridge, and see old Barnstaple lying on a stream which cannot be compared in beauty with its sister river. But for my part, I could never find anything in Barnstaple which repaid the trouble of going there; and I know no way of leaving Bideford more pleasant, or more harmonious with the aspect and associations of the town, than to get into a boat at the old quay just below the bridge, and drop down slowly with the tide till the wide waterway grows wider from the coming of the Taw, and the ocean bursts into sight, and rising over the burrows, where the high-piled Pebble Ridge groans and murmurs under the fretting of the heavy Atlantic swells, you see the grey old tower of Northam church upon the hillside, and spare a moment to think of Amyas Leigh, and the house of Burrough, where Kingsley placed his imagined hero in the dwelling of a stout seaman, Stephen Burrough, who, for his own sake, must not be entirely forgotten. And perhaps as we sweep down with the tide, beneath Appledore and the Hubbastone, and all the other famous scenes which the genius of one writer has linked imperishably with the noblest of our memories, we may remember that February evening when the bells of Bideford were answering the bells of Northam for joy that Mary, Queen of Scots, was dead, while Mrs. Leigh, widowed and alone, paced up and down the terrace walk at Burrough, watching for that ship which she could have picked out miles away among a whole fleet of sails; when suddenly there came the thunder of a gun at sea; and all the folks of Northam rushed out to the churchyard to see what might be coming in.

"There was a gallant ship outside the bar. She was running

Barnstaple.

in, too, with all sails set. A large ship; nearly a thousand tons she might be; but not of English rig. . . The strange sail passed out of sight behind the hill of Appledore; and then there rose into the quiet evening air a cheer as from a hundred throats. Mrs. Leigh stood still and listened. Another gun thundered among the hills, and then another cheer. It might have been twenty minutes before the vessel hove in sight again round the dark rocks of the Hubbastone as she turned up the Bideford River. Mrs. Leigh had stood that whole time perfectly motionless, a pale and scarcely breathing statue, her eyes fixed upon the Viking's Rock. Round the Hubbastone she came at last. There was music on board, drums and fifes, shawms and trumpets, which wakened ringing echoes from every knoll of wood and slab of slate. And as she opened full on Burrough House, another cheer burst from her crew, and rolled up to the hills from off the silver waters far below, full a mile away. Mrs. Leigh walked quickly toward the house and called her maid,— 'Grace, bring me my hood. Master Amyas is come home. . . .' And Mrs. Leigh, with Grace behind her, started with rapid steps towards Bideford. . . . As they came down Bridgeland Street. . . . they could see the strange ship already at anchor in the river. They had just reached the lower end of the street, when round the corner swept a great mob of sailors, women, 'prentices, hurrahing, questioning, weeping, laughing. Mrs. Leigh stopped; and behold they stopped also.

" ' Here she is !' shouted some one. ' Here's his mother !' "

" His mother? Not their mother !" said Mrs. Leigh to herself, and turned very pale; but that heart was long past breaking.

I make no apology for this long quotation, or for suggesting to my readers the recollection of the great and moving scene that followed. For of a truth these are the true and real associations of Bideford; and till men have forgotten much

Цукотъ.

that they now value, there will always be some who cannot
look up Bridgeland Street in the dusk of a winter evening
without seeing Mrs. Leigh turn to go homeward, holding Amyas
tight by one hand and Ayacanora by the other.

But whilst we have been calling up all these old stories our
boat has touched the golden sands at Braunton, and landed us
on a waste which, if the truth must be told, is not easy country
for a cycle.   But the distance is short before we strike the road
again ; and so ride on through Braunton village, famous for the
singular fact that it was a sow and her litter which led St.
Brannock to the pleasant spot beside a stream where he planted
the old church ; and on to Ilfracombe, a place which has
grown so large of recent years that it seems to have lost all its
old West Country flavour, and to have become cosmopolitan
like Cowes or Brighton.   What, I ask myself, are these crowds
of people doing on the shores of that cove which once resounded
with the cries of misery uttered by that Tracy who took refuge
here from the remorse he felt for the murder of Thomas
à Becket.   All along the coast his wailings used to be scattered
by the salt wind, and the folk in lone cottages upon the cliffs
crossed themselves as they heard his moaning borne by their
dwellings on the stormy winds.   Not much is told of the
anguish of this lonely soul, or the torments of remorse he passed
through in the sea cleft where he spent the remnant of his life
in fruitless repentance for a deed which his descendants have
expiated ever since.   Who has not heard of " the weird of the
Tracys, with ever the wind and the rain in their faces."   Such
is the burden laid by the Church on the remote descendants of
him who struck down the turbulent Archbishop ; but there is
little recollection in modern Ilfracombe of all this tragedy.
Nor is it easy to find in the gay town, which seems to live for
pleasure, much trace of the small but ancient port which for
many centuries played its little part in ocean commerce, and
had its share, as we may well suspect, in those questionable

dealings on the sea for which its lonely situation well
fitted it.

In other seaports of the West it is pleasant and appropriate
to follow out old history, for nothing in the modern aspect of
those towns supplies too great a contrast. But how can the past
come back on Ilfracombe? What could the old days have in

Harbour, Ilfracombe.

common with these new cut drives round ancient cliffs, these
band-stands and asphalted walks and winter shelters which oust
the sea-birds from their nesting places? It is all new wine in
Ilfracombe. Let us not try to store it in old casks, but rather
hew them up for firewood, and leave the new world to be
wholly new.

Taken frankly as a modern watering-place, Ilfracombe is certainly very beautiful. It nestles in a deep hollow among lofty tors, so humped and twisted that they seem to be still heaving from the impact of some huge subterranean convulsion. But, on a fine spring morning, when a strong west wind is blowing inshore, the green sea, ruffled over with white breakers, flies nobly flashing round the bay beneath the Capstone Rock. The cove is full of jagged black reefs ; the green water surges over them and breaks in dazzling foam. The wind is keen and exhilarating ; it sings with a sharp whistle round the rocky clefts, and yet is neither cold nor piercing, but simply salt and fresh as a thousand leagues of ocean can make it. The gulls skim to and fro across the sunny waves ; and out at sea a couple of brown fishing boats are tossing heavily in the rough water.

Such is a glimpse of Ilfracombe seen early in the morning when only wise people were out of bed, a last glimpse ere starting on the toilsome road to Lynton. That is a road indeed ; and if any one consult me about the best way of travelling it, I say emphatically that way is best which makes one use one's legs the least. For human muscles were not meant to drive a cycle over such inclines ; though when I say that, justice compels me to add that I have seen two ladies riding the road with ease. This leads me to point out, if a fact so obvious be worth mentioning at all, that hilly countries are not trying to those who know how to ride them. But however one may travel this famous road it is one that ought not to be missed, if only for the sake of Watermouth Castle, that grand and beautiful domain that lies among sweet woods low down by the shore of a rocky cove. There are few sights in lovely Devon fairer than the intersection of the valleys just beyond the castle, a labyrinth of winding field paths under deep plantations and threading meadow-lands so rich and verdant that one hardly sees the pheasants paddling away through the lush grass.

[To face p. 384.

A slow, sure-footed creature.

Watermouth is the gem of all the journey; but Combe-
Martin is beautiful too; and it is, moreover, famous in a way as
being one of the few places in this country where silver mines
have been worked with some show of profit. "Now how hilly
soever or mountainous soever this county be," cries Prince,
adding apprehensively, in evident anticipation of the complaints of modern cyclists, that such hilliness is "an argument
of a serene and wholesome air," which is certainly quite true,
"yet its mountains themselves, barren as they seem, are not
without their peculiar advantages, their very bowels being far
richer than those countries which can show much more painted
faces." One wishes that old Prince, for whose rhodomontade
we have learnt to feel something like affection, had thought
less about the bowels of his county, and considered more its
surface. Had he deigned to write of roads, we might not now
be left to lose our wind and temper simultaneously by climbing
up the hill of Paracombe, or to grow pale with terror as the
coach swings cautiously down into the abyss of Lynmouth.
But Prince had no care of roads. Probably he rode an
ambling mule, a slow, sure-footed creature which chose its own
pace and was never hurried, but browsed along at such a rate
as one might travel even now in Devon without affliction if one
had the necessary patience.

But Lynton is near at last; and I see the road dropping into
the Alpine valleys with regret. For Lynton is the last town of
all this pleasant journey, which has brought us through so
many famous places and so many more which are undeservedly
forgotten, but are still eloquent of the past when they find a
patient listener. There are people who maintain that, of all
the country we have seen since we started from old Axminster,
this is the loveliest, and that no town or village on that long
route can boast the beauty of Lynton or of Lynmouth. To
every man his preferences: but I give the palm to Clovelly
when loveliness is in question; while, for grandeur of coast

scenery, I hold that one must seek it in Cornwall on the northern
coast.   Yet there is no question at all of the surprising beauty
of these wild hills and densely wooded glens.   Were it possible,
I should wish all strangers to turn off the main road while still
three miles from Lynton, and crossing a bare common make

Lynmouth.

their way by rough paths which skirt the exquisite cliffs of
Wooda Bay down towards Lee Abbey, where a deep inlet cuts
far into the high cliff, and the rounded hill drops down towards
it garbed with brown woodlands and wide lawns of fern and
rocky bluffs, where the shadows lie long on fresh spring morn-
ings and the ivy trails as richly as if no storm-wind ever

whistled down the fertile valley. Not far beyond this lovely
bay lies the valley of rocks, a wild and desolate waste of
shattered and riven stone, out of which one peak, the Castle
Rock, drops sheer into the sea from a vast and dizzy height,
and is moreover so finely broken with jutting cairns of granite,
over all its grassy slopes, that it recalls the wilder scenes we
have left behind in Cornwall, and might be a crag upon the
coast line near Tol Pedn or Pardenick. The valley is full of
savage dignity and grandeur; and on this coast where magnificence of rock forms is comparatively rare, and the headlands
sweep down for the most part rounded and grassy to the sea,
it forms a welcome interlude among the long succession of
what are rather spurs of moorland thrust out into the sea than
the promontories of a true coast line.

It is the varied character of the scenery at Lynton which
constitutes its greatest charm. One is never sated with the
aspects of a place which offers you, at one moment, a range of
towering headlands, and the next a deep gorge, clothed with
ferns up the whole of its steep sides, until the stone crops out
high up above the woods, and the storm-swept summit of the
hill is clothed with fern and ling and short sweet turf. You
stray down the precipice into pretty Lynmouth, a village which
makes just so much pretence of fishing as gives a decent colour
to its pursuit of visitors, and for that purpose maintains a little
quay with half-a-dozen idle boatmen lounging up and down
upon it with the movements of supers on the stage. A short
turn through the houses brings you on a bridge under which a
noisy torrent pours out upon the beach, and its valley lies
opening so straight before you that you cannot but follow it at
least a little way to see whence that water comes which flows
out seawards with such a note of triumph in its singing. And
so you are led on from one beauty to another, till at length
you reach a spot where out of a den of greenery, oak coppice,
mountain ash, low growing beeches, and what not, a little river,

no more than eight feet wide, splashes over a rocky ledge into
a still, brown pool, where it swirls round and round underneath
mossy banks, leaving eddies of foam and bubbles in the
corners, and gathers courage for the whirling course it has to
go over boulders green with duckweed, to a rocky slope so
wide that the little stream covers it like no more than a thin
film of glancing emerald, and then bounces over another fall,
and then a third, all sparkling and chequered by the sunbeams
which pierce through the green tunnel of leafage overhead, and
so is whirled along beneath an overhanging oak to a deep pool
beside a lovely space of green sward, where a second river
flashes down another rocky valley, and the two run together to
the sea.

This is Watersmeet,—a valley cleft down between such
precipices that one marvels how the sunlight manages to sound
their depths. For deep as the valley is, the stream itself has
bitten deeper in the course of ages ; and yet every trail of ivy,
every tuft of primroses on the red rocks of the cliff, every
cushion of soft moss that fills a crevice of the jutting stone,
catches and reflects the warm light, and the shadows of the
trees lie dark and cool across the water.

From this point the stream flows on more quietly, but with
added volume, till the hills sweep close together, the valley
narrows to a gorge, and the river, chafing at the rough compulsion, runs black and boiling down a rapid, fretting round
the large wet boulders, flashing into little jets and bubbles
which the sun catches as they are tossed up into the air ; surging
up with force as if it meant to sweep away the opposing rocks ;
yet turned aside by a power greater than its own, and carried
back into its black and polished channel. On the bank the
mossy boulders have ranged themselves like fantastic steps or
stairs. How the sun turns them green and gold, and lights up
their cool shelves where the hartstongues dip one above another
and the polished ivy trails and climbs behind them !

A little further on, the river finds a level reach. Instantly foam and bubbles disappear, and the stream glides on silently and smooth, a belt of brown sunlit water hardly broken by a ripple. Three hundred feet and more the cliff falls sheer from the highest crags, over which the clouds float heavily in the blue sky down to the belt of trees which overhang the river; yet the sun, declining westwards, beats down fiercely on one side of the gorge, leaving cool, brown shadows on the other. Another turn of the broken pathway, and the trees are topped by the vast sweep of a gigantic hill, which adds magnificence to a scene so full already of a beauty fit for fairyland.

Such are Lynton and Lynmouth, twin villages of which it may be said that they summarise so many charms of the West Country which elsewhere are found only singly or apart, that they make a fitting close to the long journey which has brought us through the highways and the byways of nearly the whole of the county and the duchy which constitute Western England. It has been a journey surely full of interest, even for travellers who have no more association with the West than every native of Great Britain or of Greater Britain has with all those districts of the mother-country which have been great and famous; and, beyond all others, with that one whose sea-power was mighty, while northern ports were in their infancy, and where Imperial conceptions sprang first to light. As our ocean Empire grows out of youth into noble manhood, it cannot be but that from Canada, Australia, and many another country over sea, our fellow-countrymen will look back with increasing pride and affection on that corner of England, which set hand so early and so lustily to the foundations on which they have built both strong and firmly, and will glory in the memory of those first workers just as we to-day glory in the later efforts which are bringing forth such splendid fruits. These associations are the bonds of Empire, and the throbbing in the heart of a British

subject, when he thinks of home, is a link which binds as fast as
man need wish.

> Buy my English posies !
> Ye that have your own,
> Buy them for a brother's sake
> Over seas alone !
> Weed ye trample underfoot,
> Floods his heart abrim—
> Bird ye never heeded,
> Oh ! she calls his dead to him.
>
> Far and far our homes are set, round the Seven Seas,
> Woe for us if we forget, we that hold by these !
> Unto each his mother-beach, bloom and bird and land,
> Children of the Seven Seas, oh ! love and understand.
>
> RUDYARD KIPLING.

Lynmouth from Lynton.

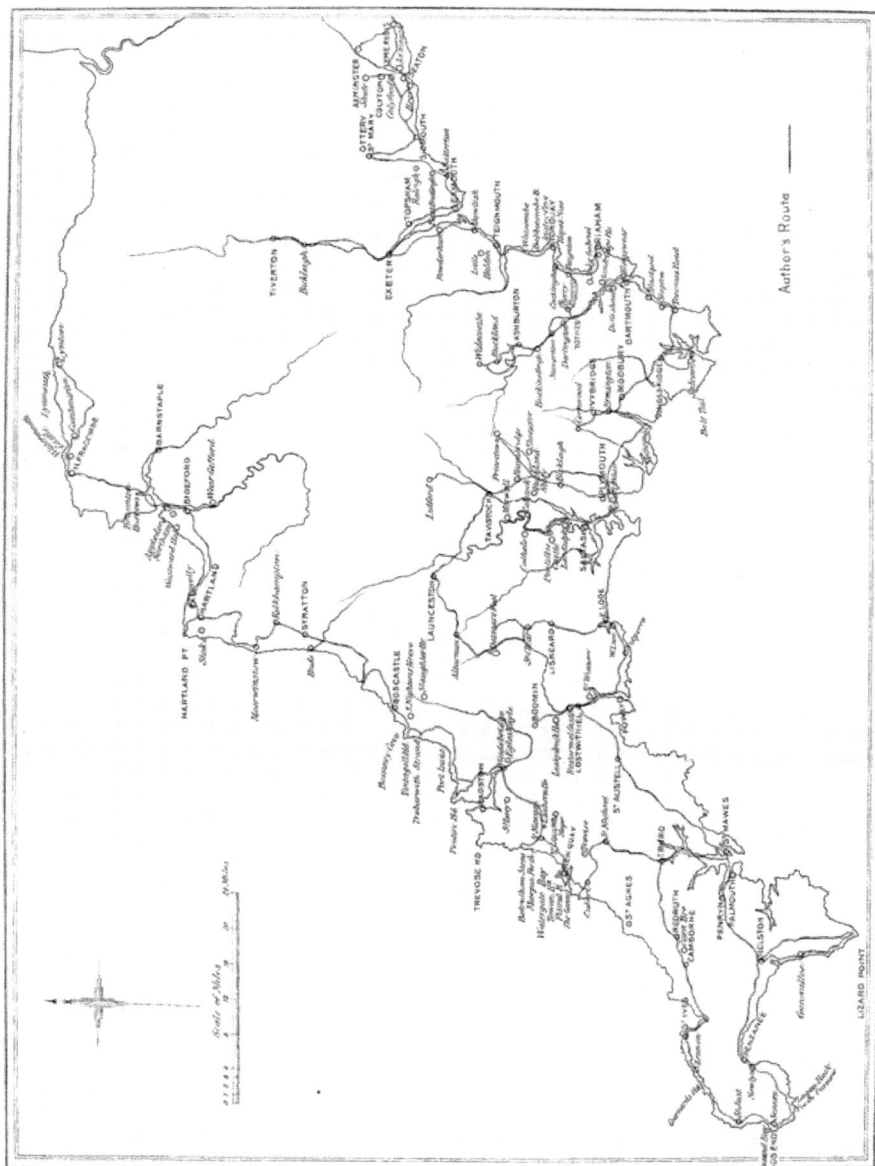

Author's Route

Scale of Miles

LIZARD POINT

LANDS END

PENZANCE

NEWLYN

HELSTON

FALMOUTH

PENRYN

CAMBORNE

REDRUTH

ST AGNES

TRURO

ST MAWES

FOWEY

ST AUSTELL

LOSTWITHIEL

BODMIN

LISKEARD

LAUNCESTON

TREVOSE HD

PADSTOW

BOSCASTLE

STRATTON

HARTLAND PT

CLOVELLY

BIDEFORD

BARNSTAPLE

ILFRACOMBE

LYNMOUTH

TIVERTON

EXETER

OTTERY ST MARY

AXMINSTER

SEATON

SIDMOUTH

BUDLEIGH SALTERTON

EXMOUTH

TOPSHAM

DAWLISH

TEIGNMOUTH

ASHBURTON

DARTMOUTH

TOTNES

NEWTON ABBOT

BRIXHAM

KINGSBRIDGE

MODBURY

YEALMPTON

PLYMOUTH

TAVISTOCK

OKEHAMPTON

NORTH TAWTON

PRINCETOWN

SALTASH

TORQUAY

INDEX

Tregeagle, 207, 338
Tregony, 255
Trethevy dolmen, 219
Trevanion, Sir J., 183
Trevilian, 303
Truro, 258

V

VERYAN, ST., 215

W

WADEBRIDGE, 335
Waller, Sir William, 193
Walsingham, quoted, 106
Warwick, Earl of, Kingmaker, 116
Watcombe, 67
Watersmeet, 384

Wear Giffard, 373
Well of St. Nun, 200
Whitesand Bay, 300, 309
Whittle, quoted, 74
Widdecombe, 88
Winnow, St., 248
Witches, 45, 154, 319, 321, 372
Withycombe Raleigh, 30
Worth, quoted, 177
Wrecking, 279, 294

Y

YEALM RIVER, 123
Yeth hounds, 87, 149
Yonge, Dr. J., 70, 71

Z

ZENNOR, 310